DIASPORA DIPLOMACY

DIASPORA DIPLOMACY:

Philippine Migration and its Soft Power Influences

Joaquin Jay Gonzalez III

MILL CITY PRESS

Mill City Press, Inc.
212 3rd Avenue North, Suite 290
Minneapolis, MN 55401
612.455.2294
www.millcitypublishing.com

ISBN-13: 978-1-937600-40-2
LCCN: 2011941247

Cover Design by Alan Pranke
Typeset by Steve Porter

Printed in the United States of America

TABLE OF CONTENTS

Acknowledgments   vii

Preface   xi

Chapter 1   Flexing Soft Power Through Mind, Heart
                 and Spirit   1

Chapter 2   The Philippine Diaspora and its Role in
                 International Relations   16

Chapter 3   San Francisco: golden gateway for
                 faithful shopping   41

Chapter 4   London: bridge to mission, care, and charity   86

Chapter 5   Dubai: port of security, sacrifice, and play   122

Chapter 6   Dhaka: garbs, games, and globalization   157

Chapter 7   Singapore: in service of God, country, and growth   191

Chapter 8   Conclusion: Philippine soft power lessons   237

References   248

About the author   259

A BIG THANK YOU

Just like my favorite *Indiana Jones* and *Star Wars* films, a global research venture of this size and magnitude would not have been possible without the five Cs—cast, crew, colleagues, credit card, and courage.

First, to my lovely wife, Michelle Hong Gonzalez, and my bubbly daughters, Elise and Coral, for tolerating my long absences, my memory lapses and the family meals that I ate while working on my laptop. They had no choice but to be co-opted into my fieldwork and writing—Michelle ended up as my photographer and videographer while Elise did some field notes and graphic design work. Coral gurgled and cooed while I typed. Their warmth, comfort and kindness sustained me throughout this project.

Second, the financial generosity of the University of San Francisco's Yuchengco Philippine Studies Program, College of Arts and Sciences Faculty Development Funds (FDF), USF Center for the Pacific Rim's Kiriyama Fellowship, the Pew Charitable Trusts' The Religion and Immigration Project (TRIP), and the Mayor George Christopher Chair in Public Administration at Golden Gate University. Special mention goes to Mona Lisa Yuchengco and her father, Ambassador Alfonso Yuchengco, for graciously endowing the Maria Elena Yuchengco Philippine Studies Program (YPSP), and then to Gerardo Marin and Jennifer Turpin for taking the risk of hiring a people-power activist-turned-professor, more than a decade ago. They gave me an academic space to plant seeds and nurture an organic garden of knowledge on the Philippines.

Third, my TRIP Gang: Loie Lorentzen, Kevin Chun, and Hien Duc Do; my YPSP Gang: Lorraine Mallare, Claudine del Rosario, Evelyn Rodriguez, Jenifer Wofford, Edith Borbon, Marissa Litman, and Mary Zweifel; my Asian American Studies Gang: Eileen Fung, David Kim, Brian Dempster, Violet

Chung, and Evelyn Ho (who lent me her i-river to digitally record interviews for a year!); and my politics gang and other USF comrades: Shalendra Sharma, Brian Weiner, Rob Elias, James Taylor, Patrick Murphy, Elisabeth Jay Friedman, Anne Barlett, Kouslaa Kessler-Mata, Doowan Lee, Heather Hoag, Spencer Rangitsch, John Nelson, and Steve Zavestoski.

Fourth, in San Francisco: Ambassador Jun Cardenas, Consul Generals Rowena Sanchez and Mariano Paynor, Consuls Tony Morales, Fred Santos, Anton Mandap, Ed Malaya, as well as staffers John Jiao, Rene Cornista, Francesca Regala, and the rest of the Philippine Consulate General of San Francisco, past and present. There were also Junjun Villegas, Dan Gonzales, Erwin Bonilla and others.

In Dubai: my cousins Guimo and Maite Gonzalez for letting me stay at their cozy Corniche home and introducing me to their vast contacts in the Filipino communities in Dubai, Sharjah, and Fujairah; cousin Galen, his wife Matet and my nephew Poch Gonzalez, who took me around when Guimo and Maite were busy; Consul Butch Bandillo and the Manahans as well as RK and Joanna.

In Dhaka: Dr. Ed Campos for housing me during my field work; Ambassador Zenaida Rabago, Consul General Alex Lamadrid, Consul Fred Borlongan, and the rest of the Philippine Embassy staff in Bangladesh; Jun Pastrana, Estela Ilagan, Arvee and Irwin Policar, Rosita Umali, Elizabeth Co. Parul, who made sure I was well fed with Bangla cuisine; and Shafiul and Bilal who drove for me. At the American International University-Bangladesh, Vice Chancellor Carmen Lamagna, Vice President Hasanul A. Hasan, Dean Charles Villanueva, Danny Morgia. Jennifer Medina, Jess Alabe, Taposh Halder provided valuable information and insights.

In London: Deputy Chief of Mission Rey Catapang, Dr. Rollie Buendia, Fr. Ino Potrido, Consul General Tess de Vega and her husband, Consul General Ed de Vega, Consuls Tess Lazaro and Bernadette Fernandez, Edith Malilin, Cecile Santos, Peps Villanueva; Chefs Felix Bayker and Randy Miravalles;

the Jury Group; the Filipino Catholic Community Prayer Group; and Street Action UK's Joe and Annabelle Walker for letting Michelle and I crash at their cozy East London home.

In Singapore: Ambassador Mindy Cruz, Consul General Neal Imperial, Rey Annabella Oliveros, Rey Navarro, Sol Iglesias, Encar Montales, Bobby Mariano, Ho Khai Leong, Rod Severino, Mars Ang, Rizo Hizon, Jayeel Cornelio, Rey Ileto, Triena Ong, Noel Perdigon, Pamela Wildheart Pilapil, as well as Clement and Luz Mesenas. The Institute of Southeast Asian Studies. The National University of Singapore and my migration colleagues, Brenda Yeoh and Shirlena Huang, who co-wrote with me and tolerated my disappearances. Former OWWA officer Josephine Sanchez, then-Consul General and now Ambassador to Malaysia Vic Lecaros and retired Trade Attache Eugene Reyes; 7101 Flavours; and OFW Pinoy Star. Special thanks to Pareng Deng Coy Miel for the hospitality and granting me permission to use his 1995 Straits Times Valentine's cartoon for the second time.

In Manila: Malou Babilonia for sharing her wonderful home and car, as well as Mada and Ina for preparing the healthy nourishments and cleaning up after my mess. The Gonzalez and Lucero clans, especially my parents Benny and Agnes, brothers Jo, Jon, Jing, James, King, sister Ji and their families. My lifetime friends, brothers, and comrades in diaspora: Emil and Kerry-Anne Bolongaita, Gambhir and Bhawana Bhatta, Bong and Cathy Bengzon, Ricky and Bambi Wong as well as Mon and Mavi Javier.

Fifth, members of the Filipino communities in the United States, United Kingdom, United Arab Emirates, Bangladesh, and Singapore who kindly shared with me their life stories and inspired me no end.

Sixth, my sincere gratitude goes to Rica Campos and Lupe Romulo for providing me with my initial key informants at the Philippine embassies in Dhaka and London who eventually became close friends. My dearest friends, Rhacel Parreñas, Malou Babilonia, my surrogate mothers, Marylou Salcedo and Barbara Bundy, my lunch buddies Lara Hansen, Annmarie Belda, and

Liza Locsin. Ashley Guevarra and her Zumba classes as well as Angelo Merino and his boxing classes at Koret which kept my aging body in sync with my forgetful mind. My teaching assistant Charles Daulo for the library sorties and online searches.

Last, to my editor, Gemma Nemenzo, and anonymous reviewers who took valuable time out from their busy schedules to provide frank comments and, at times, humorous remarks on draft chapters as well as, of course, for being tough and probing but nevertheless very collegial.

PREFACE

In many ways, this book is an accumulation of more than 20 years of observing and participating in the religious, occupational, and associational influences of the Philippine diaspora. It builds on research from my last book project, *Filipino American Faith in Action: Immigration, Religion, and Civic Engagement*, published in 2009.

My fascination with the Filipino global movement and its transnational and diasporic soft power influences began in 1987 when I first traveled outside the Philippines. My first encounter with a *kababayan* (compatriot) in another land was during the long layover at the Kuwait international airport on the way to my final destination in North Africa.

When he learned I was a kababayan, the first question that the Filipino airport maintenance worker asked me was: *Meron po ba kayong alak o baboy? Bibilhin po namin* (Do you have liquor or pork? We will buy them). These were banned items in Islamic Kuwait. I told him politely that I did not have any of those, but I offered him a pack of *tuyo* (salted dried fish) which made his eyes light up.

In Libya, I encountered tired and hungry Filipino construction workers waiting for their flight to Manila at the Tripoli airport, sweaty Filipino agronomists working in Sebha (Colonel Khaddafi's birthplace in the middle of the Sahara desert), and overworked Filipina nurses at a community hospital in Benghazi. Yet, they were all smiling when I greeted them. These images are ingrained in my heart and mind.

From then on, I developed the habit of approaching my kababayans everywhere with the universal Filipino greeting of *"Kamusta po?"* (How are you?). Many of them had developed the same habit of making conversation especially after long periods of not being able to talk to someone in Tagalog.

Their second question expressed their comfort, *"Taga saan ka sa atin?"* (Where are you from back home?). Some were suspicious though. Others were snobbish.

Shortly after I returned to Manila after that first trip abroad, I was awarded a scholarship for graduate studies in the U.S. That was it. I was formally initiated into the ranks of Filipino migrants.

I met Filipinos everywhere I traveled, lived, and worked in the U.S., from Los Angeles, California to Salisbury, Connecticut. After graduating from the University of Utah in 1992, I moved to Philadelphia and commuted to Washington, DC for work. I chatted with them on trains and planes. I attended Filipino community events. I spoke with professors and other professionals at international conferences. When I accepted a teaching position in Singapore, I continued to keep my eyes and ears open for my compatriots while working and traveling extensively in Southeast Asia, East Asia, and Australia. I always made time to chat and hear their stories and gripes.

As a Filipino migrant and social justice activist, I always wondered how I could give back to my homeland besides simply sending articles for publication in scholarly journals. I found the answer in Singapore, home to more than 100,000 Filipina domestic helpers. From 1994-1999, I spent my weekends teaching basic computer skills to *kababayans*, on their days off, at the Filipino Overseas Workers' Skills Training Program. I always looked forward to hanging out with them, exchanging stories, laughing loudly, and sometimes crying our loneliness away. I wrote my first book on the diaspora after one of them, Flor Contemplacion, was hanged for murder.

I resettled back in San Francisco in 1999. I helped propel the Maria Elena Yuchengco Philippine Studies Program at the University of San Francisco as a beacon for Filipino/a teaching, research, and community service. I interacted with the children and grandchildren of the early migrants. One day, my daughter said to me, "Dad, you always write for big people, but not for small people like me." That inspired me to write a children's book, *Countries of the*

World: Philippines, for the children of migrants who were eager to learn about their parents' homeland.

When 9/11 happened, I was called to public service by the mayor of San Francisco, so I served as immigrant rights commissioner. My new home country, home state, and home city recognized my public and community service influences with numerous awards and recognitions. From the Bay Area, I followed my insatiable appetite across the Atlantic Ocean to participate and observe Filipino migrants in the major cities of Spain, the Netherlands, Austria, Hungary, France, and the United Kingdom and then westward across the Pacific Ocean to witness them at work and play in Japan, Korea, Taiwan, Macau, Vietnam, Indonesia, Malaysia, Brunei, Thailand, and Hong Kong. I flew south to Mexico to taste and observe Filipino hospitality blended in with the Latino temperament.

I also visited my Filipino Canadian relatives in Vancouver and Toronto and interacted with others after meetings in Ottawa. In 2008, I returned to Africa with a group of Catholic university students and bumped into Filipino seamen in the port city of Durban, South Africa. I encountered many of my ocean-going "brods" and *"pare"* (mates) at the bustling ports of Manila, Singapore, Hong Kong, Fujairah, London, New York, Los Angeles, and Oakland.

It was always exciting to meet kababayans, some of whom turned out to be my childhood friends. What a small world! We swapped happy and sad stories about our adventures and families, and recalled our play-filled days on the narrow streets and slum settlements of Santa Ana, Manila. Where Filipino migrants gather socially, whether it be a remittance center, a Filipino restaurant, a freight forwarder, or a Goldilocks bakeshop, it would be doing good business. On weekends, they flowed into churches and other places of worship. They also made time for their religious devotional meetings as well as hometown association bowling and ballroom dancing. Many went back to visit and give back to their hometowns.

I have seen them in many cities and countries and could write volumes about them. But for this book I focus on my participant observations in the U.S., United Arab Emirates, Bangladesh, the United Kingdom, and Singapore. I spent between four to six weeks at a time immersed in the Filipino migrant communities in Dubai, Dhaka and London. I have lived more than two decades combined in Singapore and San Francisco.

Many members of my extended family and friends have also joined the diaspora. They kindly opened their homes for me and became my initial informants who referred me to their network of kababayans. Diplomats and attaches in the Philippine consulates of Dubai and San Francisco and the Philippine embassies in London, Dhaka, and Singapore shared their candid thoughts, reports, and databases. These men and women of the Philippine foreign service corps, as well as labor, welfare, tourism, and trade attaches and assistants are, in many ways, migrants too.

To deepen my participant observation, I read as a lector and sang with the choirs in churches, accompanied them to remittance centers, ate with them at Filipino restaurants and hawker centers, played mahjong, drank at clubs, sang karaoke, and shopped with them. I chatted with them while buying liquor at duty-free shops, at hair salons while I got a haircut, and while we waited to renew our passports. I paid my respects at Philippine embassies and consulates, took photos and videos of migrant work sites and met many for meals, *merienda* (tea or snack) or flavored *shisha* (water-pipe). They were generous with their time, gifts, food, and their thoughts.

In Dhaka, Singapore, and Dubai, I ballroom-danced with some of my sources after our meetings and watched some of the Filipino band performances, to witness them both at work and at play. I rode the crowded *abras* (water taxis) across the Dubai Creek and art-filled rickshaws to Banani Church. From my home, I walked, drove, scootered, MUNIed, and BARTed all over the San Francisco Bay from Vallejo to Fremont and from Oakland to Daly City. In London, I walked miles, took the Tube underground from Picadilly Circus to Kensington High Street, rode the red double-decker buses aboveground from East London to Trafalgar Square, the MRT, SMRT buses, and the blue Comfort cabs from Lucky Plaza on Orchard Road to Novena Church on Thomson Road.

Kababayans I had just met welcomed me with their perennial *"Kumain ka na? Halika na, huwag ka ng mahiya!"* (Have you eaten? Come on, don't be shy!). I got invited to their celebrations and get-togethers which were always marked by so much food. I observed and interviewed people at the Philippine Department of Labor and Employment (DOLE), Department of Tourism (DOT), Philippine Overseas Employment Administration (POEA), Department of Trade and Industry (DTI), Overseas Workers Welfare Administration (OWWA), and Department of Foreign Affairs (DFA). I interacted with migrant worker advocacy groups like Migrante, Gabriela, and the Scalabrini Migration Center. I also used the internet and joined migrant listservs and blogs, including that of the Worldwide Filipino Alliance. Hometown mayors and municipal officials testified to the valuable assistance they received from overseas hometown associations.

Imagining myself as the cross breed of Dr. Jose Rizal, the illustrious Philippine national hero, and the daring and adventurous Indiana Jones, I got into risky and scary situations. One that I will never forget is the questioning, fingerprinting, and three-day forced stay in Qeshm Island, Iran, as a suspected American spy. I was simply doing participant observation by joining a group of Filipino migrants who needed to exit Dubai across the Persian Gulf into Iran to exchange their temporary visit visas for employment letters.

Another that entailed less risk was when I pretended to be part of a surprise quality assurance inspection team so I could candidly observe the operations of Dhaka factories and take photos and video footages. I endured the unpredictable sand storms of Dubai, the rolling fog of San Francisco, the hot muggy traffic of Dhaka, the freezing cold of London, and the sticky humidity of Singapore. I was sniffed and cleared by bomb detecting dogs at San Francisco International Airport, Ottawa/Macdonald-Cartier International

Airport, Amsterdam Airport Schiphol, Kuwait International Airport, to Chhatrapati Shivaji International Airport. But somehow, the passportless *tuyo* (salted dried fish) in my carry-on always made it through customs inspections and homeland security.

Trust-building and consent were never a problem. Some of my key informants admitted that they were "undocumented," others showed me their fake passports and documents. They took me to their safe havens. I think being raised in a mixed class neighborhood in Manila *na naka-pag abroad* (who was able to go overseas) helped a lot. To many of us, English is merely our second language so I had to accommodate whichever language of passion they wished to use. I utilized an appropriate blend and intonation of Tagalog and English to communicate with a range of generations and socio-economic classes. With many, I had to rapidly code-switch words, phrases, idioms and sentences from Tagalog to English. I observed and reciprocated their non-verbal communication cues too.

In terms of verbal adaptation and situational accommodation, I constantly shifted intonation, phrasing, and word selection from *sosyal* (snobbish) to the rich and nouveau riche expatriates, to *hindi sosyal* (not snobbish) to the down-to-earth and those I knew had a middle-class or less affluent upbringing. My Tagalog, English, and Taglish sentences were filled with *po* and *opo* (politeness words), *paki po* (please), and *salamat po* (thank you). I used "mam" and "sir" as well as "boss", "bossing," "pare", "mare", "brod", and "sis" liberally. I also called them by their social titles, for instance: "Doctor", "Engineer", "Father", "Sister", "Architect", "Attorney", "Director", "President", "*Kapitan*" (Captain), or "*Konsehal*" (Councilor), in both my written and verbal exchange. Many reciprocated by calling me: "Doc", "Commissioner" (or "Commish"), "*kuya*" (elder brother), "*kapatid*" (brother), "*manong*" (elder), and "Prop" (short for propesor). Conversely, some of the Tagalog and Taglish conversations I had with my informants induced me to construct my sentences to begin or end with "*putang ina!*", the equivalent of "f*ck". This was the discourse of the streets I grew up with. I gave them lots of patience, respect, and understanding. I injected my Filipino humor and weird chuckle. I introduced myself to them by sharing not only the professional reason I was doing the interview but also a five-minute version of my own sojourn.

Talking about my migrant story creates an instant kababayan bond, a close kinship. We shared many trials and tribulations only fellow expats would understand. "*Bahala na*! (It's up to God!)" is what they usually utter when they do decide to leave the homeland. I also talked to non-Filipinos to get the 'other' perspective on their Filipino co-worker, spouse, friend or partner. Guided by a structured interview outline, I compiled voluminous field notes, recorded more than 100 audio interviews, took around 6,000 photos, logged thousands of miles of air and land travel, recorded more than a hundred hours of video clips, and administered a survey which garnered more than 1,500 respondents in San Francisco. The videos, pictures, and audio recordings help me remember them and also make my description richer since I could tell the tone of their voice, the background noise or music, the color of objects and what they were wearing, what was happening in the surroundings. I wrote and transcribed through their Philippine English, American twang, British accent, Banglish, Singlish, Tagalog, Ilocano, Visayan, and Taglish. I followed up with some using the internet and phone.

I am certain that my participant observation of Filipino migrants and their soft power influences will continue long before this book is published and read. After all, there are still more than a hundred other countries where generations of Philippine migration stories are accumulating and waiting to be told. The internet, through YouTube, Twitter, Facebook, and blog sites, has also become a real-time monitoring tool, allowing me to stay in touch with the global diaspora.

Diaspora Diplomacy: Philippine Migration and Its Soft Power Influences makes a unique, original, and crucial contribution to global migration and international political studies in the following ways:

- It draws on multiple mainstream academic disciplines and sub-fields including history, sociology, political science, international relations, labor studies, Asian studies, Philippine studies, cultural studies, economics, ethnic studies, geography, peace and conflict studies, and religious studies to underpin the research on transnationalism, globalization, diplomacy, migration, and diaspora;

• It blends various theoretical and conceptual frameworks to understand the religious, economic, and cultural influences of new migrant communities in global cities and their contribution to foreign policy and international politics, security, ethnic conflict and peace;

• It brings together academic scholarship and migrant narratives that are seldom in dialogue, especially in connection with the Philippine diaspora; for instance, diaspora and migration theories with international politics/ relations theories;

• It implements a unique ethnographic approach which combines the power and versatility of field notes and interviews, short clip videos, action photography, resulting in rich, thick, and analytical stories; and

• It goes beyond current published academic studies in the book market on Philippine and Asian migration with unprecedented breadth across geographies and boundaries, e.g., Filipinos and Filipinas in North America, Europe, South Asia, Southeast Asia, and the Middle East.

Each chapter begins with gripping literary vignettes taken from the ethnography that will hook and draw the reader. The city case studies are arranged in order of their geographic representations—San Francisco, USA for North America; London, UK for Europe; Dubai, UAE for the Middle East; Dhaka, Bangladesh for South Asia; and the city state of Singapore for Southeast Asia. All chapters present colorful narratives describing varying manifestations of religious Filipinization, occupational Filipinization, and associational Filipinization (*kasamahan* and *bayanihan* influences) adapted to each societal context.

CHAPTER 1

Flexing Soft Power Through Mind, Heart, and Spirit

The global perception of the Philippines is heavily influenced by the major television news networks. Watching the coverage from the West for the last 20 years has been frustrating. BBC, CNN, and FOX seem to downplay much of the good news and often play up the bad news: violent volcano eruptions, massive flooding after typhoons, overloaded ferries sinking, political scandals, terrorist bombings, al-Qaeda cells, and insurgent kidnappings. The latter three eventually moved the U.S. State Department to issue strongly worded travel warnings to American citizens about the personal risk of doing business or going on tours to the Philippines.

United States Department of State, Washington DC—

This Travel Warning updates information on the security situation and reminds Americans of the risks of travel to the Philippines. Terrorist groups and radical insurgents continue to plan multiple attacks throughout the Philippines. This Travel Warning supersedes the Travel Warning for the Philippines dated March 23, 2005.

The Department of State urges American citizens to consider carefully the risks of travel to the Philippines and continues to warn against all but essential travel throughout the country in light of heightened threats to Westerners. The Department also continues to urge Americans who choose to travel to the Philippines to observe vigilant personal security precautions, and to remain aware of the continued potential for terrorist attacks, including those against U.S. citizens..... (http://manila.usembassy.gov/wwwhtr25.html)

Countering this negative publicity is a daunting, often frustrating, task for Philippine government officials, especially those who work at diplomatic postings abroad. Who in his right mind would take the risk of going to Manila or Cebu as an investor, more so a tourist?

Yet, over the last ten years, whenever I board flights from San Francisco to Manila, Manila to Tokyo, Singapore to Manila, Los Angeles to Manila, Manila to Hong Kong, Dubai to Manila, or Manila to Kuwait, they are fully booked—almost year round! Most of the passengers are Filipino. My travel agent told me that there is no such thing as peak or low travel season anymore. State Department warnings notwithstanding, the number of foreign visitor arrivals to the Philippines have not gone down. Planes were full even at the height of the global economic downturn or the swine flu pandemic.

Eight months after the June 2006 State Department travel warning, San Francisco, California Mayor Gavin Newsom and a 140-member delegation went on a goodwill and business mission to Manila, San Francisco's sister city. All of them were U.S. citizens; more than half of them were Filipino Americans. Despite the official federal government advisory and repeated warnings, Newsom chose to heed the credible assessment of Dennis Normandy, a Filipino American who chairs the multi-sectoral, multi-ethnic San Francisco-Manila Sister City Commission. Normandy reassured the mayor that travel to the Philippines was safe, a view echoed by the FilAm (short for Filipino American) community in San Francisco.

Newsom's delegation included FilAm municipal government officials and representatives of major multinational companies, such as General Motors, Orrick Sutcliff, Citibank, LexisNexis, Stanford Hotels, New Bridge Capital, and Costco. There were also FilAm delegates from the University of California, San Francisco Symphony, AsianWeek newspaper, and a group of doctors.

The mayor and his San Francisco-Manila Sister City delegation brought with them 180 wheelchairs for distribution to Manila's physically challenged and a US$10,000 cheque for the Philippine Philharmonic Orchestra. There was little coordination with the U.S. Embassy in Manila and the State Department in Washington, DC. The San Francisco-Manila Sister City Commission communicated directly with the Philippine Departments of Tourism and Foreign Affairs as well as the Manila Mayor's Office.

[Thirty eight cities from all over the Philippines have opted for "town twinning" or "sister city" with more than 100 global cities, from Angeles City's ties with Las Vegas, to Zamboanga City's link with Zaragosa (Spain). Manila maintains 16 other sister cities partnerships besides San Francisco.]

The following summer, I visited my alma mater, De La Salle University on Taft Avenue in Manila, to listen to the visiting Assistant Secretary of State for East Asian and the Pacific Affairs Christopher Hill speak on "US-RP trade and military partnerships" before a packed conference room. I found his talk thoroughly disappointing. Filled with technical facts and figures that could be easily downloaded from the U.S. Embassy or the CIA Factbook website, Hill did not mention anything about Filipino Americans, even though his office had just released a report estimating that there were four million of us. Are U.S. officials in Washington really this out-of-touch with reality?

After his speech, I stood up and politely pointed out to Hill the significance of exchanges such as San Francisco-Manila Sister City ties and reminded him about the gargantuan role FilAms have been playing in U.S. public diplomacy. He agreed and thanked me. I suspect that after the talk, the Assistant Secretary of State may have fired his speechwriter or, at least, given that person a tongue lashing.

How international relations have moved away from how U.S. government technocrats see it to the way Filipinos in the diaspora are influencing and recasting the practice of diplomacy, is the focus of this book. It discusses the remarkable and untapped soft power that international migrants possess and how governments, non-governmental organizations (NGO), business, and international organizations could tap into this valuable resource to enhance international cooperation and development. Through the narratives of the experiences of the large Philippine diaspora, I examine how this widespread community performs numerous acts of public diplomacy that bridge the distance between their homeland and their adopted home countries.

The need for more aggressive international relations for developing states

Why should diplomacy through diaspora be a concern for scholars and practitioners of international relations? The answer is simple: there are over 200 million migrants in the world and mainstream theories of international relations have not adequately explained their role and influence in global ties, particularly in terms of their soft power. Very few international relations textbooks take this phenomenon seriously.

Moving away from the norm, Mayor Gavin Newsom of San Francisco, California, relied on what he viewed as more accurate and realistic advice from his city's Filipino migrants to travel to Manila over mainstream media exaggerations and State Department warnings. Ironically, international relations theory and practice continue to point to the supposed pragmatism of hard power—large military presence, high GNPs, and so forth—which developing diaspora states, such as the Philippines, do not have. What the Philippines offers, however, are the on-the-ground and culturally sensitive knowledge from its army of millions of Filipino migrants in diaspora.

What I am exposing and consequently espousing, is **diaspora diplomacy**, a more aggressive international relations path for developing states, which supersedes the dominant and America-centered focused ideas that eminent Harvard professor Joseph S. Nye, Jr. promotes in his influential work, *Soft Power: The Means to Success in World Politics*. Professor Nye and many other western scholars already provide excellent policy guidance for President

Barack Obama, Secretary of State Hillary Clinton, and Secretary of Defense Robert Gates on how America currently utilizes soft power and the continuing relevance of multilateralism.

Other political theorists point out why America should use soft power instead of hard power, particularly in combating terrorism. Another group discusses the best practices of soft power and policy suggestions from America's many European allies, especially the United Kingdom. Not to be out-thought, a number of reputable Washington, DC and London foreign policy think-tanks have come out with suggestions on how to channel American soft power and public diplomacy to winning the "hearts and minds" of Islamic states and the Middle East region. More recently, Nye argues that the smart soft power leadership of famous individuals like Winston Churchill, Lee Iacocca, Lyndon Johnson, and Jack Welch is what the world needs.

Is there a role for the more than five million Americans in diaspora in [the government's] shift from a hard- to soft power approach? It is still unclear. Professor Nye is presently distracted by his new role as U.S. Ambassador to Japan. I believe, however, that the hundreds of millions of migrant construction workers, engineers, chefs, nurses, nannies, entertainers, doctors, bankers and so on, have had a significant effect on not just economic globalization but on averting a clash of politics and cultures. Migrants, as pastors, imams, monks, congregants, task managers, and association presidents, have shown themselves to be respectful leaders and patriotic followers. They do not have to head name-brand companies or be famous politicians.

My perspective and objective in writing this book deviates from the arguments of Professor Nye, et al., as well as the influential Washington, DC-based Public Diplomacy Council, the Institute of World Politics, the London-based Foreign Policy Center, and many others. They focus too much on how a hegemon -- its leaders and state apparatus -- should reinvent and soften themselves. Unlike them, I seek to make temporary or permanent, document or undocumented migrants more visible to the theory and practice of international relations by showing how migrants already do public diplomacy — creating inter-faith harmony, occupational stability, and civic-minded associations in destination countries through sustained non-combative, consensual, and peaceful ways. Thereafter, I make recommendations for the soft empowerment of both developing as well as developed countries. After all, there may also be useful and humbling lessons for my American homeland from perceived marginal global players – like Filipino chefs in London, Filipino parishioners in Dhaka, Filipino basketball players in Dubai, Filipino students in San Francisco, and Filipino domestic helpers in Singapore – in the international system.

Soft power has received a mix of serious and not so serious attention from politics and government scholars in the past. In my international relations classes in the Philippines in the 1980s, Reaganism and Thatcherism were the way forward; the rest of the world was expected to follow. Hard power theories touting coercions and threats were in. To American and British foreign policy pundits, hard power was what brought down the Berlin Wall, therefore it was the most effective approach.

In the classroom, my professors made sure that we immersed in the classical schools of realism, liberalism, and idealism. They wanted us to understand the harsh global context of our less influential, developing nation state particularly under these hard power conditions. It did not matter to them that these concepts were too western-centered, thus the wrong analytical fit. What was more important to my early mentors was that we knew the games nations played, who made the rules, and most of all, that our country was a tiny fish in a large pond.

Given this bleak scenario, we always wondered if it was even possible for our diplomats and government officials to coerce and threaten countries, especially the powerful ones. What type of diplomacy should we craft to make this possible? After I graduated from college, I realized that the first question should actually be: is it even feasible for just any Filipino to go abroad? Whoever said that we live in a borderless world has not tried traveling on a Philippine passport. Like many who come from developing countries, entering another country is challenging. I never really thought it was possible for me, given my family's financial situation. But my international relations classes made me dream of a job in the elite Philippine Foreign Service corps.

In the real world, there is hierarchy of passports just like there were the "haves and have nots" in my old Manila neighborhood. As a citizen of a "small fish" country, getting a foreign visa meant having to show the foreign consuls substantial bank deposits as proof that I had no plans to stay illegally. I felt I was being treated as a guilty person until I was able to prove otherwise. When I finally got to leave, I was always intimidated when approaching immigration counters. To make matters worse, my non-machine-readable brown passport guaranteed extra scrutiny. Some culturally challenged immigration officers even asked why a person who looked "Chinese" could have a very Spanish name. Besides passports, nobody outside the country accepted my Philippine pesos. It was like I was holding on to Mickey Mouse or Monopoly play money. To be recognized overseas, I needed to buy international currencies, particularly the almighty U.S. dollar. Fifty pesos for every dollar!

Ironically, my frustrating experience with this discriminatory international context took an unexpected turn after I traveled on an all-expenses paid junket to Libya, my first overseas trip. Upon my return from North Africa, a Fulbright exchange scholarship to a university in the U.S. was waiting for me.

At my American graduate school, I was exposed to more international relations concepts, among them, neorealism, neoliberalism, constructivism, feminism, this time from the belly of the hegemon. After completing my advanced studies, I finally got to do real field missions for bilateral and multilateral governmental and nongovernmental agencies before settling into an academic career.

I did a teaching stint in cosmopolitan Singapore where I was made to feel inferior by rich Asians whose main interaction with Filipinos was as their domestic helpers. Eventually, I became a U.S. permanent resident, then a U.S. citizen, and then a public official sworn to defend the U.S. Constitution after the horrific attacks of 9/11. I started using a blue passport and was no longer required a visa to enter almost any country in the world, rich or poor. I also started earning in U.S. dollars. What a difference! Nevertheless, like many migrants, half of me continued to be intrigued by the basic survival tactics and influence of millions of brown passport holders which included kin and friends. After all, I am both a Filipino and an American.

Through the decades I remain fascinated by those basic precepts of international relations, this time as a teacher and now a citizen of an influential nation-state. From my California vantage point, it is relatively easy to make young minds understand the global affairs and policies of the U.S., a situation very different from when I was a student in Manila. As Americans, we dictate the tempo of global relations. I was now part of the "big fish." Now, I wondered how these analytical frameworks were going to help American scholars and practitioners understand international ties driven by a diaspora of millions from the developing world particularly the Philippines. It became my personal and professional mission to find answers.

My concept of diaspora diplomacy is rooted in my reflections on the applicability of the principles of international relations to the global outlook of the developing world. Poor countries really have no choice but to exercise soft power. Let me tell you why.

Political realism and hard power

Political realism is the core of hard power. What pragmatic international policy prescription does realism have for developing countries like Ecuador, Botswana, Cambodia, or states with small armies and serious balance of payments issues? From the classic realist writings of Sun Tzu and his *Art of War*, Thucydides' *History of the Peloponnesian War*, E. H. Carr's *The Twenty Year's Crisis*, and Hans Morgenthau's *Politics Among Nations*, one learns from the experiences of China, the U.S. and the other great powers that the world is filled with "chaos" and "anarchy," where nation-state survival underlies the quest for increased security through military and economic power. A hegemonic stance needs to be the ultimate goal of every territory.

In basketball, this translates to the play, "offense is the best defense." Unlike basketball, however, where dominating is as simple as getting the 7-foot, 325-pound behemoth Shaquille O'Neal near the basket to score and sow fear among defenders, multiple hegemons create a situation of bipolarity or multipolarity. The realist policy prescription therefore to countries big or small is: nurture a sizable army and a robust GNP. But a large majority of the other supposed players in the international system, including developing nations such as Ecuador, Botswana, and Cambodia, will neither have the tanks and missiles nor the hefty budget surpluses to play this realist game and thus will be relegated to watching on the sidelines. The Philippines realized this when China, which always had a hegemonic claim on anything in the South China Seas, created permanent structures on Kalayaan Islands. The Philippine government could only sit back helplessly and watch.

Neorealists, like Kenneth Waltz in *Man, State, and War*, offered a slight amendment to classic realism's core thought by believing that states' actions can be better explained by the pressures of global competition, which limits and constrains their choices. Economically, developing nations are not naïve to the fact that the rules of global competition are stacked in favor of wealthy countries and their exclusive clubs like the 30-member Organisation for Economic Co-operation and Development (OECD). In terms of security, United Nations action is determined by the Security Council which is controlled by the veto-wielding permanent five: China, the U.S., France, Russia, and the United Kingdom. Thus, developing countries only have insignificant, hardly competitive roles in the international system.

Neorealism confirms that countries such as Nepal, Burundi, Jamaica, the Philippines, Vanuatu, Syria and their cohorts are in the competitive global arena but these less developed economies will be the ones wiping the sweat off the back of gladiators who have the military and economic prowess that will determine the fate of geographic regions and even the entire planet. Nicaragua, Mali, Bangladesh, East Timor, Macedonia, or even the United Arab Emirates will not have any military or economic capacity to join this "power balancing" fray. Realist concepts such as détente, containment, and nonproliferation are not meaningful to them. The eight years of the Bush Administration were spent pursuing America's global "War on Terrorism" which has hammered *real politik* bluntly to developing countries—if you are not with us then you are against us!

The inadequacies of realism and neorealism lead to liberalism, which offers a better hope for those in search of a more comfortable developing country framework from scholars of international relations. Advocates of liberalism argue that the global anarchy and resulting state insecurity, which realism exaggerates for its convenience as a crucial theoretical jump off point, actually creates the necessary preconditions for the formation of cooperative norms, regimes, and institutions. In *Power and Interdependence: World Politics in Transition* and in many of their publications thereafter, neoliberals Robert Keohane and Joseph Nye posit that cultural and economic cooperation are the keys to an interdependent world where not only state but also non-state and sub-state actors are recognized as important players in the international system. Non-state or sub-state actors include influential leaders, nongovernmental organizations, and multinational corporations. These transnational actors together with state actors create a complex web of formal and informal connections and ties leading to global integration.

Although neoliberalism seems a more realistic description of the complex interdependence among international actors than what realism provides, it still does not fit snuggly with the political, economic, and social situations in most developing countries. Hard power still seems to be the bottom line.

The entrepreneurs and citizens of Tajikistan, Estonia, Chad, Colombia, Iraq, or Burma have neither the investment capacity to breed multinational corporations, such as Starbucks, McDonalds, Saab, Sony, and Nokia, nor the expansive resources to spawn NGOs, such as the Bill and Melinda Gates Foundation, Asia Foundation, Amnesty International, Freidrich Neuman Stiftung, and World Wildlife Fund. And even if they are able to be competitive domestically, there is no guarantee that they will survive the rougher global market. The Asian tiger economies are plausible breeding grounds for these competitive civil society and business actors but they are more the exception than the rule. Memberships in international nongovernmental organizations (INGO) and intergovernmental organizations (IGO) give voice to developing countries but the power and influence remain in the hands of the G-8 or the Global North.

Most importantly, even though neoliberalism elucidates on the significance of transnational actors to global affairs, it fails to take into account the transnational linkages and networks through contemporary migration. Nowadays, discussions of transnationalism in international relations are dominated by economic or corporate globalization. The global supply chain and same-product-brand consumption connect the world. Comparatively, migrations enable transnational connections that are somewhat different from business entities and NGOs.

Peace studies, feminism, constructivism, postmodernism, and Marxism present alternative views to realism and liberalism's overall suggestion of crafting policies around either political security or economic cooperation. However, they too manifest deficiencies. For instance, Marxism and the world systems theorists argued that just like human societies, global societies are class-structured. Thus rich countries are at the core of global politics and production, and poor countries are at the periphery. How then do poor countries free themselves from this structural arrangement? Marxists prescribe that all the poor countries unite. Such unity, however, is hindered by the economics, cultures, and politics of many developing countries which are tied to core countries through their elite, upper-class surrogates. Rich classes in both developed and developing countries are able to communicate and collaborate via air travel, long distance phone calls, and the internet. The poor classes in developing countries are not able to unite since they do not have the money to exchange information. When considering alternative views of global relations, what then is the role of diaspora members coming from the lower strata of society who are bridging poor-class to poor-class disconnection?

Is there hope from new variances of idealism? Like liberalism, classic idealism sees states as capable of rational and peace-building behavior as opposed to realism which looks at states as irrational, power-hungry actors. It is based on the universally agreed upon code of international ethics, morality, law, human rights, nonviolence and the core assumption that states with similar democratic philosophies do not fight one another. Scholar-politician Woodrow Wilson was one of its proponents, along with Gandhi, Bertrand Russell, and Henri de Saint. Filipino martyrs like Jose Rizal and Benigno Aquino Jr., who inspired nonviolent campaigns against social injustices and authoritarian regimes, belong to the same genre.

Idealism helped propel American public diplomacy that created the United States Information Agency (USIA), the United States Agency for International Development (USAID), and the Peace Corps. Public diplomacy employs peaceful and nonviolent approaches to international affairs and aid. For more than four decades, USIA ran a variety of programs (or propaganda) ranging from Voice of America, to symposia, lectures, study tours, summits, exhibitions, to library donations, and to the Fulbright Hays educational and cultural exchange scholarships, before it was downgraded and merged with the U.S. State Department in 1999. Public diplomacy, however, is still soft power as advocated by the U.S. State Department.

In the last decades, the theory and practice of public diplomacy expanded to encompass the power and influence of television, sports, the internet, pop icons, movies, songs, food, information, and commercial products. Theoretically, this equates to the cross-breeding between neoliberalism and idealism-formed neoidealism. As a result, Americanization and

McDonaldization or "international political marketing" and "place branding" have become synonymous terms.

Hollywood is also considered to be a big contributor to American soft power. In the past, indigenous religions such as Buddhism and Hinduism were the main staples of the "big three civilizations" of Asia—India, China, and Japan—but recently, civil society groups have supplemented these Asianizing religious soft power approaches with "Bollywood", "Confucius Institutes", and other "charm offensives." But what about developing countries that do not have the technological sophistication and bank accounts to internationally advertise, market, and popularize its culture and society? Their only recourse is to exert their soft power as exporters of temporary and permanent migrants who spread their national culture globally as unwitting public diplomats.

Soft Power and Developing Countries

Based on the growing literature, and from my studies and experiences, I was able to discern three streams of thought on how a developing country's soft power and influence could be theorized and practiced: internationalism, transnationalism, and diasporism.

Internationalism, the classic approach, continues to be beholden to most western scholarship and their hard power advocates. With armies and GNP still in the forefront, they wish to encourage internationalism through tedious and bureaucratic formal ties between national governments and international organizations respecting state borders but at the same time using supranationality.

Another strategy, heavily influenced by migration specialists, is to accept transnationalism which is the use of formal and informal political, social, and economic linkages between and among non-state and sub-national actors transcending nation state boundaries.

My own participant observation elucidates a third approach -- diasporism, from cultural studies, which is driven mainly by individuals and communities in diaspora, through their chosen faiths, occupations, and associations. In practice, diasporism intersperses with national government's internationalization efforts as well as business' and NGOs' transnationalization initiatives. While migrants from developing countries must first face restrictive international borders, once they are able to incorporate and settle in, they become conduits of ethnic influence and diplomatic relations for their country of origin—soft power in action.

Diasporism has been going on for centuries so its sociological character has evolved through time. From Asia, the most pervasive ones have been the Chinese and Indian diasporas which have been forming overseas communities for thousands of years, outlasting the European and Arab ones. Present-day diasporas emanate from new sources in Africa, Latin America, Europe, and Asia. They are most visible in ethnic enclaves in global cities.

A high ranking United Arab Emirates official appeases the liberal Philippine media.

CHAPTER 2

The Philippine Diaspora and Its Role in International Relations

Why is the Philippine diaspora important to the study of contemporary international relations and diplomacy? Because, as alluded to earlier, it is one of the fastest growing and thus one of the most significant soft power movements in the world today. In the last century alone, the Philippine diaspora nation has grown to more than 8.5 million strong in 182 countries, while over a quarter of a million seafarers (one-quarter of the world's total) are plying the planet's oceans and seas. Filipinos live, work, socialize and worship in more than a thousand cities and ships. The aggregated diaspora population is twice the size of New Zealand's and is equivalent to the total population of Switzerland.

Its economic influence is quite significant. In 2007, Filipino migrants remitted more than US$ 14 billion, which is the equivalent of Afghanistan's Gross Domestic Product (GDP) and more than the national income of 63 developing economies. That same year, overseas Filipinos also shipped more than one million balikbayan boxes (care packages) all over the archipelago. The U.S. accounts for one quarter of the migrant stock and half the total remittance and balikbayan box volume. There are one million Filipino workers in the Kingdom of Saudi Arabia. From the high seas, hardworking Filipino officers and engineers, deck and engine crew, on all kinds of commercial cargo ships, tankers, cruise liners, and some U.S. military vessels sent back to their families in 200 hometowns more than US$2.2 billion in 2007. Their remittances have insulated the country from the global economic crisis, growing at a 3.7 percent rate in 2008. In essence, the diaspora has become the Philippines' WMD or Wealth from Massive Dispersion.

Besides the U.S., Figure 2.1 shows the accumulating number of Philippine diaspora diplomats and their remittance contributions from the United Kingdom, United Arab Emirates, Bangladesh, and Singapore vis-à-vis selected regions of the world. Their non-monetary influences will be highlighted in the succeeding chapters.

Figure 2.1: Philippine diaspora diplomatic corps and their foreign remittance impact

(2007, in thousands, U.S. $)

	Number of diplomats	Remittance volume
By case countries		
United States	2,802,586	6,179,656
United Kingdom	203,035	597,572
United Arab Emirates	529,114	519,754
Bangladesh	976	98
Singapore	156,466	320,853
By selected regions		
North America	3,653,007	8,244,349
Europe	953,519	2,351,691
Middle East	2,181,579	2,172,417
East and South Asia	1,219,445	1,543,180
Total 182 countries		
All land-based	8,459,967	12,213,565
All sea-based	266,553	2,236,363
All land and sea-based	8,726,520	14,449,928

Note: Single country and regions, land-based only. Because of foreign currency outflow restrictions, most of Bangladesh remittances are channeled via Hong Kong.

Source: Remittance estimates are from Bangko Sentral ng Pilipinas (Central Bank of the Philippines), stock estimates are from Philippine Overseas Employment Agency (POEA).

Five decades of continuous out-migration, along with their second- and third-generation descendants and networks, have become the core of Philippine diaspora diplomacy. In every international city I visited—from Tripoli in Northern Africa to Sydney in Australia, from Vienna in Europe to Kuwait in the Middle East -- I was able to talk to Filipinos. They have more community gathering places, both informal and formal, than Philippine diplomatic missions. They are most visible in churches and other places of worship. During my visits to Melbourne and Sydney, I discovered that the Philippines is the fifth largest source of new migrants in Australia behind the United Kingdom, New Zealand, China, and India. In 2007, Philippine Overseas Employment Agency estimated that there are 462,935 temporary and permanent migrants in the land Down Under. When I visited my Filipino Canadian brother, Jing, and his family in Toronto, I learned that the Filipino community in Canada has grown to close to half a million. In Vienna, I learned from the Philippine Embassy that there are more than 60 registered Philippine social, cultural, professional, and political organizations servicing more than 30,000 migrants.

The Filipino diaspora started out as a drizzle in the 1980s and then turned into pouring rain in the 1990s. The turn of the millennium ushered in a flood of books about the Philippine diaspora in the U.S. and in other parts of the world, radically shifting the theme of Philippine and Filipino/a studies writings in the past that had been dominated by political, economic, and other hard power concerns. These new books include: R. Bonus' *Locating Filipino Americans: Ethnicity and the Cultural Politics of Space* (2000), V. Rafael's *White Love and Other Events in Filipino History* (2000), C. Choy's *Empire of Care: Nursing and Migration in Filipino American History* (2003), Y. L. Espiritu's *Home Bound: Filipino American Lives Across Cultures* (2003), E. N. Ignacio's *Building Diaspora: Filipino Cultural Community Formation on the Internet* (2005), M. Manalansan's *Global Divas: Filipino Gay Men in the Diaspora* (2003), and B. Vergara's *Pinoy Capital: The Filipino Nation in Daly City* (2009).

Sociologist R. Parreñas' *Servants of Globalization: Women, Migration, and Domestic Work* (2001) and *The Force of Domesticity: Filipina Migrants and Globalization* (2008), went beyond the America-centeredness by focusing on her sociological sorties among Filipina domestic helpers in Rome, Italy and Filipina entertainers in Tokyo, Japan. Her latest work updates T. Osteria's *Filipino Female Labor Migration to Japan: Economic Causes and Consequences* and N. Constables' *Maid to Order in Hong Kong: Stories of Filipina Workers* which were pioneering books published more than a decade ago.

My book, *Philippine Labour Migration: Critical Dimensions of Public Policy* (1998) began with a section on Philippine-Singapore relations and ended with the need for more soft power ties. Aside from these books, extensive scholarly research on Philippine soft power relations and migration in other parts of the world, particularly the United Kingdom, the United Arab Emirates, Bangladesh, and Singapore (which I cover in this book), has been sparse. Conceptually, most scholars take off from economic, sociological, anthropological, and historical perspectives; from a political science perspective, no one has looked at the diaspora from the soft power argument and framework I have chosen.

What is lacking in scholarly literature is made up for by Philippine diaspora movies, such as "Debut," "Dubai," "Milan," "Miss Pinoy," "The Flor Contemplacion Story," "The Sarah Balabagan Story," "Love Me Again (Land Down Under)," "Japayuki: Maricris Sioson Story," and "Caregiver." These movies reveal to a broader audience how Filipinos and Filipinas in the diaspora influence the countries they work in and the social costs of their sacrifices to their families back home.

Diaspora Diplomacy, Philippine style

Philippine diaspora diplomacy is people-propelled rather than product- or propaganda driven. It is the collective action of Filipinos emanating from various geographic locations and organizations.

Diaspora diplomacy enables the Philippines and other diaspora states to influence another country's culture, politics, and economics. Dual citizenship legislation which allows dual loyalties, in effect, institutionalized dual influencing. Public policies nurturing diaspora diplomacy allows the Philippines to be smart and aggressive without being hegemonic and arrogant. Realists write about the exercise of hard power such as mutually assured destruction (MAD). Diaspora diplomacy, on the other hand, is the launch of Weapons of Mass Dispersion and achieving a different form of MAD, More Acceptable Diplomacy. Thus, the Americanization and Anglicanization of Manila by U.S. and British franchises are counterbalanced by the Filipinization of certain segments of mainstream societies in San Francisco and London. For example, Filipino diaspora members successfully lobbied mainstream politicians for markers to honor the Philippine national hero, Dr. Jose Rizal, in public parks in Seattle, Washington, Singapore, and Wilhelmsfeld, Germany.

The primary driver of diaspora diplomacy is home and family. To many Filipino migrants, however, the structure of home and family have become complicated. A typical household may now include, aside from the basic family unit of spouses and children, siblings and in-laws, uncles and aunts grandparents, nieces and nephews, and grandchildren. But it could also extend outwards to friends, strangers, churches, charities, hometown associations and other organizations. Household income generation is based on this extended kinship structure; each family member of legal age is expected to contribute to household expenses which may include the education of the children, the medical expenses of grandparents, and mortgage.

Beyond the home, extra income can help rehabilitate or construct schools, chapels, and roads in the Philippines. Migrants accomplish their family obligations while at the same time contributing to the betterment of their homeland. Given these extended meanings of household and income, it is not surprising to see Filipino migrants consider their churches as part of their families. Many feel that they are being sent out to the world as church members who need to spread the word of God so they assume such roles as pastors, lay workers, bible readers and choir singers, among others.

Governments of developing countries with very limited budgets for bilateral relations are able to outsource their diplomatic functions to migrants who share their culture to the societies where they live and work. The Philippines has 87 diplomatic missions and opened seven more in 2009, but these still does not cover the more than 2,000 cities globally where Filipinos are present. Thus, Filipino migrants have taken up the role of ambassadors of Filipino culture and traditions. Through their many organizations, they assist in diplomacy by working independently or alongside efforts by the Philippine diplomatic corps. Since migrant workers use time outside of work and church to socialize and interact with the "locals" in their adopted countries. They contribute to the cultural sophistication and diversity of the latter through their religious events, musical groups, sports tournaments, and the like.

Filipino migrants highlight the importance of non-state actors and their networks in marketing Filipino culture and know-how, side-by-side with official diplomatic missions. Since the passage of the Migrant Workers and Overseas Filipinos Act of 1995 (Republic Act or RA 8042), diplomacy has been outsourced to the millions of Filipino migrants, now in more than 150 countries. Given the large outflow, Filipino migrant settlements, overseas franchises, and community centers have grown to outnumber Philippine diplomatic posts and honorary consulates. Thus, in varying degrees, Filipino migrants and their organizations have, in many cases, a greater impact than the Philippine government on the politics, economics, and societies of their host countries.

These migrants have also improved tourism in their homeland. Increased tourist arrivals do not happen by accident, as illustrated in Figure 2.2. According to my best friend, Benito Bengzon, a high-ranking official at the Philippine Department of Tourism, the Filipino diaspora's soft power has definitely contributed to the growth of tourist arrivals into the country despite U.S. State Department travel warnings. No wonder the Philippines was voted the "2009 Most Popular Destination in Asia" at the World Travel Fair in Shanghai, China.

Figure 2.2
Top ten country tourist arrivals, 2008

Rank	Country	Number	Market share
1	Korea	611,629	19.48%
2	United States	578,246	18.42%
3	Japan	359,306	11.44%
4	China	163,689	5.21%
5	Australia	121,514	3.87%
6	Taiwan	118,782	3.78%
7	Hong Kong	116,653	3.72%
8	Canada	102,381	3.26%
9	Singapore	100,177	3.19%
10	United Kingdom	87,422	2.78%

Source: Philippine Department of Tourism, 2008.

A Changed Diplomatic Corps

Before the passage of RA 8042, the basic function of Philippine diplomacy was to promote the economic, political, cultural, and consular interests of the republic. Foreign Service Officers (FSOs), Foreign Service Staff Officers (FSSOs), and Foreign Service Staff Employees (FSSEs) comprised a very snobbish, elite corps that associated only with the same snobbish, elite Filipino expatriate community, the powerful local politicians and the wealthy socialites in their country of posting. Eating with Filipina domestic helpers at a park was unglamorous to them. Many felt they had earned this diplomatic stature since they had passed a rigorous Foreign Service Officers exam. When posted overseas, they received all the diplomatic courtesies and immunities of the host country, and earn 10 times more than their civil service counterparts in the Philippines. They traveled on diplomatic passports which automatically got visas and paid no taxes to the host government based on reciprocity agreements and treaties. They were detached from the bulk of the diaspora except through routine consular work -- passport renewals, repatriation requests, and visits to the jailed. But Philippine Republic Act 8042 changed the nature of their ritzy, glitzy lifestyle.

I was teaching at the National University of Singapore when the event that triggered the passage of the law occurred. It became clear to me during those times that diaspora has a direct effect on international relations, even close ones between ASEAN (Association of Southeast Asian Nations) partners.

Flor Contemplacion, a Filipina domestic helper in Singapore, was hanged for the double murder of a fellow care worker and the Singaporean child she was caring for. Doubts about Flor's culpability led to a serious diplomatic row between the Philippines and Singapore. This will be analyzed more extensively in the Singapore chapter.

There were allegations that the Philippine government did not do enough to defend and protect her because she was "just a maid." Flor symbolized the plight of the millions of Filipino diaspora diplomats that needed better care, protection, and social safety nets. She was looked at as a martyr. In the wake of the controversy, the Secretary of Foreign Affairs of the Philippines resigned. The Philippine Congress responded with RA 8042. From then on, a series of diaspora-friendly measures were enacted.

In 1997, a Comprehensive Tax Reform Law was passed exempting the income earned by overseas Filipinos from Philippine taxation. Overseas Filipinos gained an elected representative in the Philippine Congress. Overseas absentee voting, retirement incentives, and dual citizenship laws were also enacted formalizing a Filipino global nation. Consequently, the Philippines has become the largest labor, faith, and cultural exporter among the ten ASEAN member states.

Philippine Diaspora Diplomacy and the "Filipinization" of Global Cities

The force of Philippine diaspora diplomacy comes from its capacity to influence, charm, persuade, and assert, in order to solidify ties. It is not meant to dominate, but is instead creating two-way, open, consensual, and respectful relations.

In my two decades of living in the U.S., I have been studying how this evolving "Filipinization" process facilitates transnational integration, adaptive spirit and inter-generational cohesion. If Americanization is the output of U.S. public diplomacy internationally, then varying degrees of Filipinization results from Philippine diaspora diplomacy in global cities. Our ethnic visibility through our local businesses, media, arts, pop culture and other public spheres are some of the manifestations of success.

In this book, Filipinization is defined as the process by which temporary and permanent Philippine migrants' worship, get together, and earn money in their adopted country (*kasamahan*) and how they help each other, contribute to their new communities, and assist their families and hometowns in the Philippines (*bayanihan*).

Filipinization by kasamahan involves mostly inward-focused kinship. This includes forming formal and informal groups, such as a Filipino church choir, prayer or bible study group, bingo socials, mahjong sessions, and regional societies leading to communal feelings of togetherness, companionship, fraternity, sisterhood, solidarity, pride, and competitiveness.

Filipinization by bayanihan is the predominantly outward-oriented linkages, associations, bridges, and connections. These involve transforming kasamahan to encompass volunteer activities, civic involvement, community partnerships, political advocacy, protest marches, clean-up drives, money remittance, disaster relief work, donating and fundraising. Filipinization may be more pervasive in some countries than others depending on many factors including number of migrants, their status and standing, and homeland or home base context.

Filipino migrant communities globally adapt varying forms of bayanihan and kasamahan to deepen their soft power influences and consequently, convert them into meaningful religious, economic, and political participation. I categorize Filipinization further into three types: (1) religious Filipinization or the bayanihan and kasamahan influences emanating from churches or places of worship, as well as spiritual energy, passion, action, and advocacy; (2) occupational Filipinization or the bayanihan and kasamahan influences associated with their work, labor, English proficiency, inter-personal communication skills, formal education, informal training as well as the sending care boxes or remitting money; and (3) associational Filipinization or the bayanihan and kasamahan influences that come from their participation in cultural shows, organizations, Philippine independence day commemorations, and informal gatherings.

Sociologically, many western scholars view the Philippines as a paternalistic society and see these soft power influences as driven by the Filipino migrants' extended patriarchal relations with their church, their country, and their hometown. This was validated recently in a March 2009 exchange I had with the eminent sociologist of migration, Saskia Sassen, at a University of San Francisco conference on "Religion and Globalization in Asia." I wanted to remind Professor Sassen of three facts that prove the Philippines seems to be more a matriarchal society. First, the Philippine electorate through a direct vote has twice entrusted the highest political office in the land to two women. Second, half of the Philippine overseas migrants are women who are the breadwinners of their families. Third, the Filipina wives of overseas workers control the bank account and household budgeting.

Instead of simple patriarchy or matriarchy, what I observed in my global sojourns was that migrants' lives are consciously or subconsciously guided by a more complex web of religious, occupational, and associational relationships based on *utang na loob* (debt of gratitude) to church (*simbahan*), hometown/ province (*bayan/probinsiya*), and families (*pamilya*). These are reflected in the many sayings that Filipino migrants have internalized and repeated to me during our talks.

Many Filipino migrants emphasized to me that faith and prayers helped in every step of the migration process and they show their gratitude to God by going to and supporting their churches in their adopted countries and back home. Their religious behavior is guided by the saying, *"nasa Dios ang awa, nasa tao ang gawa."* God sympathizes, but it is up to people to do the work.

Others told me that they work hard to be able to pay a debt of gratitude to the place where they come from and the country they now live or work in. Some added that their occupational drive is founded on, *"Ang hindi marunong lumingon sa pinanggalingan ay hindi makakarating sa paroroonan."* A person who forgets where he comes from will not get to where he wants to go.

Most of them said that they are very open to adapting to a new culture and language, but also like to share with non-Filipinos the love they have for their family traditions and native language. *"Ang hindi marunong magmahal sa sariling wika ay higit pa ang amoy sa mabahong isda."* He who doesn't know how to love his own language smells worse than a pungent fish.

Religious Filipinization: Influencing Through Spirit and Action

Globally, churches are the most visible spaces influenced by Philippine migrant soft power. Catholic, Protestant, Evangelical, and Independent churches see Christian migrants as church planters, missionaries, or tentmakers (from the fact that the apostle Paul supported himself by making tents while living and preaching). Overseas Filipino workers (OFWs) and overseas Filipino immigrants (OFI), are able spread the word of Jesus Christ and showcase their Christian faith where formal religious missions and professional missionaries have failed or are unable to go and work effectively. Geographically, Philippine migrants are able to highlight Christianity in under-evangelized areas, referred to by Christian tentmaker ministries as the critical 10/40 corridor, covering Northwest Africa, the Middle East, South Asia, and Southeast Asia.

In the many countries where they have settled, Filipinos recognize faith and spirituality as their anchor and source of kasamahan and bayanihan soft power. They use churches for their missionary diplomacy—spreading their faiths and practices. They bring with them their religion-reinforced Filipino traits and actions, such as *samba* (worship), *dasal* (prayer), *panata* (vow), *bahala na* (leave it up to God) fatalism, *utang na loob* (debt of gratitude), *pasalamat* (gratitude), *damay* (sympathy), *paggalang* (showing respect), *maawain* (being merciful), *mapagpatawad* (forgiving), *sakripisyo* (sacrifice), *matulungin* (helpful), lingkod (serve), *pagmamahal* (love), *pagbibigay* (giving), *maintindihin* (understanding), and *hiya* (shyness). I found Filipino migrants in the U.S. United Kingdom, United Arab Emirates, Bangladesh, and other countries transplanting their vibrant spiritual socialization and people power action from the Philippines. Not a big surprise, after all, democratic Philippines has the largest Christian population in Asia: 84 percent Roman Catholic, eight percent Protestant (mostly evangelical/Pentecostal), and three percent Iglesia Ni Cristo. Only three percent of the population is Muslim. The Philippines' El Shaddai is one of the fastest growing and influential Catholic charismatic groups in the world, according to *Time* and *AsiaWeek*.

I was not surprised when the 1991 International Social Survey Program reported that Filipinos are the most religious people in the world. In the Philippines, it is common to see worship, devotion, and prayer in many forms, in public or private places with no restrictions.

Filipinization through religious kasamahan is manifested in Filipino migrants' forming of churches, renewal of faith, introduction of new religious traditions, spreading of inter-faith respect, and praying and meditating in church or public spaces. Whether it's Novena Church in Singapore, Saint Abraham's in Tehran, Saint Remi in Brussels, San Agustin Church in

Barcelona, Westminster Catholic Cathedral in London, Saint Patrick's Church in San Francisco, Saint Joseph's Cathedral in Hanoi, Saint Ignatius Church in Tokyo, or Notre Dame Cathedral in Paris, every Saturday and Sunday, Filipino migrants help fill the pews.

Because of the more than 150,000 Filipinos in residence, Saint Joseph's in Hong Kong has three Tagalog masses every Sunday, and both English and Tagalog masses are packed. Very long lines form to get in every Sunday and once inside, it's standing room only. The church has a statue of San Lorenzo Ruiz, the first Filipino saint. The Filipino Catholic Chaplaincy has masses, bible studies and a conglomeration of inter-generational charismatic and devotional groups: Couples for Christ, Divine Mercy devotees, El Shaddai, Followers of the Good Shepherd, Lay Ministers, Legion of Mary, Mary, Mother of Christ, Music Ministry, Sacristans, and a Youth Group. Migrant Filipino priests and nuns were also there for their faithful in diaspora.

The Philippines' second largest church with close to two million members, the Iglesia ni Cristo is not too far behind in setting up congregations and worship services overseas. They are spreading the teachings of an independent Philippine Christian church through 97 ministries based in the U.S. and Canada, and 17 outside of North America. At the Daly City service I attended, it was standing room only.

Filipino evangelical groups are also making their presence felt in the various international cities, from the Filipino International Christian Church in Orlando, Florida, to the Victory Christian Fellowship in Dubai, United Arab Emirates. Spreading the word of God from a Filipino perspective has gone global with its many migrant diplomats.

Thus, Philippine migrants unconsciously become part of a global religious crusade, from Global South to Global North and from Christian states to non-Christian countries. Heralded by Popes as the "new apostles for the church," they are helping spread the word of God through their participation in Catholic, Protestant, and independent services and festivities in their host countries. They weave their own Filipino spiritual practices into these local faith communities through such strategies as the introduction of familiar iconography to Tagalog language services. This approach is a peaceful way to integrate Philippine culture into mainstream communities.

Ironically, modern-day Filipino sojourners bring with them to Europe and the U.S. their hybrid Hispanic, Anglo-Saxon, and indigenously inspired religious belief systems and spiritual practices that are the results of Spanish and American colonization. Through the church, a societal institution with which they are culturally comfortable, Filipino migrants are able to deal effectively with acculturative stress, assimilate culturally, and contribute social energy to the communities with which they come into contact. At the same time, their Filipinized churches have also become safe spaces for negotiating and challenging identity, ethnicity, and nationalism. Filipinized locations are where Filipino migrants have been encouraged and allowed by church leaders, some whom are Filipino and some not, but are willing to accommodate new styles to replenish membership numbers, to express Filipino-style Catholic, Charismatic, Evangelical, Masonic, independent, and even indigenous (baybaylan) spiritual practices, symbols, songs, dialects, chants, verses, etc. Therefore, Filipino migrants contribute to changes in the spiritual contours of global cities not only through their presence (e.g. by taking over empty churches) but also by their influence on local religious practices. As generations of Filipino parents, grandparents, children, siblings, grandchildren, and other relatives go back and forth, the practices, symbols, and songs also move back and forth from their hometown churches in the Philippines to their new churches.

But Philippine religious influence through their diaspora diplomats does not end with kasamahan. They normally render bayanihan by praying and meditating and then rendering civic action and volunteer work among the underprivileged and social injustices they face. I have seen Filipino diaspora diplomats meditate and then send money back to their families and help in the social, cultural, economic development of their hometowns. At the countries

I visited, I saw Filipino migrants replenish reduced memberships at American and Anglican Catholic and Protestant churches.

In the U.S., I attended the awareness raising and political action events organized by the activist Daly City United Methodist Church in San Francisco. Led by the fiery Filipino pastor, we were able to lobby successfully for U.S. Congressional hearings and United Nations human rights review of extra-judicial killings in the Philippines. The church organized a multi-faith service which galvanized Catholics and Evangelicals from all over the country.

From the more than 60 registered Filipino organizations in Austria, 14 were faith-oriented -- the Pandan Association in Austria (PAA), Antique Christian Community (ACC), Couples for Christ, First Filipino Bible Fellowship, Grace Church Filipino Christian Fellowship, Iglesia Ni Cristo, International Baptist Church of Vienna, Jesus is Lord Fellowship , Pfarre Saint Johann Kapistran (Philippine Sunday Mass), Sambayanan ng mga Pilipinong, Katoliko sa Vienna, Seventh Day Adventist, Vienna Christian Fellowship, Vienna Christian Center Filipino Fellowship, and Yahweh El Shaddai.

Occupational Filipinization: Influencing Through Mind and Money

Given their skills, training, education, work ethic, and English comprehension, Philippine migrants can greatly influence kasamahan and bayanihan occupational practices, products, and services in many international cities. Generally Filipino and Filipina migrants, as global workers, are valued for their respectful English communication skills (*marunong makiusap*), responsible (*responsable*), cheerful disposition (*masayahin*), industriousness (*sipag*), ability to blend in and be a team player (*marunong makisama at lumaro),* creative abilities (*maabilidad*), easily trained or taught (*madaling turuan*), as well as their can-do (*kaya natin ito*) and never-say-never (*susubukan ko po*) attitudes, among others.

These traits also draw international investors to do business in the

Philippines, with outsourcing contracts, investments, and by setting up call centers. Many global companies go to the country to recruit workers, since the Philippines produces more than half a million college graduates per year across a range of disciplines from arts to engineering. Nearly 150,000 graduate from business-related programs, while another 100,000 are from engineering or information technology (IT) programs. According to the Business Processing Association of the Philippines, the country is one of few that offer this rich pool of high quality and hardworking English-speaking college graduates each year.

Even high school graduates who did not finish college have relatively good English proficiency and competitive skills and talents. When they go abroad to work, they help both their host country and their family and hometown needs. The remittances and their development impact is the most tangible evidence of their transnational bayanihan influence.

This comes as no surprise since the Philippines is one of the largest English-speaking nations in the world, with a literacy rate of 92.6 percent, by UNESCO standards. There are more English speakers in the Philippines than in the United Kingdom. Universities, colleges, and technical institutes produce world-class doctors, nurses, engineers, teachers, managers, technicians, scientists, accountants, lawyers, etc. In many countries, labor deficiencies at critical sea-based and land-based occupations are filled by skilled Filipino migrants, such as the crew on commercial and military vessels; domestic workers in Singapore, Hong Kong, Malaysia, United Kingdom, Italy; health care and allied work in the U.S., Canada, Australia, Austria, and the United Kingdom; tourism and retail employment in Saudi Arabia, the United Arab Emirates, Qatar, Kuwait, Oman, and Bahrain as well as Spain, Italy, and Mexico; light manufacturing contracts in Taiwan and South Korea; garments industries work in Sri Lanka, China, India, and Bangladesh; as well as entertainment and hospitality gigs in Japan. Both developed and developing country economies benefit as illustrated by the succeeding cases from the United Kingdom and Bangladesh.

The high performing economies of Singapore, Hong Kong, Malaysia, United Kingdom, and Italy would not be possible without double-income productivity from families. Filipino migrants in these countries provide the necessary child care and household cleaning to allow mothers and fathers to both seek gainful employment. Longer life spans and aging populations have also created an urgent demand for hospital and home health care in the U.S., Canada, Australia, Austria, and the United Kingdom. Thus, the inflow of Filipino doctors, dentists, nurses, physical therapists, and other health care professionals into the public and private health care systems of these countries.

Second- and third-generation Filipino migrants have also followed their parents into these high paying occupations. In the 1970s, Philippine construction workers on contract with multinational engineering companies helped build the infrastructure, from airports to malls, of petroleum-states like Saudi Arabia, the United Arab Emirates, Qatar, Kuwait, Oman, and Bahrain. Now, the current wave of migrant workers comprise the sales personnel at duty free shops and food concessions in those airports, mega shopping malls, international hotels, and chain restaurants. After saving money from employment in the Middle East, some Filipino migrants move on to Western Europe and North America.

In Japan, male Japanese executives are compelled to spend very long hours in their work places. To help them unwind and recharge, Japanese clubs, bars, and hotels recruited more than 70,000 mostly young Filipinas for entertainment jobs in 2004. These jobs are really a mix of singing, dancing, modeling, talking, massaging, flirting, eating, consuming, and pouring alcoholic drinks. There are now close to 200,000 Filipina entertainers in Japan working in clubs in the northern city of Hokkaido to Okinawa in the south.

Some Philippine migrants are also into business and investments in their new homelands and infuse bayanihan influences via individual philanthropy or through their corporate social responsibility initiatives. In 2002, the U.S.

Census Bureau Survey of Business owners reported over 125,000 Filipino-owned firms that employed about 132,000 workers, and generated nearly $14.2 billion in revenue. This figure was higher by 48 percent than that of the 1997 survey. Filipino entrepreneurs invested in health care and social assistance, professional and consulting services, and scientific and technical services.

According to a 2008 Philippine Overseas Employment Agency report, close to 100 teachers left for the U.S. in 2007. That same year, 6,633 nurses and 210 IT workers were processed for jobs in Saudi Arabia, significant growths from previous years. Meanwhile, Taiwan's annual recruitment of caregivers increased to 14,716 in 2003, which brought up the number of Filipino migrants there to more than 74,000 by 2007. The need for domestic helpers continues to rise in Hong Kong and went up to 22,127, a 13 percent growth, in 2006. Italy's hiring of Filipino domestic helpers increased by 764 percent, from just 573 in 2006 to 4,951 in 2007. Spain likewise increased its hiring of Filipino domestic helpers in 2007, from 600 to over 1,500.

Filipino celebrities and media personalities are also major sources of Philippine soft power. Beauty queens, TV and movie actors such as Rob Schneider and Tia Carrera, as well as TV news presenters like CNN's Veronica de la Cruz in the U.S., BBC's Rico Hizon in Singapore and the Al Jazeera's Veronica Pedroza. In Europe there's MTV Europe's host Trey Farley and Philippine-born Bond girl Rachel Grant. There are Filipinos and Filipinas in sports. In boxing, there's pay-per-view world boxing champion Manny Pacquiao and Olympic gold medalist swimmer and adobo loving Natalie Coughlin. And let's not forget World Billiards Champions Efren "Bata" Reyes, Alex "The Lion" Pagulayan, Ronnie Alcano and on the women's side, Rubilen Amit. One of Europe's greatest football players was Filipino FC Barcelona striker Paulino Alcantara. They are also big name scientists like the University of Utah's Biologist professor Baldomero Olivera who was named 2007 America's Scientist of the Year. A spiritual celebrity is El Shaddai's charismatic leader, Brother Mike Velarde, who has been named one of Asiaweek's most powerful people in Asia. Filipina Mutya Buena of the

Sugababes brought in the first British Phonographic Industry (BRIT Awards)'s pop music award recognition while The Black Eyed Peas' Allan Pineda Lindo has won a prestigious Grammy Award for his Philippine homeland. Leah Salonga has her voice etched on Disney songs and appeared in New York's Broadway as well as London's West End. She has also won a coveted Tony Award for Miss Saigon. Many of them are Philippine-based but there is a significant number that have emerged from the diaspora.

Associational Filipinization: Influencing through Heart and Helping

Beyond church and work, Filipino migrants influence global cities and societies through their associations (*samahan*) and vibrant gatherings (*pagtitipon*). Their memberships in local NGOs, interest and advocacy groups, and other civil society gatherings or celebrations transform their kasamahan influences (bonding social capital) into bayanihan influences (bridging social capital) or willingness to help others (*nakahandang tumulong*).

In the Philippines and abroad, Filipinos and Filipinas are making waves as leaders in the global environmental movement. Greenpeace warrior Von Hernandez was awarded the 2003 Goldman Environmental Prize, the equivalent of the Nobel Prize. Not to be outdone is Time Magazine's 2003 Asian Woman heroine, actress Carminia "Chin-chin" Gutierrez for her work on environmental issues.

In some countries, Filipino associations are even more pervasive than Philippine consulates and embassies. There are more Ilocano hometown associations, for example, than Philippine diplomatic posts in the U.S. and Canada. Many Philippine towns and cities receive more remittance dollars from former residents, their hometown associations and school alumni associations, than from bilateral official development assistance (ODA) from donor agencies like the U.S. Agency for International Development (USAID), Canadian International Development Agency (CIDA), Australian Agency for International Development (AusAID), UK Department for International Development (DFID), or Japan International Cooperation Agency (JICA).

Filipino associations in the U.S. and Canada also give out more high school scholarships benefiting Filipino American, Filipino Canadian, and Philippine youth than their governments. Cebuano, Ilocano, Kapampangan, Bicolano, Pangasinan, and Quezonian hometown associations in the U.S. organize more beauty contests than Donald Trump's Miss America Organization. Titles at stake range from Miss and Mrs. Pangasinan International, Miss Philippines America, Mrs. Ilocandia, Miss Sampaguita, Little Miss Philippines, Miss Bicolandia, Mrs. Philippines, among others.

There are 24 Philippine overseas elementary and high schools scattered all over the Kingdom of Saudi Arabia, more than the American, British, Dutch, and other western international schools combined. Filipinos in Saudia Arabia host one of the largest and tightly contested diaspora beauty pageants in the world, "The Miss United OFW Saudi Arabia." How is it even possible for them to hold a beauty pageant in the land of the burqa?

In my field work, I found most Filipino migrants blend in with whatever (*bahala na*) or any (*kahit ano*) ethnoscape they face, especially because as far as concerned, they are European, Asian, and American enough to do so. Unlike Asian and other ethnic migrant communities who tend to stay close to each other, I did not find contemporary Filipino migrants centering their associational life in highly visible ethnic business and linguistic enclaves like a Chinatown, a Japantown, a Little Italy, or a Latino District. They do not find it necessary to do so.

While it would be ideal to have a Filipinotown, a Filipino grocery or a Filipino restaurant in every city, Filipino migrants can survive without them. They have no problem eating Mexican menudo, Spanish paella, American hamburger, and Chinese dimsum. To most new migrants, ethnic enclaves play a major role in their socio-cultural networking and civic connections to mainstream societies. They also seek to draw the mainstream into their "ethnic towns" for business and socials. Filipino migrants' "centers" or "spaces" for associational Filipinization via kasamahan and bayanihan that I immersed myself in are much more interwoven with whatever mainstream or minority neighborhood they are in. There are clusters but they will not have the size and scale of a typical ethnic town.

Instead of enclaves or neighborhoods, Filipino migrants have gathering places, such as the Philippine embassies and consulates, grocery stores and other business spaces that they patronize. In London, I took the bus and train with some migrants hailing from different Philippine provinces who began their Sundays eating breakfast at the McDonald's in front of the Kensington High Street Tube station. We then stopped by Earl's Court to allow two of them to send some money through Sunrise Remittance at the Filipino supermarket before attending the Filipino Catholic Community Group prayer meeting at Sacred Heart Church in North London.

In San Francisco, London, and Dubai where there are more than a hundred thousand of them, Filipino migrants' socialization patterns also revolve around their provincial and regional origins. Thus there are Pasiguenans of Northern California, the Naga Metropolitan Society, the Aklan Association and the Marinduque Association, among many others.

Map of the Philippines

The Philippine archipelago is divided into three main island groups: Luzon, Visayas and Mindanao. These are then segregated administratively into 17 sub-regions, which are further divided into 80 provinces, and further, into 120 cities, 1,511 municipalities, and 42,008 barangays (villages). Language and dialects could also be the basis for the segregation of communities from one another—the Philippines has more than a hundred. This is why there are so many Philippine home province and hometown (cities and municipalities) associations in global cities.

Home province associations subdivide into hometown associations. For instance, the home province association called Pangasinan International Charitable Foundation based in California is an umbrella organization for the following Pangasinan hometown associations: Balungao Association of America, Banians of the USA, Inc., Bonuan International, Dagupan Association of Stockton & Vicinity, Dagupenians Association of America, Inc., Dagupenos Charitable Foundation International, Inc., Federation of Dasol Associations of America, Laoac Association of Northern California, Mangaldan Association of Northern California, Rosales United Club, San Carlenians of Pangasinan, USA, United Binalonians, Urdaneta Association of America, Inc., and Villasinians of America, Inc. These associations organize dances, language and dialect classes, beauty pageants, raffle draws, bingo and bowling nights, sports festivals, picnics, and neighborhood cleanups, preserving cultural capital from the Philippines and adding them into whatever society and culture they settle in, temporarily or permanently. Their fundraisers benefit old and new home base, homeland, and international causes.

The most popular devotional associations revolve around national spiritual symbols like the Santo Niño de Cebu (Christ Child), the Virgin Mary, Nazareno (brown/black images of Christ), and San Lorenzo Ruiz (the first Filipino saint). There is also a natural merging of the hometown associations and spiritual organizations during the feast days of a town, as statues or images of the town's patron saint are commonly displayed. For instance, members of Bicol hometown associations from London to South Carolina are also core members and organizers of traditional fluvial events celebrating its divine provincial patron, the "Nuestra Señora de Peñafrancia." The Bicol Association in the U.K. hosts Sarong Bangui celebrations in honor of the Our Lady of Penafrancia at Westminster Cathedral Hall yearly. I joined the Bicol Association in Vienna on a rented ship reenacting the fluvial trip on the grand Danube River.

The Sinulog festival is one of the grandest and most colorful festivals in the Philippines, held yearly on the third Sunday of January in Cebu City to honor the Santo Niño, or the child Jesus, who used to be the patron saint of the entire province of Cebu. The festival is essentially a dance ritual that commemorates the Filipino people's pagan past and its acceptance of Christianity. In Macau, the first Philippine fiesta was held on January 3, 2001 at the Saint Joseph Parish Church. On its second year, the idea of a Sinulog was hatched. In 2003, the Sinulog in China made its debut on January 19. The affair was a success beyond all expectations. It was bigger than anyone expected. Bishop Lai officiated at the Mass. Enthusiastic for its tourist potential, the Macau government threw its support behind it.

Worldwide professional associations of Filipino migrants include organizations of nurses (e.g., Philippine Nurses Association), engineers and architects (e.g., Marianas Association of Filipino Engineers and Architects), teachers, doctors (e.g., Philippine Medical Association), lawyers (e.g., Philippine Lawyers Association), executives (e.g., Filipino Association Singapore), and public employees (e.g., Pacific Gas and Electric Filipino Employees Association). Educational and alumni associations in the U.S. represent high schools (e.g., Morong High School Alumni Association), universities (e.g., University of the Philippines Alumni Association), and combined regional schools and universities (e.g., Samahang Ilocano). I also found multitudes of Filipino cultural, sports, history, performing, literary, as well as visual arts associations. There are more than 10,000 active Order of the Knights of Rizal members globally.

In the sprawling Kingdom of Saudi Arabia, where there are more than one million Filipino migrant workers but no churches, masses, rituals and festivals are permitted. Nevertheless, there are around 200 Philippine associations registered with the Philippine Embassy in Riyadh and the consulate in Jeddah. The largest numbers are in professional associations as well as sports and martial arts clubs. There are professional associations for computer technicians (e.g., Association of Computer Enthusiasts), engineers (e.g., Philippine Society of Mechanical Engineers - Jeddah Chapter), nurses (e.g., Filipino Nurses Society in Saudi Arabia), and even ex-soldiers (e.g., Philippine Guardians Brotherhood).

The major cities of Jeddah and Riyadh are the hubs for weekend and weekday sports and martial arts warriors and their families. There are Filipino recreational clubs for darts (e.g., Expat Darters of Saudi Arabia), bowling (e.g., Filipino Tenpin Bowlers of Jeddah), tennis (e.g., Pinoys Netters Club 102), badminton (e.g., Jeddah Slashers Badminton Club), chess (e.g., Riyadh Chess Club), basketball (e.g., Pinoy Basketball Club), and volleyball (Volleyball Association of Riyadh). There are also groups that meet for karate, like the OFW Karate-Do Association, aikido, like Asian Martial Arts Ultimate Combat Aikido, and taekwondo, like the King Tiger Taekwondo Association, and other forms of martial arts.

CHAPTER 3

San Francisco: Golden Gateway for Faithful Shopping

"What? You're getting married and leaving for the States? What about your younger siblings? Who will help send them to college? Don't forget to go to church, *ha*? *Magdasal ka*! [Pray!]." These were my mom's worried pleas before I left Manila for San Francisco.

I am not the first in my clan to get these worried queries and sweet reminders. My two paternal granduncles, Lolo Pepe and Lolo Kikoy, were the earliest diaspora diplomats in my family. They must have gotten similar admonitions from my great grandparents when the "two boys" left our rural hometown of Baliuag in Bulacan Province in 1914, stowed away on separate ships and arrived in America.

With just two dollars in his pocket, Lolo Pepe started with odd jobs at Brooklyn pool halls and hotels, sharpened his American English (rather, New York Brooklyn) accent, and eventually rose to become a very proud New York City commuter train conductor. Lolo Kikoy followed a year after. Both returned to Manila as *pensionados* (retirees with U.S. social security pensions) in their mid-70s. Even after 50 years in America, Lolo Pepe and Lolo Kikoy never married and never became U.S. citizens.

Growing up, I remember Lolo Pepe, who lived to be 107 years old, surreptitiously passing money to my cousins and me when our parents' backs were turned. He had saved a lot and received his pension in U.S. dollars. The exchange rate then was already an imbalanced US$1.00 = PhP30.00.

My maternal grandparents, Lolo Pidring and Lola Lulu, also became late-life diaspora diplomats. In the early 1980s, they arrived in San Francisco and stayed with relatives. Lolo Pidring was looking forward to working at the San Francisco International Airport when he was run over by a commercial truck one very foggy morning on his way home from church. He was declared "brain dead" at the hospital and passed away peacefully at the Lucero's ancestral home in Cubao, Quezon City. Lola Lulu, a former high school principal, assumed the tough matriarchal role. She made sure that six of their ten children had sufficient funds to come to the U.S. on tourist visas, marry for green cards, and eventually raise families in the Los Angeles area. She even wrote a cheque for my college application fee.

On June 24, 1988, I landed at the San Francisco International airport with two bulging suitcases, the rosary mom gave me in my left pocket, and two hundred dollars—my lifetime savings combined with money collections from relatives -- in my wallet. More importantly, I had a full scholarship to an American graduate school. When I graduated, I sent money to my brother, nieces, and nephew for their enrollment, even as I was sending my own daughter to school.

What was common to all of us? We were determined to earn money as migrants and share our good fortune with our loved ones – a chain of *utang na loob* (debt of gratitude). This is how my own diaspora diplomacy story began.

In this chapter, part of my goal is to retune the international discourse on the bilateral- to reflect more of the transnational soft power influences, with San Francisco representing the on-going pattern of reverse colonization in many U.S. cities where Philippine diaspora diplomats are making their mark. I then talk about the religious influences of Filipinos and Filipinas in their various churches and elaborate on Filipino American faith, their community advocacy and Congressional activism. I discuss the diaspora's occupational influences through Philippine-educated engineers and health care professionals from downtown San Francisco to Silicon Valley. I also write about their contributions to the economy and their shopping capacity. Finally, I elaborate on Filipino associational influences from San Francisco's fast growing Philippine studies program, Filipino American student organizations, fraternities, Philippine cultural nights, and hometown associations and their beauty pageants. I conclude with some *kasamahan* and *bayanihan* lessons learned.

Colonizing the colonizer

Colonized, the Philippines hosted two of the largest U.S. military installations in the world. At their peak, Clark Air Base and Subic Naval Base had 35,000 and 40,000 servicemen, civilians, and their dependents, respectively. They ensured America's control and colonization of the air and sea lanes over the Pacific Ocean and South China Sea. Operating like independent city states within a nation-state, they were glaring manifestations of post-[Philippine] independence American hegemonic influence and presence in the Philippines as well as the Asia Pacific region. In a bold move, the Philippine Senate voted to close them down in 1991, ending around 100 years of large- scale American military presence and more than 400 years of foreign bases on Philippine soil.

In spite of this large-scale downsizing, America's former colony continues to be one of its most important strategic partners in Asia, militarily and economically, particularly in the global war on terrorism and markets-driven globalization. The U.S. and the Philippines continue to honor a 1951 Mutual Defense Treaty with annual *Balikatan* (Shouldering the Load Together) joint operational exercises.

Presently, there are only 500 U.S. military personnel under a 1999 Visiting Forces Agreement (VFA). But they are doing critical anti-terrorism assignments as advisors and trainers to the Armed Forces of the Philippines (AFP) particularly in Mindanao (Southern Philippines) as part of Operation Enduring Freedom (formerly Operation Freedom Eagle). Their mission is to help the Philippine government quell terrorist threats like the Jemaah Islamiyah, the Abu Sayyaf, the New People's Army, the Rajah Solaiman Movement, the Moro National Liberation Front, and the Moro Islamic Liberation Front.

Even with the significant reduction of U.S. military presence in the Philippines, the two Pacific Rim allies enjoy very close economic ties, with around US$16.3 billion in total merchandise exchanged between them in 2007. This is approximately 15.5 percent of the country's total merchandise trade volume for that year. According to the Philippine Department of Trade and Industry, around 15 percent of Philippine imports in 2007 came from America, and about 17 percent of the country's exports went to the U.S. Worth more than US$8.5 billion, Philippine export earnings from the U.S. market was ranked number one in the same year followed closely by Japan (US$7.3 billion).

The Philippines ranks 29th in the U.S. export market and the 34th largest supplier. Important Philippine export products are wheat and animal feeds, semiconductor devices and computer peripherals, coconut oil, automobile parts, electric machinery, garments and textiles. Conversely, the Philippines acquired raw and semi-processed materials for the manufacture of semiconductors, electronics and electrical machinery, transport equipment, and cereals and cereal preparations from the U.S. Historically, the Philippines has always enjoyed a favorable trade surplus with its former colonial master.

Over the last decade, Makati, Quezon City, San Juan, Mandaluyong, Davao, Cebu, Baguio, and many other metropolitan cities have become chosen hubs for American business process outsourcing (BPO) and Voice over Internet Protocol (VoIP) services, or call centers for short. These Philippine-based contractors do American English- accented customer relations globally, ranging from travel services, health care, technical support, education, customer care, financial services, and online business to customer support, online business to business support. The country's top U.S. clients include American Express, Vonage, Capital One, Ambergris, Dell, AT&T, IBM, among the many Fortune 500 companies who have decided that the quality of customer care and tech support from Filipinos is at par if not exceeds U.S. standards. These American companies have created hundreds of thousands of jobs and, in doing so, have agreed to be influenced by Philippine-style business culture and customer service.

More than half a million American citizens came to the Philippines in 2008, a more than 18 percent increase from the previous year. Tourism arrivals in Manila have grown over the past 100 years as the number of Filipino Americans (FilAms) increased. Philippine TV, movies, and sports have FilAm faces. The Philippine Basketball Association will always remember the likes of Eric Menk of Tanduay, Shell's Chris Jackson, Purefoods' Noy Castillo, Ginebra's Alex Crisano, Sta. Lucia's Rob Wainwright and Tanduay's Rudy Hatfield. While star playmaker Ryan Reyes of HenkelSista's has made his mark on the Philippine Basketball League (PBL).

In America, FilAms have become the second largest Asian American population and the third largest immigrant group. In fact, there are more Filipino Americans than Japanese Americans and Korean Americans combined. Department of State estimates in 2007 placed the number of Filipinos in America at more than four million, concentrated mostly in the major metropolitan areas of California, Hawaii, New York, and Texas. Comparatively, this figure is around the same size as the entire population of the Republic of Singapore, about half the residents of Greater London, and almost equal to the total number of persons living in the United Arab Emirates.

Missing in the official reports from the State Department are the stories of how Filipino and Filipina migrants in the U.S. influence both the Philippine and American economies significantly, particularly how they are presently "colonizing" San Francisco and many other major U.S. cities.

Their economic power is immense. Using U.S. and Philippine banks and remittance agencies, they sent more than US$6.2 billion to the Philippines in

2007. This is equal to U.S. foreign direct investments for the same year, and is half of the US$12.2 billion global remittance total officially recorded by the Philippine central bank. Filipinos in California alone sent more than US$2 billion.

Filipino migrants channeled more money than what the U.S. Congress authorized in economic and military assistance. Also in 2007, more than half a million *balikbayan* boxes (hundred-pound care packages) arrived in the main ports of Manila from cargo ships from the U.S. Filipinos in the U.S. have also poured in millions of dollars into Philippine tourism, housing developments and business start-ups. While the numbers of McDonald's and Starbucks franchises in the Philippines continue to multiply so have popular Philippine restaurants in California: fifteen Goldilocks franchises, ten Jollibee franchises, and seventeen Red Ribbon franchises.

There is a FilAm Center at the San Francisco Public Library and you can rent the latest Filipino flicks at the Daly City Public Library. There are streets in San Francisco named after Filipino heroes—Mabini Street, Rizal Street, Lapulapu Street, Tandang Sora Street and Bonifacio Street. Filipino historical landmarks are found in downtown thoroughfares like Union Square, Market Street, Mission Street, and Kearny Street in Chinatown. Moreover, Philippine *patis* (fish sauce) or *toyo* (soy sauce) are available at almost every local Albertson's or Safeway supermarket.

Filipinization in American pop culture is becoming more noticeable especially in California. When deejays play The Black Eyed Peas' *Bebot* and *APL Song* on trendy radio stations, they help mainstream the Filipino language. Both are by Filipino migrant Allan Pineda Lindo, better known as Apl.d.Ap, one of the four mainstays of the Grammy Award-winning group. Other rock stars helping put a Filipino face to American music are Metalica's lead guitarist, Kirk Hammett and Journey's lead vocalist, Arnel Pineda. Then there are showbiz celebrities with Filipino roots: Enrique Iglesias, son of Julio Iglesias and Filipina socialite Isabel Preysler; Lou Diamond Philips, Rob

Schneider, Phoebe Cates, Enrique Tia Carrera, Dante Basco, Paolo Montalban, Brandon Baker, Samantha Marie Becker, Shannyn Sossamon, Lexa Doig, and *Inside Edition*'s Victoria Recaño.

Television has its Filipino faces as well: KTVU's Lloyd La Cuesta, FOX's Bob De Castro, CBS News' Hazel Sanchez as well as Malou Nubla, two-time Emmy Award winning television host, and CNN's Veronica Delacruz and Elaine Quijano. In pop songs and on stage, Leah Salonga has made a Filipino mark with her singing in Disney movies (e.g., *Aladdin* and *Mulan*) and acting in Broadway hit musicals (e.g., *Miss Saigon* and *Les Miserables*).

Filipinos in America have made their presence felt by supporting some of their own in popular TV shows: Filipino-Hawaiian singer Jasmine Trias become a finalist in FOX's highly rated "American Idol" while Filipina American dancer Cheryl Bautista-Burke won the championship of ABC's hit show "Dancing with the Stars" twice.

Then 15-year-old Charice Pempengco became a phenomenon after appearing in Ellen DeGeneres' and Oprah Winfrey's prime time TV shows and went on to sing with top names in the music world. Charice has since become a bestselling recording artist as well.

Descendants of Philippine migrants have made an impact in American sports. Among them are Victoria Manalo-Draves, who in 1948 became a two-time platform diving Olympic gold medalist and the first American female athlete in modern Olympic history to win six medals in one Olympics; Natalie Coughlin, also a multi-gold Olympic medalist in swimming; International Boxing Federation flyweight champion Nonito Donaire; Tim Asis Lincecum, the San Francisco Giant's brilliant all-star pitcher who has won the National League's Cy Young Award twice, and Erik Spoelstra, the Miami Heats' coach, whose mother hails from the province of Laguna.

Reaching out to their big Filipino fan base, the San Francisco Giants and 49ers, the Oakland As and Raiders, the Golden State Warriors, and the Sacramento Kings designate Filipino Heritage games annually with discounted tickets and celebrities, like world boxing champion Manny Pacquiao, making guest appearances. The Oakland Raiders even have a Tagalog page on their web site.

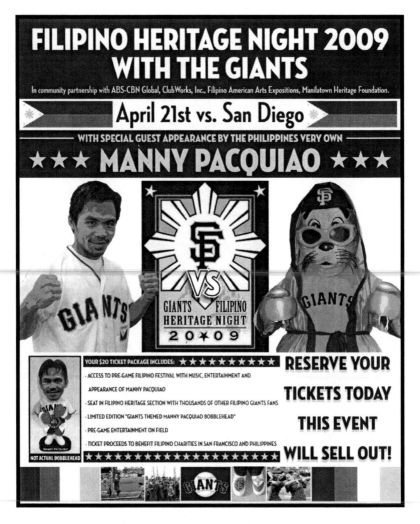

Soft power in America's favorite sport

Because of diaspora diplomacy, there are more officially sanctioned festivities in the U.S. for Philippine Independence Day than U.S. Independence Day in the Philippines, even though there are 250,000 Americans there.

In the Philippines, the July 4th American Independence Day celebrations are spearheaded by the U.S. Embassy in Manila and the U.S. consulates in Cebu and Davao. The June 12 Philippine Independence Day is commemorated by Filipino communities and local governments at all the major U.S. cities where they have settled. In San Francisco, for example, the Philippine Consulate invites the community to a dress-up party, and there is a flag-raising ceremony at the Mayor's balcony, and cocktails at City Hall. Atlantic City's Philippine Independence Day commemorations drew a crowd of about 15,000 when Hawaii-born Angela Perez-Baraquio, the first Filipina and the first Asian American to be crowned Miss America, was the special guest.

There has also been a trend towards sister city relations between U.S. and Philippine cities. Of the 38 currently existing, 26 involve California cities. In 2008, 10 San Francisco Bay Area cities had 12 sister cities in the Philippines, the highest number in any geographic region in the U.S. San Francisco and Fremont have two Philippine sister cities each, Manila and Abra for the former and Jaipur and Lipa for the latter. The rest of the Bay Area sister city commissions are Daly City-Quezon City, Milpitas-Dagupan City, Palo Alto-Palo, San Mateo-San Pablo City, South San Francisco-Pasig, Union City-Pasay City, and Vallejo-Maquio. Other active U.S.-Philippine sister city commissions include Los Angeles-Makati, San Diego-Cavite, Seattle-Cebu, and Salt Lake City-Quezon City. Manila, the Philippine capital, is the most popular among U.S. cities with four American sisters—San Francisco, Santa Barbara, Sacramento, and Honolulu.

Religious Filipinization

In my book, *Filipino American Faith in Action,* I pointed out that churches are the most common places where Philippine migrant religious influences

-- both *kasamahan* (bonding socio-cultural capital) and *bayanihan* (bridging socio-cultural capital) – are most felt. This is the best place to witness how they colonize the colonizer.

In a brief exchange with eminent globalization and migration professor Saskia Sassen, I was surprised that western scholars like her still think that Filipino Catholics in the U.S. are just meekly blending in with mainstream American Catholicism. They appear to do so in the beginning particularly when they have no choice. I had to explain to her that as their numbers grew and they assumed more leadership roles, Filipino diaspora diplomats in San Francisco have made inroads in the way America practices and interprets Catholicism. Sometimes they play by the rule book as dictated by the Archbishop but most of the time they push the envelope when his back is turned.

Filipino migrants have introduced their own iconography, music pieces, singing styles, language, homilies, liturgies, priests, nuns, saints, practices, food, drinks, celebrations, holy days, devotions, groups, and reading materials into church leadership, bible studies, and mass content. In fact, they now dominate two churches that San Francisco's early European immigrants established: Saint Patrick's, set up by the Irish, and Saint Boniface by Germans. The Irish are only at Saint Patrick's now on March 17th, Saint Patrick's Day. The rest of the other 364 days, it is a predominantly Filipino American Catholic church.

Although there are documentation that Filipinos were brought to coastal towns of California and Louisiana via the Manila-Acapulco Galleon trade (1565-1815), the mass migration of Filipinos to the U.S. began in the 1910s, around the time my granduncles arrived in New York. Lolo Pepe, Lolo Kikoy and many Filipinos who came to America helped increase church attendance rates especially among Catholic Churches in the major gateway cities of San Francisco, Honolulu, Los Angeles, Seattle, New York, and Chicago. In Hawaii and the west coast, they were mainly agricultural laborers while in the east coast they were hotel, restaurant, commuter train, recreational hall, and odd-job workers. This trend spread to other U.S. cities. The end of World War

II and the passage of the 1965 Immigration Act, increased immigration to the U.S. thus filling up Catholic churches.

According to the U.S. Catholic Conference of Bishops (USCCB), the three San Francisco Bay Area Catholic dioceses, i.e., Oakland, San Francisco, and San Jose, are ranked fourth, fifth, and sixth in Filipino parishioner population size after the massive Dioceses of Los Angeles (first), Honolulu (second), and San Diego (third). The USCCB states further that there are more than 100,000 registered Filipino Catholic parishioners in the Archdiocese of San Francisco out of an estimated population of more than 400,000 Catholic residents. Statistically, as shown in Figure 3.1, this meant that one out of every four Catholics in the area is of Philippine descent.

Figure 3.1
Filipinos in San Francisco Bay Area Catholic Dioceses

Diocese	Filipinos	Percent of total Catholic population
Oakland (4th)	103,722	19%
San Francisco (5th)	100,519	25%
San Jose (6th)	76,060	13%
	280,301	18%

Source: United States Conference of Catholic Bishops (2003).

Established in 1853, the Archdiocese of San Francisco is one of the oldest ecclesiastical dioceses in the western U.S. It is the home to more than 100 churches and religious sites, including the Cathedral of Saint Mary of the Assumption, the National Shrine of Saint Francis of Assisi, Missions Dolores and San Rafael, Saint Patrick Seminary and University, as well as Holy Cross Cemetery. There are also more than 80 Catholic elementary, middle, and high schools as well as colleges in its jurisdiction.

From the 1980s to the 1990s, many San Francisco Bay Area Catholic churches, including my Lolo Pidring's and Lola Lulu's favorite Saint Anne's of the Sunset Church, have filled up with devoted Filipino parishioners, especially south of San Francisco and across the bay in the neighboring Catholic Diocese of Oakland. Saint Andrew's Church and the Our Lady of Perpetual Help Church in Daly City, and Saint Augustine Church in South San Francisco all have Filipino priests preaching to memberships that are more than 80 percent Filipino. Tagalog masses are held at Saint Patrick's Church and Saint Boniface Church in San Francisco as well as Holy Angels Church in Colma. Thus, Tagalog masses, Philippine feast days, novenas, and devotions are held all over the Archdiocese. The popular charismatic renewal movement El Shaddai meets every week at the Star of the Sea Church in the Richmond District (www.sfarchdiocese.org).

The Diocese of Oakland is home to 560,000 Catholic residents. Of this number, more than 103,000 are Filipino Catholics or one out of every five. The diocese administers over 47 elementary and middle schools as well as nine high schools serving over 19,000 students. There are also seven Catholic colleges and seminaries in the diocese's ecclesiastical jurisdiction, including: the Graduate Theological Union, Holy Names University, Queen of the Holy Rosary College, and Saint Mary's College of California. Tagalog Sunday masses are held at Cathedral of Christ the Light in Oakland, Our Lady of Good Council Church in San Leandro, and Saint Paul Church in San Pablo.

Although established only in 1981, Catholic mission work in the Diocese of San Jose is as historic as the ones in neighboring San Francisco and Oakland. The ecclesiastical diocese of San Jose serves a diverse community of over 600,000 Catholics, roughly 76,000 are Filipino Catholics, or one out of every ten. It is home to 52 parishes and missions, three university campus ministries, and 38 schools, making it the second largest education provider in the county after the San Jose Unified School District. The diocese has a large and active office of Filipino ministry which organizes novenas, masses, and fiesta celebrations for the Our Lady of Antipolo (also known as Our Lady of

Peace and Good Voyage) in the month of July, the San Lorenzo Ruiz in the month of September, and the Santo Niño de Cebu in the month of January.

For Filipino Catholics in the Archdiocese of San Francisco, historic Saint Patrick's on downtown Mission Street is the closest thing to a Philippine national church on American soil. Formerly an Irish American parish, the church is now almost entirely staffed and populated by Filipinos. All the priests, nuns and ninety percent of the altar servers, ushers, and collectors are Philippine migrants. Filipino religious icons, posters, and practices are also evident inside the church. Not surprisingly, Saint Patrick's has become a place where Bay Area Filipino migrants participate in religious and social traditions transported from their motherland. Saint Patrick's is one of the few places where Filipino Catholics can attend devotions particular to the Philippines, such as the Simbang Gabi, the early-morning masses celebrated during Christmas season. It is usually after such devotions that food is served to the congregation, whether it is breakfast after Simbang Gabi or an early evening snack after a novena to the Santo Niño de Cebu. There are also shrines, devotions, and lighted candles for the San Lorenzo Ruiz, the first Filipino Saint, and the Black Nazareno of Quiapo, Manila. Filipino migrant faithful have transported to the U.S. their church-linked organizations, including Couples for Christ, Singles for Christ, El Shaddai, Knights of Columbus, Knights of Rizal, Carmelite Lay Orders, Philippine bible and prayer groups, as well as Marian devotions. Popular healing priests and nuns from the Philippines visit regularly along with visiting blessed statues and images of Christ, the Virgin Mary, and the holy family.

At the Holy Name of Jesus Catholic Church also within the jurisdiction of the Archdiocese of San Francisco, Philippine diaspora devotees of the Blessed Virgin Mary held an inaugural mass to open the Shrine of the Blessed Virgin Marys on February 11, 2007. Droves of people, Filipino and non-Filipinos pilgrims seeking inspiration, spiritual renewal and strengthening of spirits, gathered at the church. The pilgrims knelt before thirteen Marian images at a one of a kind "Shrines of the Blessed Virgin Mary", eight from around the world and five from the Philippines. They included Our Lady of Ireland, Our Lady of Loreto from Italy, Our Lady of Mount Carmel from Israel, Our Lady of Guadalupe from Mexico, Our Lady of Lourdes from France, Our Lady of Fatima from Portugal, Our Lady of Akita from Japan, Our Lady of La Vang from Vietnam, Our Lady of Antipolo from the Philippines, Our Lady of Manaog from Pangasinan Philippines, Our Lady of Penafrancia from Bicol Philippines, Our Lady of Solitude of Porta Vaga from Cavite Philippines, and Our Lady of Compassion and Protection. The last one is the most popular Marian image with the Filipino American community of the San Francisco Bay Area.

Aside from Catholic churches and religious organizations, other major beneficiaries of the Filipino inflow to San Francisco are the Archdiocese's many Catholic schools. As early as September 1963, 38 of the 45 elementary schools in the city reported a total of 680 Filipino children in attendance. The schools with the largest numbers were: Sacred Heart Elementary (78), Saint Paul (42), Star of the Sea (41), Saint Peter (38), and Saint Monica (28).12 In the 1980s and 1990s, San Francisco's religious elementary and high schools experienced surges in Filipino enrollment as the children of migrants from the 1960s and 1970s reached school age. New arrivals and their families also contributed to the increase. By 2000, Corpus Christi Elementary School had become more than 75 percent Filipino in terms of its student body. Several other elementary schools have student populations that are close to 50 percent Filipino, including the Church of the Epiphany, Church of the Visitacion, Saint Elizabeth, Saint Emydius, Saint Finn Barr, Saint John the Evangelist, Saint Kevin, Holy Angels, and Our Lady of Perpetual Help.

Some of the Catholic high schools in the San Francisco Bay Area currently have student populations that are between 20 and 25 percent Filipino, including Saint Ignatius College Prep, Archbishop Riordan, Mercy High, Bishop O'Dowd and Sacred Heart Cathedral Prep. Catholic colleges and universities, including the University of San Francisco and Santa Clara University, have also experienced rapid growth in Filipino student enrollment. Saint Patrick's

Seminary and University in Menlo Park also reported a significant number of students who are of Filipino descent training for the priesthood and enrolled in graduate theological and religious programs.

U.S. President William McKinley's "benevolent assimilation" policy on its Asian colony brought many American Protestant groups there to build churches and "save" the Filipinos from the distortions of Roman Catholicism. They were eager to heed the President's call to "civilize and Christianize those savage Filipinos". Little did these Americans know that while they were "saving" them, converted and baptized evangelical Filipinos would bring Protestantism back to America, precipitating a reverse "benevolent assimilation." Although smaller in number and distribution to their Filipino Catholic counterparts, their presence and growth are still worth examining.

Filipino Protestant agricultural workers who came to the U.S. began attending services and bible studies with the various American Christian Protestant churches in Hawaii and California. As their numbers grew, they also began to establish their own Christian Protestant and Independent church congregations. Just as in the Philippines, many Filipino Catholics in the U.S. crossed over and joined Protestant and Independent churches. Philippine migrant Methodists, Congregationalists, Presbyterians, Lutherans, Baptists, Adventists, Anglicans, Episcopalians, Mormons, and Witnesses when they arrived also joined American evangelical and Protestant congregations. Philippine independent Christian groups came as well, including the Iglesia Filipina Independiente (Aglipayan Church or Philippine Independent Church) and the Iglesia ni Cristo.

Daly City is a bustling suburb adjacent to San Francisco. Because it is home to the largest concentration of Filipinos outside of Manila, it has become a virtual Philippine province. The proliferation of businesses focused on the preparation, creation, and consumption of Filipino food is an indicator of the size and scope of this community. Numerous Filipino restaurants have established businesses in town, and several Filipino and Asian supermarkets also carry everything needed to create a Filipino meal, from essential ingredients to prepared foods. One can practically smell sinaing (cooking rice) and today's ulam (main dishes) being prepared as one walks through the streets of Daly City.

In this city where Filipinos have become the majority, the Philippine-based Iglesia ni Cristo (INC) has also staked its claim. According to its teachings, God called upon a Filipino preacher and biblical scholar named Felix Y. Manalo in 1914 to shepherd the last group of His chosen people. God gave the assurance that He would help and strengthen Manalo as he pursued this important task. From the time Manalo got this divine order, the INC has grown from a one-man crusade into a dynamic, international independent religious movement.

The INC's doctrines are fundamentalist and bible-based. Much of its theology effectively refutes the doctrines of other churches, especially the Catholic Church, to which a vast majority of Filipinos, even in the U.S., belong. Presently, the INC claims millions of members in 70 countries. Adherents view this dramatic development—and the church's expansion to Daly City—as the fulfillment of God's plan.

An unassuming building near Serramonte Mall serves as home base to the Daly City locale of the INC, where close to 1,000 brethren attend services. More than 50 percent of them are first-generation Filipino migrants. At Grand Evangelical Missions, or GEMs—monthly events designed to introduce visitors to the church's doctrines and membership—the church welcomes newcomers with open arms and plates overflowing with Filipino food, balancing the serious-minded bible lessons with more lighthearted fellowship. By missionizing with Filipino food, the INC has made effective social connections that eased the way for spiritual conversion. Notably, while most prospective members are first- or second-generation Filipinos, some are not. Thus, food also serves as a medium for indoctrinating non-Filipinos to Philippine culture—one might say that it helps to Filipinize Americans.

The events of one particular GEM that we attended typify the way in which Filipino food functions as a social medium within the church.

Food and Religion

During one of our University of San Francisco Religion and Immigration Project research team visits, we observed a GEM, in the chapel, with a lesson about the INC's belief system. The lesson was taught through selected readings from the bible and explanations by the ministers, but also through the disciplined model of behavior that is embedded in the rigid organization of people and things in the room. Men and women sat on separate sides of the room and were guided to their places by gender-appropriate attendants. The demeanor of worshippers was overwhelmingly solemn—there was no socializing; one quickly got the message that the chapel is a sacred place whose purpose is to house serious worship activity. Male and female choir members sat quietly, moving in unison whenever movement was called for. Their robes rustled slightly as they stood on cue and opened their hymnals at the same time, as if they were psychically linked.

After this serious, formal lesson, INC members invited us and the other visitors down the hall to a casual buffet lunch. Churchgoers streamed out of the worship area and into the hallway. By the time they reached the social hall, where a veritable feast had been laid out, the quiet crowd had turned animated and noisy. Loud talk and laughter filled the room, where several rectangular folding tables placed end to end formed a vast buffet of restaurant-purchased and homemade Filipino and American food. Large aluminum trays piled high with *pancit bihon* (Chinese noodles), *pritong manok* (fried chicken), and Filipino-style spaghetti from local restaurants were placed alongside homemade dishes in smaller, individualized containers. Filipino *pinakbet* (vegetable stew), Spanish-influenced *mechado* (beef stew), Malay-Indian influenced *kare-kare* (oxtail stew) and other favorite dishes from various

Philippine towns and provinces spoke both of the congregation's geographic diversity and love of food.

As we entered the social hall, our hosts sprang into action like a well-rehearsed team, staking out a table and enough metal folding chairs for each member of our group. One woman sat at the table and reserved seats with our purses and jackets, while the rest of us did battle with the crowds at the well-stocked buffet. We made our way to the food tables and scooped a little bit of rice, *pinakbet*, and *pancit* onto our plates. One of our companions urged us to try some of the other, home-cooked dishes. "This is *bopis*--it's my favorite! You've got to taste it!" she insisted, passing a serving spoon. Made with pork heart, lungs, and other innards, *bopis* is an acquired taste, and is thus not commonly found at mass gatherings like this one. The rarity of this dish makes it all the more appealing, however, since its taste and smell have a singular link to the Philippines. Our attention was also directed to a paper plate laden with bits of sweetened yam. We noticed that our companion's plate was heaped in layers, with several fried sardines perched atop a generous pile of rice, noodles and vegetables. Back at our table, we ate and talked about food: recipes, condiments, and the best local sources for Filipino ingredients, but also the memories that Filipino food conjured about "home." Speaking in Tagalog, the church members and guests reminisced about food and life in the Philippines. Here, the church's hospitality created a comfortable and inviting environment for Filipino immigrants hungry for familiar sounds, smells and tastes. Based on the locale's rapidly growing membership, it is obvious that these sensory enticements are effective missionary tools. Also, as this example shows, by stimulating people to speak Tagalog and conjuring reminiscences of the Philippines, Filipino food can actually help expand the presence of the Philippines in the U.S.

Religion and Political Action

Filipino migrants have integrated their unique form of kasamahan religious influence in San Francisco. In *Filipino American Faith in Action*, I also pointed out that they have used their churches for bayanihan influences— drawing other Filipinos, their families and friends to do civic engagement and political activism. They have successfully lobbied the Presidency and the U.S. Congress—to act favorably on two critical concerns: the Filipino World War II Veterans equity bill and the extra-judicial killings in the Philippines as part of the global War on Terrorism. The Filipino World War II Veterans equity struggle is very personal to me.

Before leaving Manila, I had to embark on a farewell ritual—visiting my closest friends and relatives. The latter was critical since I wanted to collect some much-needed pocket cash from the elders, aside from getting their blessings. I visited my paternal grandmother's brother, Lolo Tony, who lived in Biñan, Laguna Province, one of my family's hometowns.

Tears filled my eyes when Lolo Tony gave me a parting gift -- a black Santo Niño statue he had carved out of a water buffalo's black horn. Making it must have been very painful on his aging hands since Lolo Tony never really fully recovered the wounds he sustained when he was fighting for the U.S. Army's Philippine Scouts in World War II. Saying goodbye, he playfully winked, grabbed my hand, placed a folded five hundred peso bill on my palm, and closed my fist. The Santo Niño gift, he said, is a reminder for me to pray always and to include in my prayers his wish for a U.S. citizenship and veterans benefits.

General Douglas MacArthur and President Franklin D. Roosevelt had promised both to the thousands of Filipinos who heeded their call to serve under the U.S. Armed Forces of the Far East (USAFFE). At the time of USAFFE's formation, the unit consisted of 22,532 troops, 11,972 of which were Philippine Scouts like my Lolo Tony and my mother's father, Lolo Pidring. When the war ended, however, an ungrateful U.S. Congress passed two Rescission Acts which invalidated MacArthur's and Roosevelt's vow.

In 1990, U.S. President George H. W. Bush signed the Immigration and

Naturalization Act granting them U.S. citizenship rights to Filipino veterans. Lolo Tony finally got what he and I had been praying for and arrived in California as a proud American veteran in 1992, the year I graduated. Having no money, he and his wife had to survive on social security income. They were not given benefits equal to other U.S. veterans. As more veterans started arriving. the FilAm community and their churches mobilized to lobby and influence the politics not just in San Francisco and Sacramento but in the U.S. Congress and the White House Oval Office.

In Saint Patrick's, as in other churches, veterans and youth combined their petitions, novenas, and venerations with the community's prayers to icons of popular devotions in the Philippines. Images of the Mother of Perpetual Help, the Divine Mercy of the Holy Infant Jesus, the Santo Niño of Cebu, San Lorenzo Ruiz and the Black Nazareno of Quiapo, Manila, are present at St. Patrick's.

According to Monsignor Fred Bitanga, the pastor, the veterans are not just regular Sunday churchgoers, they actively volunteer during mass and church functions doing a variety of roles. They have also provided financial and material support to the church and its causes, even with their meager incomes. The Filipino veterans are also active members of the church's many lay organizations. In recognition of the spiritual importance of the veterans' secular cause, the pastor of the church sits on the board of directors of the San Francisco Veteran's Equity Center.

Aside from the other Catholic Churches in the vast Archdiocese of San Francisco and Diocese of Oakland, the San Francisco Filipino American Seventh-Day Adventist Church in Pacifica, Iglesia ni Cristo's San Francisco Bay Area locales, Faith Bible Church of San Francisco, Filipino Jehovah's Witness congregations, Filipino ward of the Church of Jesus Christ and Latter Day Saints, Saint Francis and Grace United Methodist Church in San Francisco also have faithful Filipino veterans and youth among their congregations who participate actively in their masses and bible studies, church organizations and functions, perform community outreach, donate funds, and receive counseling and support. The veterans who are not able to travel to religious spaces continue to pray in their homes and are visited regularly by ministers, pastors, and church members, who also bring them food and other necessities. Besides offering prayers, church leaders and their congregations have appealed to their local and Congressional representatives to act on the veterans' issue. They joined other Filipino American community-based organizations in protests in front of City Hall and the Federal Office building. Church members have also raised funds to help fly veterans to Washington D.C. to meet with Congressional staff and testify in hearings. They were hosted by Filipino Methodist, Catholic, Iglesia ni Cristo, and Jehovah's Witness families there.

On January 17, 2009, 60 years after the 1946 Rescission Acts, newly elected U.S. President Barack Obama signed the US$787 billion American Recovery and Reinvestment Act of 2009, also known as the "Stimulus Package", which included a $198 million earmark for the remaining veterans and their families. Those who have become U.S. citizens got US$15,000 each while non-citizens received US$9,000. This historic insertion would not have been made possible without the consistent lobbying of Filipino diaspora diplomats from all over the country. A bulk of the pressure have been directed at California and Hawaii House and Senate Congressional delegations who have been bombarded over the last 20 years with Filipino and Filipina constituent faxes, phone calls, letters, petitions, and e-mails. These led House Speaker Nancy Pelosi and Senate majority leader Harry Reid to agree with the strategy of Senator Daniel Inouye and Representative Bob Filner to take the risk of including a veteran's equity provision in a bill that would surely be passed by Congress. Unfortunately, Lolo Tony had passed away before this law was passed. But I am happy that the president I campaigned and voted for rescinded the rabid act that took away what was due him and the rest of the family.

Another illustration of effective Filipino religious *kasamahan* turned *bayanihan* influence was the fight that reached the halls of the U.S. Congress against extra-judicial killings in the Philippines. In 2006, the extra-judicial killings of United Church of Christ Pastor Pawican, United Methodist Church Pastor Sta. Rosa, and Iglesia Filipina Independiente Bishop Ramento raised to 25 the number of church leaders slain by suspected military operations as part of the Philippine chapter of the U.S.-led global War on Terrorism. This includes: 10 clergy, six lay workers of church-based programs, seven members of the United Church of Christ in the Philippines (UCCP) and two members of the United Methodist Church (UMC). All were slain heeding the call of their faith and working for poor and oppressed communities. They were killed as part of a larger global plan to eliminate members and supporters of the CPP-NPA, a Philippine terrorist group in the U.S.-Designated Foreign Terrorist Organizations List. Hence, annual U.S. military assistance to the Philippines' "War on Terrorism" directly contributed to these extrajudicial deaths. Philippine evangelical churches took the lead in successfully lobbying the U.S. Congress on this human rights issue.

Together with many civil society groups, church leaders and members from the Philippines not just prayed for the extrajudicial killings to stop. They also appealed for investigations and actions from local to national politicians, all the way to President Gloria Macapagal Arroyo. Protestant churches also banded together to appeal to the international community, including their "mother" churches in the U.S. In May 2006, distraught attendees at the General Assembly of the United Church of Christ in the Philippines (UCCP)—the church which has been the hardest hit in terms of the number of victims—called for the holding of a Human Rights and Peace Summit. At the summit, hosted by UCCP in cooperation with the NCCP, the UMC, IFI, the Ecumenical Bishops' Forum (EBF) and the Benedictines for Peace, the ecumenical and inter-generational participants (included youth participants) called for a thorough independent investigation by the United Nations High Commissioner for Human Rights to determine the truth and to hold accountable those responsible for these extra-judicial deaths.

Through phone calls and the internet, their pleas for help were received on the other side of the Pacific Ocean where their Filipino American Protestant brothers and sisters in Christ helped amplify their concerns to their U.S. church leaders. It became more compelling since many firs-generation Filipino American UMC migrants personally knew the victims and their families. Thus, in June 2006, an inter-generational gathering of pastors and lay persons at the annual UMC California-Nevada Conference, overwhelmingly accepted, approved, and supported Resolution 58: "The Philippines: Disappearances, Extrajudicial Killings, and Human Rights Violations" expressing solidarity with the UMC in the Philippines, the UCCP, the NCCP, and the many other church and secular voices in the common cry for justice and peace in the wake of a spate of harassments and assassinations and reported and documented killings and summary executions of church leaders, both clergy and laity, and peace and human rights advocates, including journalists. The Secretary of the California-Nevada Annual Conference sent copies of Resolution 58 to political leaders in the Philippines and the U.S.

Moved to act, former NCCP social worker Wilson DeOcera, Pastor of the Daly City United Methodist Church and Chair of the Filipino Caucus at the California Nevada Conference helped raise awareness and rally support by co-sponsoring an unprecedented inter-faith and inter-generational worship service (Pagsambang Bayan or People's Worship) mourning the death of peace and justice in the Philippines. Besides UMC members, the Daly City church's worship area was filled with young and old members and supporters of PANA Institute (Institute for Leadership Development and Study of Pacific Asian North American Religion), and Pacific Asian American Ministries of the United Church of Christ. Youth from the Filipino Community Support (FOCUS-Bay Area), Filipino Community Center (FCC-San Francisco), BAYAN USA, families from the Liwanag Cultural Center in Daly City, and students from the area's colleges and universities were also present.

The e-mail invitation reached many non-Filipino faith communities— African American, Asians, Latinos evangelical church members— and some even came from New York. They joined a very solemn ecumenical candlelight vigil and procession that was covered by the Filipino American and national media. At the service, the inter-faith, inter-generational gathering of clergy and lay persons sadly reflected on the unsolved murders of the past five years of hundreds working for social justice in the Philippines. It was the first time pastors of Filipino descent from the Iglesia Filipina Independiente, the UMC, UCC, Baptist, Episcopal, and other Filipino evangelical congregations came together as one in the San Francisco Bay Area.

After their invocations, the church leaders strongly condemned the murder of Bishop Ramento and the other wanton killings, and urged their respective religious congregations to write formal protest letters to the Philippine Ambassador to the U.S. in Washington, D.C., the U.S. State Department, and their U.S. congressional representatives. After the Daly City service, Filipino American leaders and members of the Episcopal Church's asked then newly installed Presiding Bishop, the Most Reverend Katharine Jefferts Schori, to immediately write a letter to Philippine Ambassador Willie Gaa expressing "deep concern among U.S. denominations over the deplorable number of extra-judicial killings."

To emphasize the seriousness of this issue to the international UMC congregation, none other than Bishop Beverly J. Shamana, head of global United Methodist Church and chair of the UMC's General Board of Church of Society, joined the 17-member Cal-Nevada United Methodist Philippine Fact-Finding Team/Solidarity and Pastoral Visit mandated by Resolution 58. The February 2007 mission had heavy representations from very concerned UMC Church pastors and lay members from the San Francisco Bay Area, especially those with many Filipino migrant congregants.

In Feb 2007, the UN Special Rapporteur Philip Allston conducted an independent investigation and came out with comprehensive recommendations. Its most important recommendation was to ask the Philippine President Gloria Macapagal Arroyo, as Commander in Chief of the Armed Forces, to eliminate extra-judicial executions from the country's "war on terror" counterinsurgency operations. The UN report also requested the Philippine Government to direct all military officers to cease from making public statements linking political or other civil society groups to those engaged in armed insurgencies. Any such characterizations belong solely within the power of the civilian authorities.

Publicity on the ecumenical gathering in Daly City moved U.S. Senator Barbara Boxer and California Congressman Tom Lantos to call for separate congressional meetings and consultations. Senator Boxer chaired the special session of the Senate Foreign Relations Committee which heard testimonies from State Department officers and civil society organizations from the Philippines and the U.S., including the General Secretary of the UCCP, Amnesty International, and the U.S. Institute of Peace. A copy of the NCCP report was circulated.

One of those who shared his views at the Congressional meeting was Chris D., a second-generation FilAm who, along with his family, attended the Geneva United Methodist Church. He was a student at San Francisco State University and had learned about these human rights violations from his professors and fellow FilAm students at a League of Filipino Students teach-in. He was at the Pagsambang Bayan at Daly City UMC. Chris admonished political and military leaders in both his homelands for tolerating and encouraging the extra-judicial slayings especially the evangelical pastors. Their spirit-filled testimonies and candlelit vigils convinced the U.S. Congressional leaders to link the partial release of the 2008 U.S. military aid to the Philippines with the Arroyo administration's adherence to human rights and international laws.

Hearing the voices of their constituents, including Filipino faithful and their fellow Protestant church members, 49 Democratic and Republican members of the U.S. House of Representatives sent an urgent compliance reminder to President Gloria Macapagal Arroyo in August 2007. The bi-partisan letter stated: "Since the extra-judicial killings in the Philippines continue unabated, and given the fact that there are many unanswered questions about the role of the Philippine government and military in these deaths, we respectfully request your strong and immediate leadership in investigating and prosecuting those individuals and/or groups, including those in the AFP [Armed Forces of the Philippines] and PNP [Philippine National Police], responsible for these killings, and in eliminating the underlying causes of the violence."

In November 2007, the World Council of Churches (WCC) also sent a fact-finding delegation headed by WCC general secretary Reverend Samuel Kobia. The mission included Sophia Adinyira, a justice of the Supreme Court of Ghana and a member of the (Anglican) Church of the Province of West Africa; Reverend Sandy Yule, the national secretary for Christian Unity of the Uniting Church in Australia; and WCC program executive for Asia Mathews George Chunakara. Given all the bilateral and multilateral pressure, extrajudicial killings declined in 2007—a sign that their prayers had been answered. It was also a signal to the US. that it needs to rethink and re-examine the wide-ranging human rights and moral side-effects of its military and economic aid to countries enforcing America's "Global War on Terrorism."

Occupational Filipinization

Philippine diaspora diplomats' occupational *bayanihan* and *kasamahan* soft power influences are manifested by their working for San Francisco Bay Area corporations, health care centers, and shopping malls. They have made occupational imprints in almost every type of job in government, business, and civil society.

This is largely attributed to the Philippine diaspora diplomats multicultural heritage—an Americanized, Hispanicized, and Asianized educational and cultural background which has paid off handsomely in terms of greater access and influence to higher skilled and higher paying San Francisco Bay Area jobs compared to Latino and other Asian ethnicities, and even Caucasians. But few know that the occupational inroads and sacrifices they have been making in California has a more than a hundred year old history beginning with farm workers to present day computer engineers.

In a survey I conducted in 2006 with 1644 respondents from the San Francisco Bay Area, my random sampling showed that 20 percent were in the legal, accounting, and consulting professions, and another 20 percent were working for the high-paying health, information technology, and engineering sectors. There were also those who were retired, unemployed, and homemakers. Seven out of ten reported that they held one job, while two out of ten indicated that they worked two jobs. One out of every four individuals surveyed had been working in the U.S. for between one and five years.

Because of its century-old migration history, it is not surprising that some Philippine diaspora diplomats have quietly etched their names in business, arts, science, military, literature, and medicine scenes of the most powerful nation in the world.

Here in San Francisco, I met Philippine-born and educated entrepreneur and engineer Diosdado "Dado" Banatao. Sometimes nicknamed the "Bill Gates of the Silicon Valley," he is regarded as a visionary influence not just in the U.S. but in Asia and Europe. His graphic acceleration inventions and chip technology research have helped lower the cost of personal computers while increasing its efficiency and performance.

Silicon Valley covers 1,500 square miles of the southern portion of the San Francisco Bay Area. It covers three large Bay Area counties, San Francisco, Santa Clara, San Mateo, and stretches from downtown San Francisco, down Highway 101, past the biotech campuses of South San Francisco and the corporate campuses to the IBM software labs in south San Jose and on to the telecommunications work in Morgan Hill.

In this technology region of the California, Dado Banatao went to graduate school at Stanford University and thereafter developed several key semiconductor technologies and startup companies. In 1997, he received the Ernst & Young, Inc. Magazine's Master Entrepreneur of the Year Award. He gives back to his two home countries by establishing scholarship funds to encourage Filipino students to study science and engineering. Dado continues to mentor young venture capitalists from the Philippines. He is the managing partner of Tallwood Venture Capital and chair of the University of California-Berkeley's College of Engineering advisory board.

Also cashing in on Silicon Valley technology are Filipino multi-millionaires Elizabeth Rivera who owns RiveraTech Multimedia and Rodolfo Dorilag who owns Micro-Integration Engineering. Filipino diaspora diplomats like Dado, Elizabeth, and Rodolfo have made the U.S. technology sector more competitive internationally.

But you do not have to be a Dado Banatao to have an occupational influence. Even simple and regular people make their own little marks on San Francisco's employment market. Just like in London, I found the city's health care system well impacted by the trademark care, training, energy, diligence, discipline, and laughter of Filipino diaspora diplomats.

My buddy from Santa Ana, Ricky W. and I would visit his convalescing 88-year old mother, Rose, at the Laguna Honda Hospital, which is dominated by Filipina nurses. Just like Laguna Honda, the nursing, administrative, housekeeping staff combined at San Francisco General, Pacific Medical Center, Saint Luke's Hospital, Saint Mary's Hospital, and even Seton Medical Center in nearby Daly City are about 30-50 percent Filipino. There are many Filipino volunteers at these hospitals too. Ricky was one of them.

At Kaiser Permanente, where three generations of my family go for health care, there are a lot of Filipino clerical, nursing, lab technicians, radiologists, maintenance, and medical staff too. Our physician, Dr. Eric Capulla, is a Philippine- and U.S.-trained specialist in internal medicine. We converse with everyone in Taglish. Our encounters always remind my family of our medical visits to the Makati Medical Center in Metro Manila. The Filipino nurses and doctors treating and caring for us here were educated and trained at the same schools and hospitals as those who cared for us in the Philippines.

Thanksgiving 2008: My fiancee and I visited my brother, James, who was working the Turkey Day shift at CP Japantown, a posh retirement community near downtown San Francisco. While James played his guitar, Michelle and I sang and danced with the elderly Asian and European migrants. Some were rarely visited by their families; many already had dementia and Alzheimer's, and were taking a cocktail of drugs that have made them very demanding, depressed, and confused. But that afternoon they were smiling, clapping, and singing tunes they could recall from the distant past, from classic children's songs like "Old MacDonald Had a Farm" to John Denver's "Leaving on a Jet Plane." The charming five-story complex is able to fulfill its promise of 24-hour assistance to more than 180 residents with the help of its caring, patient, and cheerful staff of Filipino migrants, from receptionists, to caregivers, to kitchen staff, food servers, to housekeeping, to activity coordinators like James.

Filipino diaspora diplomats are sought after in the U.S. health care industry for their naturally caring and charming approach to their occupations. James' boss intimated to me on the way out, "The skills combination, education and training of your brother is one of a kind."

Earning and Shopping at Serramonte Mall

Encountering a Philippine migrant, as a customer or employee, in one of its shopping malls around the San Francisco Bay area is a very high possibility. After all, the region is home to more than 300,000 of them. Their presence, selling charm, and buying power is felt in many U.S. labor and consumer markets. Highly skilled jobs in the workforce have led to high income levels. The 2000 U.S. Census provided empirical data to support this fact, noting that Filipinos (along with Asian Indians) have the highest median family incomes among all ethnicities due to their highly prepared technical and educational backgrounds. Their capacity to make significant *bayanihan* and *kasamahan* contributions to America is anchored on their being highly educated and employable, resulting in higher individual and family incomes compared to the average for the total U.S. population, as illustrated in Figure 3.2. They are a young and highly productive segment of the U.S. population—sixty-three percent of them are "Generation Y'ers".

Figure 3.2
Filipino population compared to U.S. population, 2004

	U.S. Filipinos	U.S. Population
Education		
High school	90.8%	83.9%
Bachelor's degree	47.9%	27.0%
Masters, Doctorate degree	8.2%	9.9%
Employment rate	68.8%	65.9%
Income		
Median family income	$72,165	$53,672
Individual per capita income	$25,534	$24,020

Source: U.S. Census Bureau (2004).

In a survey I conducted in 2006, I found half of the respondents (or 823 out of 1,644) declaring salaries from $30,000 to $60,000, yearly. This earning capacity is five to ten times above the 2006 U.S. Poverty Guidelines for individuals (making $6,600 a year). Diaspora diplomats in the San Francisco Bay Area are relatively well off vis-à-vis other ethnicities. According to U.S. Citizenship and Immigration Services sponsorship guidelines, their income levels essentially allow them sponsorship of between 7 to 16 family members from the Philippines. Notably, nine percent of those questioned were in the high six-figure earning level.

The sizeable earnings of Filipino and Filipina diaspora diplomats in the San Francisco Bay Area makes it feasible for them to maintain twin homes, in the Philippines and United States, especially with a much lower cost of living in the Philippines and stronger exchange rate for the dollar to the peso (now approximately US$1.00=PhP45.00). But for what expenses are their remittance used? Housing assistance in the form of monthly lease payments or mortgages is the most popular reason for sending money. The second is the education of the next generation back in the Philippines--some of whom will eventually join the diaspora. The third most common reason for sending money home is for elderly support and medicines.

Filipino migrants work hard and shop hard. This is most evident just watching them at the gigantic strip and complex malls of the San Francisco Bay Area. One of them is the Serramonte Center in Daly City, categorized as a super regional shopping mall open 7 days a week, 11 hours a day.

At this massive suburban shopper's paradise, every third person you will meet is of Philippine descent, hardly a surprise since the population of Daly City is predominantly Filipino. Serramonte has become an inter-generational Philippine community center where Filipino schoolkids hang out and their lolas and lolos socialize with each other. Tagalog is used alongside English as a language of transaction from the small kiosks to the huge McDonald's where Filipino customers meet Filipino cashiers. Philippine dialects like Ilocano, Cebuano, and Bicolano, also come in handy at times.

Many first- and second-generation Filipino migrants from around the area find their first job at the chain and retail stores of Serramonte. This is why close to half of the employees at the gigantic Target is Filipino, helping sell products made in countries from Bangladesh to Haiti. Not intimidated by retail giants like Forever 21 and Macy's, a Philippine-based apparel store, Bench, is there pitching clothes that fit and look better on not just Filipino but Asian Americans. While retail giant Mervyn's collapsed during the height of the economic downturn, Bench continued to thrive and prosper. At the food court, Manila Bay Cusine's freshly cooked *chicken adobo, pansit bihon, lumpiang sariwa*, and *pork barbeque* are the alternatives to quick meals from Burger King, Panda Express, and Orange Julius.

Around the fringes of Serramonte mall are churches that Filipino residents attend: Saint Augustine's Catholic Church, Daly City United Methodist

Church, Iglesia ni Cristo, Philippine Independent Church, among others. There is ballroom dancing at the nearby community center and the basketball and tennis courts are filled with Filipino regulars from youth to seniors. The Daly City public library probably has the best collection of Philippine DVDs in the U.S. From my many trips to Serramonte over the past 20 years, I saw how consumerism, community, and church have evolved together in the Philippine migrant's daily life.

Associational Filipinization

In the succeeding paragraphs, I highlight the contributions and impact of Philippine diaspora diplomats as manifested in their hundreds of colorful and vibrant *kasamahan* and *bayanihan* groupings and gatherings that have become part of San Francisco's cultural capital and social calendar.

At the beginning of the millennium, Harvard politics professor Robert Putnam came out with his best-selling book, *Bowling Alone,* arguing that social and civic capital formation has declined in the U.S. Like-minded scholars extended his point further to eight other advanced democracies in *Democracies in Flux.* By extension, their political neorealistic thought backed by page after page of historical data doused water on any neoidealist thinking on the power and growth of civil society groups. However, probably because of Putnam and his allies' mainstream ethnic socialization which created racial blind spots, they seemed to have missed out on new migrants to the U.S. and the western states they studied. More importantly, the new forms of bonding and bridging of social and civic capitals new Philippine migrants build and propagate affect both the domestic and international spheres.

As of 2005, there were more than 400 Philippine hometown associations in the San Francisco Bay Area. These hometown associations organize dances, language classes, beauty pageants, and neighborhood cleanups. They also organize fundraisers for local and international causes. In doing so, they are using social and cultural capital formed in the Philippines and fostered in churches in the U.S., then imparted to American society and culture.

Yearly doses of Filipinization do not just happen in June during the Philippine Independence Day celebration and parade on downtown Market Street. Since 1988, October is recognized as Filipino American History Month or Filipino American Heritage Month in San Francisco and throughout the U.S. Every December, there is a Parol (Christmas lantern) stroll and contest on Mission Street. There is also the colorful Santacruzan at San Francisco's Bessie Carmichael Elementary School in May which is about the time many hometown associations celebrate the feast day of their towns' patron saints. San Francisco Quezonians make time for a Pahiyas every May. Cebuanos look forward to feast of the Sinulog festival praising the Santo Niño de Cebu every January, the most popular Philippine icon. San Francisco Bicolanos do a smaller version of the Peñafrancia festival every September.

Figure 3.3
Philippine diaspora organizations in the
San Francisco Bay Area

Type	Number	Percent
Hometown/Regional	170	41
Spiritual/Religious	37	9
Professional	36	9
Cultural and recreational	34	8
Filipino American social clubs	31	8
Political and civic	26	6
Senior's and elderly	22	5
Veterans	19	5
Educational/Alumni	16	4
Philippine development	13	3
Lion's clubs	7	2
Total	**411**	**100**

Source: Philippine Consulate General of San Francisco, as of January 2005.

One of the hometown association ambassadors representing America in the Philippines is Mrs. Ilocandia Queen. The U.S. Ilocano National Association (USINA) based in San Francisco has successfully sponsored the contest since 1993 as a way to raise money for Filipino American scholarships as well as for its elderly members' health care, death, and disability needs. Past winners of the Mrs. Ilocandia Queen Contest have been sent to their hometowns to deliver money for the building of health care centers, repairs to the public markets, and construction of libraries at municipal schools. The beauty queen's price includes a roundtrip airfare is paid for by the USINA.

Next in number to these vibrant Filipino hometown associations are energetic spiritual and religious organizations (nine percent), which derive from a broad array of churches in the Philippines. The most popular ones revolve around national spiritual symbols such as the Santo Niño de Cebu (Christ Child), Virgin Mary, Nazareno (brown/black images of Christ), and San Lorenzo Ruiz (the first Filipino saint). There is also a natural merging of the hometown associations and spiritual organizations during the feast days of a town, as statues or images of the town's patron saint are commonly displayed on such occasions. For instance, members of hometown associations from Bicol province are also core members and organizers of traditional fluvial events surrounding its divine patron, the Nuestra Senora de Peñafrancia. Non-Catholic spiritual groups also have their organizations in the U.S., including the San Francisco Filipino Full Gospel Assembly and the National Association of Filipino American United Methodists.

Professional associations of Filipino migrants (making up nine percent of Filipino groupings) include organizations of nurses, engineers, architects, teachers, doctors, lawyers, executives, and public employees. Some are organized around the largest public and private institutions in America, such as the Filipino Postal Employees Association of San Francisco, Filipino American Government Employees of Northern California, and Fil-Am Communications Employees of SBC Pacific Bell. The Fil-Am Chevron Employees Association has even set up its own separate United Way fund for the Filipino community. The Filipino Employees Association of Pacific Gas and Electric Company commit themselves to making a positive impact on the company, their members and the Philippine and Filipino American communities it serves. They sponsor community benefit events and awareness raising talks, and award scholarships to deserving college-bound students of Filipino descent annually.

The Philippine Consulate in San Francisco has identified 34 Filipino cultural, sports, history, performing, literary, as well as visual arts associations. They include the Fil-Am Music and Arts Society, the Mabuhay Golf Club, and the Fil-Am Basketball Association. The Filipino American Democratic Club and Filipino American Republican Club represent political interests from both ends of the spectrum. Older Filipino migrants find comfort and camaraderie in 22 San Francisco seniors' and elderly organizations, including the Filipino Seniors Club. They can congregate and enjoy activities at the Filipino Senior Center in Oakland, for example, or the Canon Kip Senior Center in downtown San Francisco. Even before the influx of Filipino World War II veterans in the early 1990s, veterans' associations had emerged in San Francisco. Currently, forty-one area organizations represent the special interests of Filipino seniors and veterans.

Numerous alumni associations in the U.S. represent high schools (e.g., Saint Anthony Catholic High School Alumni Association in Rizal Province) and universities (e.g., De La Salle Alumni Association, Ateneo de Manila University Alumni Association, University of the Philippine Alumni Association) in the Philippines. Fraternity alumni groups include the Alpha Phi Omega Alumni Association of Northern California and the Triskelon Alumni Association of Northern California. They organize philanthropic golf, poker, badminton, tennis, basketball, and bowling tournaments. Their beneficiaries are special projects their universities and colleges helped identify back at their other homeland. Filipino alumni sponsor regular gatherings as well as special events, such as talks by distinguished fellow alumni and faculty members from their schools back home.

Robert Putnam notes that traditional American civic clubs like the Lions, Rotarians, Elks, and Jaycees have seen declining memberships. This is not the case among the Filipino migrant community in San Francisco, where the number of Lions Clubs has increased from zero in 1965 to seven in 2005. There are also seven new Filipino American Lions Clubs outside of the Bay Area. Additionally, there are newly activated Filipino American Rotarians, Jaycees, Knights of Columbus and Masonic circles. Some Filipino American organizations specialize in channeling assistance to help address development issues back in the Philippines, such as the Coalition for Philippine Renewal and Philippine International Aid. To share informational resources and cultural capital, sister city arrangements have been established between cities in the Philippines and the San Francisco Bay Area, including Fremont and Lipa, San Francisco and Manila, Palo Alto and Palo, and Daly City and Quezon City.

Educating minds and hearts to change the world

Accommodating the insatiable demand of the Filipino community for cultural education (*kasamahan*) as well the need to sustain and deepen their social justice and civic engagement (*bayanihan*) have spurred the opening of Philippine studies programs at San Francisco Bay Area schools. I had a role in nurturing this educational movement.

Eleven years after graduation, I was teaching public policy and administration at Golden Gate University when I was invited to teach a Philippine studies class at the University of San Francisco. At first I was skeptical: who the hell would be interested in such a course in America? Besides, it had been more than a decade since I have taught anything relating to my culture.

Was I was surprised when I first entered the classroom! Before me was a sea of black-haired brown faces, the sons and daughters of first-generation migrants from the 1960s and 1970s or the grandchildren of Philippine migrants from the 1940s and 1950s. They were in my class because they were told by their parents and grandparents that the only way to succeed in U.S. was to speak, act and live like the majority of Americans. In other words, they were ordered to be "white" because ethnic culture and language were considered liabilities.

As these kids got older, the more they tried to become "white," the more they realized they were not, thus began their search for their own American identity and ultimately, their ethnicity. They wanted to know about their Filipino roots and learn Tagalog. They asked a lot of "why?" questions. At the end of one of my classes, a young lady, whose parents hailed from Cebu, summed up their unwitting diaspora diplomat role in U.S. society thus: "Professor, it's cool to be Filipino, huh?" Before I could respond, she added, "We make American communities colorful!" The rest of the class laughed in agreement.

For those who came of age in the U.S. before the late 1990s, seeing the words, "the Philippines," in English-print, still surprises them. This is because, as recently 10 years ago, you could still count with one hand the number of places where "the Philippines" was published: in the ethnic newspapers from local pandesal bakeries or Asian supermarkets, and in the one or two pages U.S. history textbooks devote to the Spanish-American War. Because the out-of-home exposure to anything Filipino was so inadequate, most had no clue that the Philippines shares such a long and complicated history with the U.S. And they certainly could never have imagined such a thing as "Philippines Studies" or "Filipino Studies," which not only analyzes and disseminates this history, but places the Philippines, with its history of colonization, migration, and racial mixture and integration, at or near the center of global and diaspora scholarship.

Fortunately, this is less the case for students today, especially at the University of San Francisco (USF), where the Maria Elena Yuchengco Philippines Studies Program (YPSP) has made it possible for the next-generation diaspora diplomats to learn about the Philippines in their university courses. It is the only Philippine Studies program in the world with social justice courses like "Filipino politics and justice" and "Knowledge activism."

Created by the generous endowment of Filipino diplomat and philanthropist Ambassador Alfonso Yuchengco, YPSP established itself with financial grants to Kasamahan, USF's Filipino student organization and their long-standing Philippine Cultural Night presentation, Barrio Fiesta; the purchase of Philippine studies publications and films; financing student attendance at Philippine studies conferences and workshops; and enlisting student participation in the USF-Ateneo summer immersion program in the Philippines. Beside "Filipino Politics and Justice" and "Knowledge Activism", YPSP has expanded to offer courses in Philippine and Filipino-American histories, beginning to advanced Filipino/Tagalog, Filipino American visual art, Philippine performing arts, Asian Americans and the media, Philippine boxing and culture, and a survey course on contemporary Filipino culture and society.

Since then, the YPSP has grown and evolved, especially in response to student appeals for an education which enables them to understand how the culture, politics, religion, business, societies, environment, and economies of the Philippines are related and interdependent on Filipino relationships with and within other nations. To further institutionalize Philippine studies as an important academic field of inquiry, YPSP developed an undergraduate minor—the only one of its kind in San Francisco. Today, YPSP faculty are teaching courses, conducting research, and performing service learning on a broad range of topics relating to the Filipino diaspora as well as collaborating and linking to the rest of the world.

Unlike other universities, USF's Philippine studies courses are an integral part of university's general education core requirements for Cultural Diversity, Service Learning, and Social Science. They satisfy major requirements in the Politics, Asian Studies, and International Studies programs as well as electives in the Asia-Pacific Studies, Ethnic Studies, Asian American Studies, Catholic Studies, and McCarthy Public Service programs. A Yuchengco Fellows

Program for Young Professionals in the Media has recently been established at USF's Center for the Pacific Rim as well as an Ambassador Alfonso Yuchengco Lecture Series which is sponsoring the centennial conference: "100 Years of Filipino Presence in the United States: A Journey of Hope".

The young Filipino American diaspora diplomats of the USF Yuchengco Philippine Studies program are immersed in service learning and community activities in San Francisco's South of Market District (SOMA). They mentor and assist at-risk new Filipino migrants and their families at Westbay Multi-Services Center, the Filipino Education Center, and Bessie Carmichael Elementary School. Every year, along with their YPSP professor, YPSP students provide hundreds of hours volunteering at the Veterans Equity Center, Filipino American Development Foundation, Manilatown Heritage, Bindlestiff Studios, and Filipino Seniors Nutrition Program. Besides these non-profit organizations, they do service learning in the following city and state government offices: District 6 Supervisor, California State Senator Leland Yee, California Assembly Majority Whip Fiona Ma, and California Assemblyman Tom Ammiano, and the San Francisco Immigrant Rights Commission. They join Filipino ethno-tours of San Francisco as well as protest marches in front of the City Hall, the Philippine Consulate, and all the way to the U.S. Congress.

Recently, along with Filipino American students, faculty, and administrators from San Francisco State University, Golden Gate University, and the City College of San Francisco, YPSP students launched a successful campaign that named a South of Market park for Filipina American Olympic, two-time gold medalist platform diver Victoria Manalo Draves. They have also marched for the Filipino World War II veterans' equity issue, Lesbian, Gay, Bisexual, Transgendered (LGBT) concerns, human rights, and immigrant rights in San Francisco.

Students on a Philippine Ethno-tour of San Francisco pause at the foot of a concrete Corinthian column commemorating Admiral Dewey's 1898 victory in Manila Bay.

Established by San Francisco pioneer Filipino migrant Ed de la Cruz 40 years ago and now staffed with student volunteers and alumni from the USF, West Bay Pilipino Multi-Service Center (West Bay) is the oldest non-profit organization providing social services to the Filipinos in the South of Market, Tenderloin, and Mission neighborhoods of San Francisco. The organization is fully staffed by products of USF Yuchengco Philippine Studies Program, particularly my "Filipino politics and justice course." With their help and influence, West Bay has expanded to accept other ethnic groups in its public health, employment and housing programs. West Bay enjoys the support of the community for its 39 years of excellent track record in community services. It received numerous recognitions from different governmental agencies (Federal, State and Local) and private foundations that fund the organization.

The agency has the support and respect of City leaders and agencies.

Over the years, USF student have helped make West Bay a place where mainstream society members are able to donate money or do hands-on community service clients who are mostly at-risk Filipino youth, seniors, and their families. Through the non-profit, European Americans, Latino Americans, and other Asian Americans are able to give back to society through programs for children and youth such as after-school tutoring, homework assistance and other services to keep youth motivated in education, keep them off the streets and from violence, and provide guidance as they mature to adulthood. University of California-San Francisco, University of California-Berkeley, San Francisco State University, City College of San Francisco, and other service learning students have done thousands of hours of volunteer work at West Bay's support groups, counseling sessions, mental health information and referrals, employment assistance, crisis hotline, and many other services that only West Bay has the capacity and experience to provide.

Summary and Conclusion

Nowadays, we, the FilAms in San Francisco tantalize the appetite of our fellow Americans and tourists from all over the world with a sneak preview of the natural beauty of the Philippines through public places and exhibitions in our city.

Not too far away from where I live and work is the world-class science center—the California Academy of Sciences (CAS). It is one of the world's largest museums of natural history. When it reopened in 2008, CAS scientists and the Filipino diaspora community proudly showed off the planet's deepest living coral reef display with living plant and animal species from the Philippines. Many San Francisco Filipino diaspora diplomats helped with the project since they believe that a large chunk of their cultural pride would be on display in a breathtaking 25-foot 212,000-gallon aquarium tank. Since CAS opened, more than a million visitors a year witnessed and learned about the ecological interaction of Philippine mangroves, soft and hard corals, black-tipped reef sharks, rays, and more than 4,000 reef fishes that are native to the Philippines. The mother reef where the CAS exhibit reef was grown from is part of the Coral Triangle spanning not just the Philippines but also Indonesia, Malaysia, Papua New Guinea, Solomon Islands and Timor-Leste.

Energetic FilAm diaspora diplomats Malou Babilonia and Marylou Salcedo of PUSOD, a nongovernmental organization with trans-Pacific offices in Berkeley and Batangas, along with REEF (Reaching out through Environmental Education for Filipinos) volunteers proudly underscored that the Philippine coral reef region teems with the richest concentration of iridescent corals, fish, crustaceans, mollusks, and marine plants in the world. No Philippine government-funded tourism campaign or travel agency advertising could illustrate the natural beauty and splendor of the Philippines as an eco-tourism destination more visibly and positively.

The California Academy of Sciences exhibit has provided Filipino and Filipina diaspora diplomats in the Bay Area with a more positive and impact-filled display to counter exaggerated U.S. State Department advisories and negative news reports about their hometowns. It also helps educate America on how citizens of the Philippine practice innovative environmental preservation and justice approaches to solve their problems. On an audiovisual panel, children could listen to Malou Babilonia and me and our Tagalog-tainted English narrating basic facts and lessons about Philippine corals. At a wall panel, Philippine activists, school children, and entrepreneurs explain their role in preserving their livelihood, their reef, and the Pacific Ocean they share with America. Essentially, even though Philippine diaspora diplomats in San Francisco are thousands of miles away. We are still connected by this majestic body of water. Hence, whatever carbon emissions we produce in the U.S. adversely affects the already thin ozone layer regulating the temperature above the fragile coral reefs adjacent to our Philippine hometowns.

In sum, it is obvious from this CAS narrative and the discussion in this chapter that, as the number of Filipino migrants in San Francisco increased by leaps and bounds over the last 100 years, so have their religious, occupational, and associational soft power influences in the U.S. The soft power lessons, narratives and discourse I shared in this chapter is how I gently suggest the retuning should be of the write-ups found in both the U.S. and Philippine foreign service home and overseas offices websites and documents. There is a critical need to emphasize the remarkable work of Philippine diaspora diplomats and civil society alongside the traditional economic, security, military, and political. I have written up a small segment of the Philippine migrant influences in San Francisco. This should be considered and credited as part and parcel of Philippine soft power in the U.S. Including demographic information on the number of Americans and Filipinos and their organizations on both ends would already be a giant step forward.

The Philippine diaspora diplomat's religious impact in San Francisco is subdued and respectful but pervasive and deep-seated. Systematic migration to the U.S. over the last century from its former colony has brought a remarkably healthy mix of *kasamahan* (bonding Filipinization) and *bayanihan* (bridging Filipinization) soft power influences through their vibrant Philippine spirituality and faiths. The Filipino faithful are helping renew sagging attendances at San Francisco Bay Area churches and reshaping the contours of American Catholic and Christian practices. This is illustrated by their takeover of historic San Francisco Catholic and Protestant church spaces, like Saint Patrick's Catholic Church and the Christ the Scientist Church. They introduce new *kasamahan* spiritual practices, rituals, beliefs, icons, devotions, prayers, songs, and inter-generational groupings from the Couples for Christ to the Binhi Iglesia ni Cristo youth. They also use their Filipino American faith to foster civic engagement in the government and policies of the city. Youth and their seniors have successfully advocated and lobbied for their political and social concerns from City Hall to the U.S. Congress. They have won citizenship and veterans' benefits for aging Filipino World War II veterans, as well as successfully linked human rights provisions to further U.S. military and economic assistance to extra-judicial killings perpetuated under the global War on Terrorism.

Philippine diaspora diplomats' *bayanihan* and *kasamahan* soft power influences are also manifested in the important work they do for San Francisco Bay Area corporate firms, health care centers, and shopping malls. They are in every type of occupational field. They bring into their work spaces their Philippine brand of English, education, training, ethics, and attitude. A number of individuals have even distinguished themselves in their own fields, from nurses and doctors, teachers and activists, artists and designers, lawyers and accountants in downtown San Francisco hospitals to engineers and architects, public servants and entrepreneurs, scientists and medical technicians, soldiers and law enforcers in the Silicon Valley. At work places, most Filipinos are stereotyped as hardworking, caring, energetic, happy, helpful, and a team player. Their occupational success has translated to their significant contribution to the American economy and measured through their mall shopping mall purchases. Even during economic downturns they still manage to send billions of dollars back to their Philippine hometowns.

In terms of associational influence, the contributions and impact of Philippine diaspora diplomats are manifested in the hundreds of colorful and vibrant *kasamahan* and *bayanihan* groupings and gatherings that have become an integral part of San Francisco's cultural capital and community calendars. Their hometown and regional, spiritual and religious, professional, cultural and recreational, Filipino American social clubs, political and civic, senior's and elderly, veterans, educational, and high school, college, and fraternity alumni organizations as well as Lion's and Rotary chapters help replenish and renew transnational social and cultural capital in the San Francisco Bay region while reducing acculturative stress and inculcate values of civic engagement. Interestingly, Filipino American soft power influences have significant effects not just in their U. S. home cities but also back in their ancestral Philippine hometowns.

In general, these have been encouraged and embraced by San Francisco Bay Area citizens, governments, and businesses. To accommodate their demands and needs for cultural education as well sustain and deepen the social justice aspect, many Bay Area schools have even begun Philippine studies programs and Tagalog language classes which educate minds and open hearts to understand and change the world. One program in particular which has made a significant social justice impact in San Francisco and the Philippines is the Maria Elena Yuchengco Philippine Studies Program at the University of San Francisco. Thousands of students, one quarter of whom are not of Filipino descent, have taken the courses, and more than 200 have completed their major and minor programs. Over the past decade, they have put in thousands of hours of service learning and community work, saving U.S. government agencies and non-profit organizations millions of dollars.

Filipino and Filipina migrant contributions to Philippine relations and development should be considered and credited as an integral part of U.S. soft power. American cities are fond of sister city links. San Francisco has a successful one with the Philippine capital city of Manila. A number of other Bay Area cities have sister city linkages with other cities in the Philippines and elsewhere in the world. But what is not underscored or is unseen from "American lenses" is that almost every Filipino American hometown association in San Francisco pursues the same soft power influence (probably even more!) as a Philippine-U.S. sister city committee. For most of these hometown associations, their impact on both sides of the Pacific is consistent. This *bayanihan* model even supplements the dwindling official economic and social development assistance from the United States Agency for International Development (USAID). Philippine hometown associations contribute their own brand of cultural diversity and social capital (*kasamahan*) into the San Francisco Bay Area's already vibrant ethnic community with their Filipino beauty pageants and folk dances while at the same time helping their less fortunate townmates through scholarships, donations, sponsorships, and medical missions.

CHAPTER 4

London: bridge to mission, care, and charity

In all the countries I've been to, I interacted with a different breed of Philippine career diplomats. Sworn to serve and protect nationals in constant migratory movement—over and above the two other pillars, national security and economic diplomacy -- they even defend Filipinos who may not even carry Philippine passports anymore but continue to go to Philippine diplomatic missions for help and comfort.

In the past, the ones I've met seemed quite snobbish, with an elitist attitude. Now, in my field research in Singapore, Dhaka, Dubai, and San Francisco, I encountered a more down-to-earth, very hands-on corps of young Foreign Service Officers (FSO), Foreign Service Staff Officers (FSSO), and Foreign Service Staff Employees (FSSE). My assumption is that they recognize that their roles have changed and are now very different from that of their predecessors. As career diplomats for a diaspora state, their first and foremost mission is to respect the spirit, sweat, and heart of Philippine soft power—millions of their own kind in diaspora. They are there to help support, coordinate, and supplement the religious, occupational, and associational *kasamahan* and *bayanihan* efforts of their *kababayans*.

Ever the social scientist, I decided to test this assumption. I went to the Philippine Embassy in London one very cold January afternoon. I took the Tube from my temporary home base in East London to Trafalgar Square and walked a block to the embassy. Following protocol, I exchanged pleasantries with an old acquaintance, Rey C., who I had met when he was a young consul managing the chaos on the ground during the unfortunate diplomatic tiff between Singapore and the Philippines. Rey C. was the Deputy Chief of Mission (or DCM) in London.

I then interviewed Consul Tess L. who was in charge of cultural affairs. She was frank and candid with her assessment of the Philippine community in the United Kingdom (UK) not proprietary at all with the information I needed. She impressed me with her deep knowledge of and involvement with all Filipino community religious and social activities, from every December's *Simbang Gabi* Christmas masses to every June's Philippine Independence Day commemorations all over London and other parts of the UK.

After my chat with Consul Tess, I proceeded to the adjoining building housing consular services. There were lots of people seated patiently in a brightly lit waiting area. Some were reading information from a flat screen TV while waiting for their number to appear on the small LED panel. I noticed another young officer, Consul Bernadette F., who was diligently escorting clients up and down a steep staircase in what used to be a Victorian home.

After half an hour of people-watching, I was whisked upstairs to the office of Attache Edith M. When I was about to ask questions, an urgent ATN (assistance to nationals) case was brought in. I witnessed firsthand how the new breed of Filipino career diplomat provided calm and collected counsel to a visibly distressed Filipino male nurse who had come all the way from Manchester to seek the Philippine Embassy's help. "*Gusto ko nang umuwi…wala na po akong pera,*" (I want to go home…I do not have any money) he said in a strained, loud voice. "*Tulungan ninyo po ako…*" (Help me please), the distraught young man added. "Don't be scared, relax ka lang," Edith M. told him reassuringly.

I slipped out of the room to let them continue their exchange in confidence and went down to meet Edith's boss, Tess DV, the Consul General or ConGen— another new generation career diplomat. Mother of two but looking barely in her 30s, I found out that she is married to a high school mate of mine who coincidentally is the consul general in Barcelona. Small world! The long distance relationship must be tough for both of them, I thought. Diplomats are, in many ways, living a migrant life too.

According to ConGen Tess, the consular section's actual workspace got bigger compared to the former Embassy location in Palace Green in the classy Kensington area. "My office is quite spacious since many clients come and see me personally on a daily basis for advice on various matters ranging from legal to family and job concerns," she explained. "Filipino community leaders also tend to drop by and relay invitations to social events." This sounded like the work of my mayor in Biñan, Laguna or San Francisco, California.

While walking amongst the famous Nelson's Column and the imposing National Gallery on the way to Charing Cross Station, I could not help but reflect on what I witnessed that day: my assumption had been confirmed that this new generation of Philippine foreign service career officials. More importantly, I observed how countries of origin of migrants should be treating their overseas nationals—not as liabilities but as assets for carrying out soft power globally.

In this chapter, I proceed with some highlights of long-time transnational Filipino and British people-to-people linkages which are under-emphasized in traditional bilateral government-to-government discourse which focus on the formal military, political, economic, and cultural. Thereafter, I elaborate on the Church of England's convenient alliance with Philippine Independent Church members to help save the Queen's church. I also expound on the religious influences of Filipino Catholic priests and parishioners via traditions like *Simbang Gabi* (Christmas evening novena masses) at the grand Westminster Cathedral and many other historic London Catholic churches. Moreover, I discuss Philippine occupational influences through Filipino British chefs, nurses, caregivers, and domestic helpers in the restaurants, hospitals, and homes from Hackney to Hatton Cross. Finally, I tell the stories of associational influences from Filipino British organizations like the more than a decade-old Batangas Association of the United Kingdom (BAUK), the Filipino Catholic

Community Prayer Group in Kilburn Park, and the London-based jury system advocacy groups. I sum up with some lessons learned on their *kasamahan* and *bayanihan* influences.

Descending on Her Royal Majesty's Capital

Because of the significant increase in the number of Filipinos in the UK, both the British Ambassador to the Philippines Peter Beckingham and the Philippine Ambassador to the UK (or officially the Court of Saint James) Edgardo Espiritu like to begin interviews about bilateral relations between the two countries with this interesting trivia question: Do you know that there are five Filipino babies born in the UK every day? Maybe they should add: Do you know that there are more English speakers in the Philippines than in the UK? Do you know that there are more English speakers in the Philippines than in Australia and Canada, two of the largest British commonwealths, combined?

The honorable Ambassadors could also add this historical trivia: Do you know that the Philippines like the U.S., the United Arab Emirates, Singapore, and Bangladesh, was once a part of the British colonial empire? The Philippines was occupied by the UK more than a hundred years before American colonization. At that time, France and Britain were on opposing sides of the bloody Seven Years War and trying to gather allies to support their positions. Portugal sided with Great Britain while Spain secretly signed a pact with France. To get back at Spain, Britain mobilized troops to take over Spanish possessions in Asia. On orders from London, a fleet of Her Majesty's Royal Navy loaded with a Royal Expeditionary Force of 6,839 British soldiers, sailors, marines, and volunteers left India to attack and takeover Manila, the capital city, on September 1762.

Within 10 days, Britain had defeated Spanish and Filipino troops in the battles for Manila and Cavite. On October 30, 1762, Britain accepted the surrender of the Spanish government in the Philippines. The UK administered the Philippines until April 1764 and returned it to Spain as part of terms of the Treaty of Paris signed the previous year. It took eighty years before formal relations restarted with the arrival of the first British consul to the Philippines in 1844. Comparatively, it only took twenty years for an army of 200,000 Philippine diaspora diplomats to descend on Her Majesty's capital and its environs.

More than two centuries later, the UK and its former 18-month colony found themselves allied with another former British colony in the War on Terrorism. They had one thing in common: terrorist groups had struck their major cities—Makati and Zamboanga in the Philippines, New York and Washington, DC in the U.S., and London in Britain. The Philippines followed UK's move and sent medics, engineers and other troops to reinforce the 2003 U.S.-led invasion and occupation of Iraq. Even after the withdrawal of the Philippine military from Iraq in 2004, the Philippines and the UK continued to be military partners through Operation Enduring Freedom where the Philippines is one of 10 non-NATO participants.

Presently, political and security relations between the two countries focus on combating domestic and international terrorism, human rights issues, environment, disaster planning, international crime and kidnapping, peace building, as well as peace building in conflict areas by encouraging inter-faith dialogue between Muslims, Christians and Indigenous Peoples. In 2007, her Majesty's government provided US$5.7 million in aid to help fund the replacement and repair of around 250 bridges and national roads network all over the archipelago. The British Council is the face of public diplomacy in the Philippines.

More than fifty percent of British trade is to its key European Union partners, particularly Germany, France, and the Netherlands. Nevertheless, over the years, UK companies have also made significant investments in the power, energy, agri-business, transport, water and financial services sectors of the Philippines. In 2007, it ranked 15th out of 212 trading partners. Compared to the U.S. and Japan, the majority shareholders of the total merchandise trade traffic in and out of the Philippines, the US$830 million from Britain in 2007 is less than a percent share. The Philippine enjoys a trade surplus advantage with more than US$478 million worth of merchandise exported to the UK. Imports totaled US$351 million for the same year.

There are about 200 British companies in the Philippines ranging from big multinationals to small and medium enterprises (SME). Major British companies in the country include: Shell Corporation, HSBC, GlaxoSmithKline, Standard Chartered, Rolls Royce, and Unilever. Well-known household retail stores such as Marks & Spencer, Clarks Shoes, Dr Marten, Dunhill, and Burberry operate in the Makati shopping area. Not to be outdone, Philippine corporate staples such as the Bank of the Philippine Islands (BPI), the Philippine Long Distance Telephone (PLDT), Globe Telecom, and ABS-CBN television are visible in the Greater London area particularly at Kensington High Street and Earls Court. The Philippine National Bank (PNB), one of the oldest and largest banks in the Philippines, even has two London branches: one at Notting Hill Gate and another at Earls Court. PNB, like BPI, offers loans, deposits, and remittance services.

Nowadays, diplomats like to highlight the not-so-well-known accomplishments of UK-Philippine relations over the centuries including, its helping establish the Philippine sugar industry, the railway system, the early waterworks, the first telecommunications lines, the first ferryboats, the earliest trading companies, the first in banking, insurance, pawnshops, newspaper, betting, etc. Over 50,000 British tourists visit the Philippines annually, which is more than any other European Union country. A 2009 agreement allows seven flights per week on a B747 aircraft, which could accommodate over 500 passengers from London, Heathrow, Gatwick, and Stanstead. This will definitely increase transnational people-to-people flows between the two nations, particularly London and Manila.

There are more than 1,000 British residents in the Philippines concentrated mostly in Manila. Like the tourist arrival phenomenon from the UK, Filipino

British migrants have become a significant number of English arrival statistics. Many come as visitors but some come to their parent's homeland to be actresses or actors or to play in Philippine sports. Among the former are Bea Alonzo, Amanda Griffin; Maui Taylor, and Maritoni Fernandez, as well as actor and TV presenter Derek Ramsay.

Filipino British footballers have followed their Filipino American counterparts in basketball. They are helping revitalize football in their other homeland as key players in the Philippine National Football Team or *Azkals* (street dog). Glasgow-born James Hall of English Premier League Everton and goalkeeper Neal Etheridge of London-based Fulham Reserves have made the Philippine team more competitive especially among Southeast Asian rivals. Aggressive striker Chad Edward Alesna Gould played for AFC Wimbledon, semi-professional English football club affiliated to both the London and Surrey Football Associations. They are joined by strikers Floriano Pasilan of Fulham FC and midfielder Christopher Greatwich who plays for Ringmer of the Sussex County Football League. Christopher's brother Philip who plays for Towson University, in Baltimore, Maryland is also a member of the Philippine team. Brothers Darren and Matthew Hartmann who plays for Nottingham Forest Football Club, an English professional football club based in West Bridgford, a suburb of Nottingham. Other siblings on the team are star Azkal midfielders James Joseph Placer Younghusband and his brother Phil who have been playing with Chelsea FC since they were 10 years old.

Like the U.S., Singapore, and the United Arab Emirates, there is a significant Filipino population in the UK. In a little over two decades, the Philippine Embassy estimates that the number of Filipinos living and working in the UK has increased eleven-fold, from roughly 18,000 in 1986 to a whooping 203,035 by 2007, thereby ushering in more than half a billion dollars of remittances to the Philippines. Over the past two decades, Filipinos in the UK are the third largest source of foreign remittances to the home country, after the U.S. and Saudi Arabia. In 2007, the UK was home to the largest number of temporary and permanent Philippine migrants in Europe, where there are close to one million. Italy was second with 120,192, followed by Germany with 54,336, France with 47,075, Spain with 41,780, Austria with 29,657, and Greece with 29,344.

This is only the beginning of the Filipinization story in the Greater London area where 70 percent of them live, work, socialize, and worship. Historically, most of the Filipinos in London who came in the 1970s worked in the city's bustling hotel and restaurant industry. Then in the 1980s, demand for domestic helpers increased and many came with their British and other expatriate employers who were previously stationed in the Middle East and elsewhere. In the 1990s came the nurses and caregivers. Almost 40,000 visas were issued for Filipinos to visit the UK in 2007, and that figure is going up by 10- to 15 percent, every year. Accommodating this inflow is a more spacious British embassy inaugurated in October 2008.

The number of first- and second generation Filipino students pursuing tertiary studies in the UK is also going up. At the turn of the millennium, Filipino migrants work in a variety of sectors, ranging from IT, aviation, education, hospitality (hotels, restaurants and casinos) and healthcare, as chefs, and as house managers.

Increasingly, Filipino engineers and IT experts are being recruited to the UK in significant numbers. About a hundred engineers recruited after 2000 are working in the aeronautical and avionics companies in the servicing and maintenance departments while others are with railway companies. Several dozen IT experts also work for British telecommunication companies such as Vodafone, T-Mobile, and Orange in software development, as well as with computer companies working on e-commerce solutions.

Just as in the U.S., Filipino men and women have become familiar in British theater, cinema, television, and print media. Lea Salonga began her conquest of the world stage in London with Miss Saigon. More recently, Joanna Ampil made waves as the female lead, Maria, in Audie Gemora's production of West Side Story. Like Lea, she has impressed audiences all over

Asia, Australia, and Europe, including the Queen of England.

In film and television, there is English quiz player Olav Bjortomt, and employee of The Times who has appeared on British TV's *Fifteen to One* four times and won the World Quizzing Championships in 2003. MTV Europe host Trey Farley who has also presented in British programs like *Masters of Combat*, *Loves Like a Dog*, and *Grandstand and Live & Kicking*, acted in *Bend it like Beckham*, *The Run*, *Martyr*, and *Slow Fade*. Perhaps the biggest head turner is Philippine-born English actress Rachel Grant who was the Bond girl in *Die Another Day* and Angelina Jolie's body double in *Lara Croft: Tomb Raider*. There is also English actress-dancer Rhoda Montemayor whose mother is from the Ilocos region and whose father grew up in Pampanga province. A regular face anchoring the news is Verónica Pedrosa of CNN International and BBC World. To the disdain of the conservative Filipino community, Filipina British model Leilani Anne Dowding and her sister Melanie decided to make their mark in the UK by joining the thousands of young English girls who have posed topless in the tabloid daily newspaper, *The Sun*'s, notorious page 3 (www.page3.com). On TV, Dorset-born Leilani Dowding has done guest appearances on the *Big Breakfast*, *This Morning*, *The Weakest Link*, *Faking It*, *Celebrity Wrestling*, and *Celebrity Fear Factor*.

In the British music scene, there is pop, R&B, and soul singer Mutya Buena who was raised on adobo and rice in Kingsbury, London. Mutya is a founding member of the Sugababes, a British Phonographic Industry (BRIT Awards)'s pop music award winner. She has toured with George Michael and has a UK Top 20 ballad duet with him, *This Is Not Real Love*. Not to be outdone is Filipina British pop and R&B singer Vanessa White, a member of the British-Irish five-person girl group *The Saturdays*. Its top ten debut album, *Chasing Lights*, produced three UK top ten singles. Finally, there is Myleene Klass, TV and radio presenter, model, classical pianist, member of UK pop band *HearSay*.

The Philippine Embassy in London survey also revealed a growing number of entrepreneurs, about five percent of the sample. Interestingly, 10-20 percent of the respondents are second-generation Filipino British youth, sons and daughters of the earlier migrants, many of whom are finishing university courses. Fulfilling the Filipino British communities' many social and cultural needs are about 100 Filipino community associations/charities all over the UK that are registered with the Philippine Embassy. Keeping them abreast of local Filipino community news and happenings back in the Philippines are a number of widely circulated FilBrit newspapers: *Filipino International*, *Philippine Express International*, *Filipino Observer*, *Planet Philippines*, and the *Euro Filipino Journal*.

Religious Filipinization

During my many visits to London, I observed that Philippine diaspora diplomats have slowly and discreetly been able to make noteworthy inroads into British religious life. They are accomplishing this through their active congregational participation and financial contribution to the Church of England's newly established Filipino Chaplaincy.

Many research studies have shown that Sunday churchgoing in the UK, including both the Church of England and the Catholic Church, has been witnessing a steady downward spiral since the 1890s. If this trend continues, major UK denominations will collapse by 2030. To illustrate how alarming that situation has become, from 1969 to 1999, in just a 30-year span, Anglican Church attendances almost halved, from 3.5 per cent of the population to just 1.9 percent.

To help mitigate this serious decline, one of the strategies Her Majesty's Church has adopted is to form partnerships with new ethnic migrant congregations and their churches, particularly the ones with similar theologies and themes. Consequently, the Church of England has reached out to Philippine migrants through the Philippine Independent Church (PIC), officially the Iglesia Filipina Independiente (IFI) but also nicknamed the Aglipayan Church after its first *Obispo Maximo* (Supreme Bishop). A by-product of the 1898 Philippine Revolution against oppressive Spanish government, military, and Catholic church, the PIC has grown to close to three million members in ten dioceses, including the Diocese of the U.S. and Canada.

The Church of England and the PIC have been in conversation since 2000. Finally, in May 2006, the local London Anglican-Aglipayan partnership was formalized, creating a mutually beneficial spiritual and social arrangement. The PIC needed to provide a spiritual space for its London-based Aglipayan members and newly converted Filipino migrant recruits. As agreed, the Church of England provided Saint John the Evangelist Church at the affluent Notting Hill neighborhood for the new Filipino chaplaincy. Notting Hill is strategically located at one of the Filipino community's favorite weekend hangout places. This early English-style church is one of 19 Kensington churches built around 1842-1875 with a tall spire resembling historic Saint Mary's Church in Oxfordshire.

Saint John's used to accommodate 1,500 local parishioners. But like many Anglican churches this number has declined significantly over the decades. Desperate to balance their budget, diocesan leaders have even resorted to renting out rooms for concerts and performances, birthday parties for young children, charitable trust meetings, pre- and post-natal classes for women, Alcoholics Anonymous sessions, violin and French lessons for young people, modern dancing lessons for teenagers, and meetings of political parties. So the Filipino songs and voices that fill the main church is most welcomed and appreciated.

In May 2007, no less than the Archbishop of the PIC, the Most Reverend Godofredo David, celebrated the first anniversary mass and preached the Eucharist at Saint John's Ladbroke Grove with the blessing and encouragement of the Bishop of Kensington. The Filipino chaplaincy is helping save the Queen's church.

Doctrinally, the PIC is also the best fit among the many Philippine

Protestant and Independent Christian churches since it is in full communion with the Episcopal Church of the U.S. and through it, the entire Anglican Communion since 1963. Like Anglicans, Aglipayans see themselves as both Catholic and Reformed, thus are Reformed Catholics. Both are part of the universal apostolic church of Jesus Christ and part of a Protestant Reformation. The Church of England's Filipino Chaplaincy acknowledge both Queen Elizabeth II, as the "Supreme Governor of the Church of England" as well as the current PIC Obispo Maximo, the Most Reverend Godofredo J. David. In London, their spirits are guided by the present Archbishop of Canterbury, Rowan Williams.

The Filipino Chaplaincy is coordinated by Filipino PIC Chaplain and Associate Vicar Salvador Telen who presides at the Saturday 5:30 pm and Sunday 12:30 pm, Tagalog masses. In addition, the Anglican-Aglipayan alliance at Saint John's provides pastoral care, assistance on immigration and medical problems, and community development. They emphasize that all Filipino men and women are welcome regardless of faith and denominational affiliation. To underscore its importance to the Church of England, the Archbishop of Canterbury, Rowan Williams, and the Bishop of London, Richard Chartres, occasionally join its Eucharistic celebrations. The Church of England has accommodated the PIC's doctrine of a "One, Holy, Catholic, and Apostolic Church as adapted to the Filipino way of life." Anglicans regard with reverence and independence all the saints recognized and accepted by the PIC, particularly the Santo Niño (Holy Child) and the Blessed Virgin Mary which, to Aglipayans, ought to be venerated as the foremost of the saints.

On a Wednesday evening in mid-January 2009, I dined with five Filipina Catholics migrants, Jenny D., Rosel T., Lenlen V., Dona S., and Angie A. They had started attending services at Saint John's Church the year before. After they were assured that I was not an investigator from the British Home Office, four of them confessed they were not legal immigrants. All of them worked as domestic helpers and nannies, and they would send money every week to their families in the Philippines. Jenny and Rosel proudly showed me their laminated Church of England-Filipino Chaplaincy identification card signed by Pastor Telen, attesting to their active membership. Their Church of England IDs, according to both, have always "protected" them from public harassment and embarrassing questions from the London municipal police.

Like the five ladies, many Filipino migrant Catholics had started attending the Anglican services to take advantage of this sanctuary effect and other allied services and assistance from the Anglican Church. From the UK National Health Service offices outside London, some of them were able to secure NHS cards and services just by showing their church of England IDs.

After getting her NHS card, Dona, with the assistance of Praxis, a London charity helping new migrants on Pott Street, received free pre-natal care at the Bethnal Green Health Centre and gave birth at the nearby hospital. She is eternally grateful to the Filipino Chaplaincy for the support and direction.

The Church of England's Filipino Chaplaincy ID Card allowing some undocumented migrants to receive public and private assistance.

Another Filipina, Lenlen, said that they are also able to buy Filipino food after the masses at Saint John's, something that does not happen when they attend Catholic services occasionally. Philippine migrant rights groups, like Kadamay, Gabriela, and Migrante UK, have also been able to use the Filipino Chaplaincy as a forum to raise awareness of critical social, welfare, and labor issues in the UK and the Philippines.

Aside from the PIC, the Iglesia ni Cristo or INC (I've described their origins and practices in the previous chapter) has also made a mark on British religious contours. It has well-attended worships and congregational services in England, Scotland, Ireland, Northern Ireland, and Wales. In London, the INC has two active congregations: Battersea Congregation meeting every Thursdays and Sundays at Parkgate Road and the Camden Congregation worshipping regularly every Wednesday and Saturdays at the YMCA Indian Hostel. In other parts of England, INC members attend service at the Bournemouth Committee Prayer, Manchester Group Worship Service, Norwich Group Worship Service, and Portsmouth Group Worship Service. I also met Filipino Methodists, Baptists, Adventists, Mormons, and other evangelical and protestant members who also help boost sagging church attendance in the London Metropolitan area.

Introducing a new Christmas tradition

Although a significant segment of the UK's population subscribe to the Church of England, there are still five million Catholics who live in England and Wales' twenty-two dioceses, from Arundel and Brighton to Wrexham. This number only makes up around eight percent of the total UK population.

Like the Anglican Church, Sunday attendance and contributions, are on the decline in Catholic churches. Thus the church leadership in the UK, particularly London, is very pleased with the influx of hundreds of thousands of Philippine diaspora diplomats and their children who have become active churchgoers. The powerful Catholic Bishops' Conference of England and

Wales has been aggressive and is even a couple of steps ahead of their Anglican Church counterparts in terms of care and attention to new migrant parishioners.

For instance, it appointed the Reverend Patrick Lynch, the charismatic Auxiliary Bishop of Southwark, concurrently bishop in charge of the pastoral care of all migrants in England and Wales. Citing his favorite biblical passage, [Matthew 25:36, "I was a stranger and you welcomed me"] the Bishop, at the 2009 Migrants Mass held on the feast day of Saint Joseph the Worker at Westminster Catholic Cathedral, reminded the large group of barong-clad Filipino migrant workers, "I would like to affirm the contribution migrant workers have made to Britain especially in recent years. You have contributed culturally and economically to the nation and you have contributed spiritually and socially to the Church bringing with you your deep faith, your commitment to the family and your loyalty to the Church."

Additionally, the Catholic Bishops Conference created an office of ethnic chaplaincies supporting the needs of Filipino Catholics and 29 other ethnicities. The festivities of ethnic Catholic migrants are prominently featured on the dynamic, interactive website of the Catholic Church (www.catholicchurch. org.uk). The Church of England's website, on the other hand, still had not mentioned their ethnic chaplaincies and outreach, when I checked in June 2009. Since they have the reputation of being the most active and demanding, the pastoral care of the large Filipino Catholic community has been entrusted to a team of chaplains, unlike the other ethnicities. The team is coordinated by Vencentian priest Cirino Potrido (popularly known as Fr. Ino) who is joined by Scalabrini priest Jake Dicto (Southwark Archdiocese), Saint Paul priest Serge Magbunua (Brentwood Diocese), and Diocesan priest Agustin Paunon (London).

The Vencentian superior, after a general meeting at the Vatican, responded to the request from the Diocese of Westminster to assign ethnic priests, including Nigerian and Ethiopian. They called it the "London Project." This is how Fr. Ino came to London in 2006.

Ordained as a Vencentian priest in 1990, Fr. Ino believes priests are diplomats on the spiritual side representing the church of God, and Philippine Embassy staff members are diplomats for the political side representing government. He hears and tries to act on all the problems of Filipino migrant workers, documented and undocumented, from morality concerns to homosexuality issues. Whatever he feels needs Philippine Embassy intervention he brings to the attention of Consul General Tess DV or Consul Bernadette. Some problems Fr. Ino solves on his own, others he brings to charity groups. His general approach to counseling is to listen and "journey" with them and let them discover what their faith wants them to do. He finds ways to raise money for emergency airfare and rental loans. Fr. Ino believes that it is his destiny to be assigned as pastor to marginalized groups, from the slum community in the garbage dumps of Payatas, Manila and then with indigenous people and the poor in Mindanao and Cebu. He was instrumental in forming parish-based communities and Catholic self-help and support groups for LGBT and elderly pensioners. His peers, Fr. Jake and Fr. Serge, also have duties with their religious organizations while Fr. Agustin is concurrently assigned by the Diocese of Westminster as the chaplain for Central Middlesex Hospital on Acton Lane in London. Figure 4.1 shows where Filipino Catholic priests hold monthly Tagalog services.

Figure 4.1
Tagalog Masses in London

Catholic Church	Frequency
Stevenage Parish	every first Sunday of the Month at 5:00 pm
Saint Mary's Church at Chelsea Parish	every second Sunday of the Month at 3:00 pm
Sacred Heart and Mary Immaculate Church	every second Sunday of the Month at 7:00 pm
The Blessed Sacrament Church	every third Sunday of the Month at 3:00pm
Sacred Heart of Jesus Church	every third Sunday of the Month at 3:00 pm
Our Lady of Dolours Church	every fourth Sunday of the Month at 6:30 pm
Our Lady of Grace and Saint Edward Church	every last Sunday of the Month at 6:00 pm

Because of the number and timing of Tagalog masses monthly, a Filipino migrant is able to attend and hear masses or do a traditional *bisita Iglesia* (church visit) in his or her ethnic language if he or she chooses too. Some actually do.

Just as in San Francisco, the Filipino Catholic community in London has not only filled the pews, contributed money, introduced Filipino images and devotions, Tagalog masses, it has also institutionalized Philippine traditions particularly the *Simbang Gabi* novena (Evening mass novena). Fr. Ino, when I saw him last in 2009 told me of Christmas in London: *"Very busy ang Pasko dito sa London. Daig pa sa Pilipinas kasi kaunti lang a paring Filipino. Tapos maraming request, sunod-sunod—pa-misa, pa-bless, at pa-get-together.*

Nakakapagod! (Christmas season is very busy here in London. It is busier than the Philippines because we have few Filipino priests and its mass after mass, blessing after blessing, get-together after get-together. Very tiring!). It is not unusual to see pastors in the Ambassador or Consul General's office since Filipino Church leaders are also community leaders and are important role models guiding and reminding diaspora diplomats of their missions to their London homebase, their Philippine hometowns, and God.

Replicating the Christmas mood in the Philippines, London churches with Filipino congregations, hometown and professional association, the Philippine Embassy, along with Fr. Ino and the other Filipino priests usher Christ in their lives and into British culture through ten days of open to the public *Simbang Gabi* evening masses. For the past 10 years, they have successfully staged this longest and most popular Filipino tradition in and around the London area. They have even caught the attention of the Mayor of London's office and the national tourism bureau whom have started promoting Simbang Gabi as part of UK's celebration of cultural and ethnic diversity.

For the 2008 *Simbang Gabi*, 20 Filipino organizations, from the Bicol Association to Couples for Christ hosted the serious Eucharistic celebrations and the joyous eating that follows (see Figure 4.2). The masses began on December 15th at the Our Lady of Victories Church in Kensington, co-sponsored by the Filipino Women's Association UK and the Oxford Filipino Association and ended in a December 24th service at the Saint Joseph's Catholic Church in London hosted by the Filipino Community of Roehampton. Fr. Ino presided at seven of these thirty-three Simbang Gabi services. They were all filled with hundreds of eager hearts and spirits.

Figure 4.2
2008 Simbang Gabi Novenas in London

December	Church	Sponsor
15th at 7:00 pm	Our Lady of Victories Church, Kensington	Filipino Women's Association UK and Oxford Filipino Association
16th at 6:30 pm	Carmelite Church, Kensington	Bicol Association, Ifugao Association, Carmelites Choir and Friends
17th at 7:00 pm	Saint Joseph's Church, Surrey	Filipino British Nurses Association-Surrey
17th at 7:00 pm	Church of the Five Precious Wounds, London	Share Hope Outreach and Filipinos of Brent
18th at 7:00 pm	Our Lady of Lourdes Church, Acton	Filipino Community in Acton
19th at 6:00 pm	Saint Michael and Saint Martin Church, Middlesex	Philippine Center
19th at 6:00 pm	Our Lady Queen of Heaven, Surrey	Couples for Christ and Filipino Choir of Frimley, Surrey
19th at 7:00 pm	Farm Street Church, London	Aguman Kapampangan, Batangas Association UK, Farm Street Church Filipino Community

December	Church	Sponsor
20th at 3:00 pm	Westminster Catholic Cathedral, London	Filipino Club at Westminster Cathedral
20th at 6:00 pm	Church of the Most Sacred Heart of Jesus, London	Holloway Parishioners
21st at 2:00 pm	Sacred Heart Church, Kilburn	Filipino Catholic Community Prayer Group
21st at 3:30 pm	Catholic Parish of Our Lady and Saint George, London	Filipino Community of the Catholic Parish of Our Lady and Saint George
22nd at 7:00 pm	Our Lady of the Holy Souls, London	Filipino Community of Our Lady of the Holy Souls and Couples for Christ
23rd at 7:00 pm	Saint Joseph's Catholic Church, Wembley	Filipino Community of Saint Joseph's Catholic Church
24th at 8:00 pm	Saint Joseph's Catholic Church, London	Filipino Community of Roehampton

Source: Philippine Embassy, London, 2009.

To share this remarkable Filipino tradition to a larger base of parishioners and deepen its institutionalization in Britain, the Oval Filipino Community of the Holy Redeemer Church, the Scalabrini Migration Center -- both under the Catholic Archdiocese of Southwark and entrusted to the Scalabrini Fathers -- and the Filipino Community of Roehampton also celebrated two separate

Simbang Gabi English-language masses from the 16th to the 24th of December 2008. Fr. Jake Dicto was the main presider along with some Scalabrini priests. Parishioners of all ethnicities participated even in the Tagalog masses.

Occupational Filipinization

Did you know that at the historic Saint Mary's Hospital in Paddington, where the late Princess Diana gave birth to both Princes William and Harry and where Sir Alexander Fleming discovered penicillin, more than 10 percent of the nursing staff is Filipino?

In London, the Philippine diaspora diplomacy's greatest visible impact is in the health care system. A large segment of the Filipino migrant community works as nurses and caregivers. The UK is the third largest occupational market for Filipino nurses after the U.S. and Canada, and fourth top destination for Filipino caregivers after Taiwan, Israel, and Canada.

A 2008 Philippine Embassy survey conducted among a limited sample of Philippine diaspora diplomats revealed that 65 percent of Filipinos are in nursing and allied medical professions. Within a six-year period, more than 20,000 Filipinos were recruited into the health service, most of whom are nurses now serving in the National Health Service (NHS) while the remaining work in the independent health care sector – mostly private nursing and senior care homes.

At Saint Mary's and other UK health and senior care facilities, Filipino nurses and caregivers are highly regarded for their efficiency, high degree of professionalism, and dedication to their jobs. No less than Saint Mary's chief executive, Julian Nettel agrees. They have also won acclaim for their patriotism and loyalty to Britain in the aftermath of the London tube terrorist bombing on July 7, 2005 when the blast victims were rushed to the hospital for treatment. One of those nurses is Myrna Miaque who worked for 17 years in the Middle East before permanent immigrating to the UK and establishing her career at Saint Mary's.

I was able to interview Elisabeth Z., a self-declared born-again Christian from the province of Negros Occidental. According to her, employers like Filipino nurses and caregivers because they are easily taught, bring presence of mind to the job, and are flexible and patient. Their English communication skills are fundamental to their job effectiveness. She added that hospitals, like hers, commend their interpersonal skills which help ease patient and physician concerns and anxiety, especially under difficult medical circumstances.

Care homes in England, Wales and Scotland started hiring Filipino caregivers in 1998. Ninety percent of the 25,000 Filipino caregivers in the UK work in hundreds of privately run care homes, while the remaining 10 percent are with the NHS. New NHS guidelines increased the salary of caregivers to £7.02 per hour or £14,600 yearly. In Teignmouth, South Devon, town councilors even passed a resolution joining the community in the fight to save five Filipinos, who were taking care of dementia patients at Mayfield Hall, from being kicked out of the country when their work permits expired in 2008.

The UK's health care needs, particularly for nursing and senior care, are spread out over the NHS jurisdiction of 47 counties, 7 metropolitan counties, 26 districts, 9 regions, and 3 islands areas. Care homes frequently have problems recruiting British nationals to the jobs done by Filipinos because of low pay rates, and workers from the new EU states in Eastern Europe are not always as suited to the posts because many do not speak English well. Thus, health care administrators from London, Cardiff, Norwich, Manchester, Birmingham, Colchester, Chelmsford, Southend, Ashford, and Bristol are frequent participants in Philippine nursing conferences and expos.

Inside her spacious office I photographed ConGen Tess DV while she was administering the oath of allegiance to, Imelda Maningding, a Filipina British nurse, one of the prides of Addenbrooke's Hospital, who was reacquiring her Philippine citizenship. The scene evoked nostalgia. On one side of the room was a Philippine flag and on the other end was a beautiful rice harvest

painting which almost took up the whole wall. I joined   ConGen Tess DV
in congratulating and shaking Imelda's hand. It was for both—her dual
citizenship and her gallant service to her old and new homelands.

Sprucing and Spicing Up Menus

Honestly, which do you think would be more appetizing? Bangers and
mash for breakfast, fish and chips for lunch, and roast beef with more potatoes
and green string beans for dinner? Or, freshly cut Philippine mangoes and
papayas for breakfast, *adobo* battered Asian stuffed chicken wings for lunch,
and lamb shank over mashed potatoes laced with *caldereta* sauce for dinner?
I am fairly certain that it would be the latter. Which is what Chef Randy
M., originally from Batangas Province, will be able to whip up for you at
The Landham Hotel's restaurants on London's Regents Street. This creative
chef is one of around 5,000 Filipino migrants who are sprucing and spicing
up the menus of hotels, restaurants, department store cafés and patisseries in
Greater London. In 2007, they banded together to form the Philippine Chef
Association UK (PCAUK).

Yes, Filipino chefs are enhancing Her Majesty's cuisine. Some are not
just ordinary chefs. They are award-winning, world-class, and internationally
trained culinary masters influencing the kitchens and menus of posh hotels,
such as the Dorchester, Mandarin Oriental, Hilton, Intercontinental, Carlton
Towers, Junneriah, and Lanesborough, as well as globally renowned restaurants
like Gordon Ramsay, Nobu, Wolsey, and Mitchels and Butlers.

At Hospitality 2009, the best known and most prestigious culinary
competition in the UK, three PCAUK members won awards. The veteran
Harrods executive *sous* pastry chef Jeremiah Lagudas got a Gold award in
the "Tea pastries" competition and a Silver medal in the "Restaurant plates
sweets" category. Jumierah Carlton Tower chef Reynaldo Ayag received a
Silver award for his Buffet Centerpiece, "Dragon, fish and warrior; and
Harrod's pastry chef Felix Bayker Jr. won a Bronze Award, P1 Decorative

Exhibit-Sugar Showpiece, a Bronze Award, P1 Decorative Exhibit-Chocolate Showpiece, and a Merit Award, P7 Miniature Flower-Mini Sugar Showpiece. In 2007, chef Jun Dalmacio bagged the gold medal for a vegetarian dish at the Welsh International Culinary Championship. Edpoe Villanueva, *chef de partie* at the Victoria Hotel in London, has also received international accolades for his creations.

A native of Bacoor, Cavite, Chef Felix B. credits his kitchen ethic and culinary creativity to his education and experiences in the Philippines, supplemented by accumulated hands-on experiences and formal pastry classes. He started his hotel and restaurant career with the Hyatt Regency Manila as a Utility Steward and Dishwasher working the dreaded night shift. While still working full-time, the young Felix finished a Bachelor's Degree in Hotel and Restaurant Management in 1997 from the University of Perpetual Help in Las Piñas, Metro Manila. Right after graduation, the Hyatt's pastry chef took Felix in as an apprentice. In December 2002, The Oxford Hotel in Oxfordshire, England offered him a position which he accepted enthusiastically. He transferred to Hilton London Paddington in 2003 and stayed there for five years. The Hilton, recognizing his pastry skills, sent him to Switzerland for advanced patisserie training in "Sugar Artistik". In March 2008 he went back to study "Chocolate Artistik" on his own dime. At Harrod's Pastry Section, Chef Felix B. is sought after for his cake decorating, wedding and birthday pastries, sponges, tarts, chocolate praline, desserts, sugar showpieces, chocolate showpieces, marzipan figures and figurines, and pastillage-making.

Like Chef Randy, who works at the Artesian and Landau Restaurants, these white top-hatted cooks have mainstreamed Philippine recipes, sauces, as well as preparation and cooking techniques to enhance the flavor, décor, aroma, of food in the UK. Prior to settling in London, Chef Randy worked with the Emirates Airlines catering department from 1989-1994. He was based in Dubai then. He proudly revealed that the five Filipino chefs at the Landham Hotel are well-liked, thus retained even during economic downturns because of the high quality of their work, creativity, interpersonal communication skills, and their professionalism.

To complement the delicious food and create better ambience, Londoners could also spruce up their wedding banquet with a one-of-a-kind ice sculpture from Samuel Palaban, a famous Filipino events sculptor, known for his adventurous combination of ice with fruits or vegetables interspersed with a Philippine-accented baked chocolate cake decorated with handcrafted roses made of marzipan.

In September 2008, the Philippine Chefs Association organized the "Philippine Food Expo" at the Battersea Art Centre to underscore their members' remarkable contribution to the growth and development of UK's culinary scene.

At the event, PCA UK members showed off different Filipino foods from the three main island groupings of the Philippines—Luzon, Visayas, and Mindanao. They also did some food preparation and cooking demonstrations showcasing provincial tastes and flavors from all over the Philippines. UK-based Filipino food suppliers provided the ingredients giving them a more "authentic" regional flavor and aroma, creating a mouth-watering fusion of eastern and western cooking. The most popular ones were Far East Food Supply (Kent), Filipino Supermarket (London), Jade's Far Eastern Food (Lancashire), Lara's Filipino Groceries (London), Manila Supermarket (London), Nayong Pilipino (London), Saint Ann's Oriental (London), and Triponia's Food Store (London).

Philippine chefs in London show their food stuff

At the end of the day, executive chefs from top Greater London hotels, restaurants, and shopping centers and European culinary industry experts who attended the food expo were quite impressed. They expect to see more Filipino foods entering the highly competitive British and European markets. Jullien Perrier, executive head chef of Andaz-Hyatt Hotel, was so enamored by the blend of glamour and flavor that he offered Hyatt Hotel as the venue for the 2009 Philippine food expo.

Associational Filipinization

My memories of Batangas Province are filled with pristine beaches— Tali, Nasugbu, Matabungkay, Mabini, and Calatagan. But, what do Batangas diaspora diplomats in London do to help keep these memories alive?

To get the answer, I met with fellow La Salle alumni Peps Villanueva, past president and active member of the Batangas Association UK (BAUK). According to him, the BAUK was formed in 1993 to unite Batanggenyos through fellowships, socials, and sporting activities.

The association's first activities were parties introducing the BAUK to the larger UK society, recruiting members, and fund raising for their UK and Philippine projects. It then expanded to outreach programs for less fortunate *kababayans* back in Batangas. BAUK sends books and funds for desks, tables, and repairs to public schools in the province. It has also organized medical missions which has distributed medicines and provided immunization and check-ups for the elderly and the young. Annually, BAUK sponsors basketball tournaments, Simbang Gabi novena services, and Philippine Independence day festivities in and out of the Greater London area.

Peps added that BAUK has also facilitated the donation of much-needed medical equipment to local clinics all over Batangas. The group also sponsors an ongoing activity called "*Alay Pasko*" (Christmas offering) that distributes food hampers to indigent Batanggenyos in selected town and cities of the province. In the UK, BAUK is involved in sports and the arts. For 2006 and

2007, BAUK sponsored with the Philippine Embassy art exhibits featuring upcoming artists from the Philippines as part of the UK Filipino community's Independence Day celebrations.   The association also organized softball tournaments and fielded teams in the London basketball tournaments.

BAUK has also been a staunch supporter and lead organizer of the Simbang Gabi novenas described in the previous section. Compared to Singapore and San Francisco, British Filipino's Simbang Gabi tradition is one of the most well attended outside the Philippines. London Batanggenyos have always enthusiastically sponsored one of the nights since the annual tradition started in 1998.

To fund its various projects, BAUK held its first dinner-dance at the London Marriott Hotel Grosvenor Square on October, 1994. Since then, this annual affair has become the main source of income for the association. It also has the annual Easter Family Gathering which gives all Batanggenyos in the UK the opportunity to meet up and socialize. In 2006, BAUK members voted to adopt the Bahay Ampunan Foundation, Inc. as its main beneficiary. Located in the city of Tanauan, it is a home for the homeless elderly from all over the Philippines. BAUK has donated more than £10,000 already in addition to the goods that its members bring there but it is still not enough. In 2008, the construction of the Bahay's fence to provide security and protection to the residents was completed.

In 2008, the Philippine Ambassador to the UK Edgardo Espiritu proudly reported to the President of the Philippines that the UK Filipino community raised £22,500 (roughly PhP2.4 million) for the construction of nine classrooms in various provinces in the Philippines. There are approximately 118 associations registered with the Philippine Embassy in London (see Figure 4.3).

Figure 4.3
Philippine Associations in the UK

Typology	Number	Percent
Homeland	52	44
Religious	15	13
Hometown	14	12
Occupational/Professional	13	11
Cultural	10	8
Development/Charity	5	4
Women's Group	3	3
Sports	2	2
Second Generation	2	2
Fraternity/Sorority Alumni	2	2
	118	100

Source: Philippine Embassy, London, 2009.

Besides the BAUK, there are 13 other hometown associations registered with the Philippine Embassy in London. Filipino migrants from the provinces of Bulacan, Ifugao, Benguet, Bicol, and Pampanga also have active social and cultural get-togethers, fundraisers, and civic projects. Many other Philippine linguistic, regional, and political subdivisions have organizations who weave in the sub-cultures and dialects, deepening the diversity of British society. They include: Camilineos and Friends Association, Igorot Association, Ilocano Association, Kalipunan ng mga Kapisanang Pilipino sa Silangan (KAPIS), Mindanao-UK Group, and the Sagunto UK Association. Close to half of Philippine associations scattered all over the UK are general Philippine community associations, such as the North Staffordshire Filipino and Friends

Association (NSFFA), the North Wales Filipino Association, the Oxfordshire Filipino Association, the Philippine Association of Surrey UK (PASSION), Slough Filipino Community Association UK, and the Merton-Sutton Filipino Neighbourhood Association (MSFNA).

Every year, the Philippine Embassy, with the support of many of these organizations, co-sponsors a number of Philippine Independence Day, June 12, commemorations. In 2008, Filipino community groups, led by the Philippine Centre UK helped in a "Barrio Fiesta sa London" in Hounslow, a "Filipino Festival" in Beckton, East London, "Independence Day" at Morden in West London, Hounslow, and on High Street Kensington. In June 2009, "Barrio Fiesta sa London" celebrated 25 years of production. Not surprisingly, one of the most active professional groups is the Philippine Nurses Association of United Kingdom (PNA-UK).

Philippine diaspora diplomats in London have also formed social justice and charity organizations. The Centre for Filipinos (CF), formerly known as the Commission for Filipino Migrant Workers (CFMW), is a registered UK social and immigrant services charity. It is currently operating two centers based in the London boroughs of Camden and Hammersmith and Fulham. Receiving, donations and other monetary contributions from private and public source, CF provides temporary and permanent Philippine diaspora diplomats with new arrival information, referral service, youth work assistance, health care promotion, continuing education and training, counseling and advising, and community development.

Established in March 1985, the Philippine Centre is a voluntary non-governmental organization and a registered cultural and civic UK charity. It helps the large Filipino community program activities that elevate their sense of community, belongingness, and mutual support in the UK. Based at the Hounslow Community Association in Middlesex, the Philippine Centre strives to provide opportunities, facilities and services to foster a continuing interest and appreciation of Filipino values and tradition, culture and social norms. Its latest project to reach out to the second-generation is the Philippine Centre Youth Basketball Academy (PCYBA) which began in January 13th 2008. This project for Filipino British youth and students between the 7-18 years old involves weekly basketball coaching sessions from a qualified basketball coach with the aim of competing in one of London's many local leagues.

Mixing youth, charisma, and advocacy

Like their Filipino American peers, the students, scholars, and second-generation British Filipino men and women in the UK also infuse vitality, vigor, and social justice into Philippine *kasamahan* and *bayanihan* influences, both in their London community and their ancestral hometowns. They gravitate between the internet and live get-togethers to create a youth dimension, space, and voice in the many Filipino organizations and their activities.

According to its website, Phil-UK's second-generation Filipino British founders, Alexis Aquino, Anthony Lopez-Vito, Carmelo Macasaddu, Fe Abogadie, Rachiel de Chavez, and Roann Tubalinal, first met in 2000 during the ARC (Awareness, Respect and Co-operation) meetings held by the former Philippine Ambassador to the UK Cesar Bautista. One of the main points highlighted was the need to increase the visibility of the Filipino Community in the UK, so they created Phil-UK. Starting with online e-mail exchanges they eventually met face-to-face to start civic projects. They were mostly university students or young professionals in finance, law, media, and technology. Phil-UK members believe that "young Filipinos in the UK do not have a voice in society. This is causing us to lose our culture and our identity. It also means that we can't play an active role in shaping our community. Our aim is to enable Filipinos to be a positive and visible influence in Britain's cultural diversity. We will do this by promoting awareness and pride in our culture; by bringing together young Filipinos with projects for change; and by creating partnerships with people who share our views."

Pinoy-UK has almost similar roots. Beginning as an electronic networking group for mostly postgraduate students, researchers, and lecturers at UK colleges and university in 1995, it has metamorphosed into a number of social and social justice-oriented gatherings and exchanges. The first get-together was held in December 1995 at the Manchester Cyberia. Since then it has grown to more than 80 members, including alumni, covering Filipinos at Ashton, Cambridge, Oxford, Cardiff, King's, Lancaster, Goldsmith's, Imperial, London School of Economics, School of Oriental and African Studies, Loughborough, Leeds, Nottingham, Stratchclyde, Portsmouth, Sheffield, Southhampton, Surrey, West England, and Warwick colleges and universities as well as European universities in Amsterdam, Sweden, and Germany.

To most Philippine diaspora diplomats, attending Saturday or Sunday worship services is not enough. They influence spaces and places with charisma—including, clapping, chanting, and raising their hands and voices. This *kasamahan* behavior was emphasized in San Francisco and it also applies to London: praising and worshiping God with their larger Catholic, Anglican, Aglipayan, and Iglesia congregations but afterwards joining other religious sub-groupings for more intense bible study, quiet meditation, loud singing, or peer counseling. They organize festivals, devotions, charismatic praise, rosary sessions, processions, and traditions such as *Simbang Gabi*. Then they eat together and discuss serious issues like advocating for a jury system to be introduced in their native land.

For instance, one of the regular sponsors of the December 2008 *Simbang Gabi* is the lively and charismatic Filipino Catholic Community Prayer Group at Sacred Heart Church in Kilburn. I went with Fr. Ino to one of their regular services and discovered a very cheerful praising and prancing group. They welcomed me warmly as a special *kababayan* guest. Our get-together did not end at church; most of the members took a short bus ride to their "headquarters." Fr. Ino and I went with them. We ended up laughing, bantering, and eating. Most of them were domestic helpers and nannies. Like Jenny D., Rosel T., Lenlen V., Dona S. they were under a lot stress—no legal immigration papers and lots of family needs to fulfill in the Philippines. But they nevertheless greatly impact British family life since busy working professionals would not be able to handle their domestic chores, and child and senior care obligations without their help.

A lively Filipino charismatic prayer group sings and praises regularly at Sacred Heart Church in Kilburn.

Not as openly enthusiastic but still equally charming as the Filipino Catholic Community Prayer Group are the other Catholic groups, like the Filipino Catholic Community Organization of Saint Francis of Assisi, the Filipino Club at Westminster Cathedral, Filipino Community, Diocese of Menevia in South and West Wales, Filipino Community, Diocese of Wales, Filipino Community of Saint Joseph's Catholic Church, Wembley, and the Filipino Community of The Holy Redeemer Church. They help organize everything from somber prayer vigils and Mother Mary rosaries to celebratory Simbang Gabi and Independence Day get-togethers.

They are joined by London and UK chapters of popular Philippine Christian and Catholic groups. There is *Banal na Pag-aaral* (A Holy Study) which is a community of people who have been touched by Jesus Christ through Ate Salve. This organization's purpose is to network among fellow brothers and sisters in Christ in London, San Francisco, Singapore, Australia, and other parts of the world.

There is a London chapter of Jesus Is Lord Church (also known as JIL Fellowship or JIL Movement) which is a Pentecostal group founded by Brother Eddie Villanueva in 1978. It presently has 10,000 local congregations in 85 provinces and 1000 cities across the Philippines. Besides the UK, the JIL Church claims to have millions of members in more than 40 countries. Other heavily inter-generational religious groups are Couples for Christ; East London Rosary Crusad; El Shaddai DWXI - Prayer Partners, Foundation International, London Chapter; the Galilee Lighthouse Christian Foundation International; and the Great Missionary Ministry.

There are two very active London-based jury system advocates. I know since I constantly get their e-mail messages and every time I am in London, Tim Sipurco invites me to share my thoughts on this. I am of course very supportive since the U.S. has a jury system like the UK. Besides these two countries, I know that Australia, Canada, New Zealand, Hongkong, Japan, Russia, and 46 other democratic countries and dependencies around the world effectively utilize the jury system.

The first group is Tim's Philippine Jury Campaign International which seeks to install or incorporate juries in the Philippine justice system at the earliest possible time. Tim's group firmly believes that a strong and truly independent judiciary is a vital step towards a better Philippines. Members confided to me that they feel that a just and humane society where people are free from fear, where the government is free from corruption, where justice is served when it is due is badly needed in the Philippines.

The other deeply committed London-based jury system advocate is the

"People's Movement for the Creation of Philippine Jury." Chaired by Ana Maravilla, this UK-charity is formally registered in 2007 with the Philippine Securities and Exchange Commission. Like the Philippine Jury Campaign International, its objective is to campaign for the passing of a law of trial-by-jury in the Philippine judicial branch. In line with this objective, they welcome each and everyone, Filipino or not, to join their group and be an advocate in calling for all Filipinos to rally behind the immediate installation of a Philippine jury system. They believe that people's participation in the administration of justice ensures a just and humane society. Ana M. and her peers believe that fundamental constitutional judicial changes are long overdue. For the past 72 long years, since the establishment of the 1935 Constitution, they say that there has been no improvement in the delivery of justice in their Philippine hometowns.

Summary and Conclusion

Another reason I come to London besides fieldwork is my board membership with a UK-based international charity called, Street Action UK. I am the founding co-director of Street Action USA. Street Action raises support and builds connections for street children organizations in sub-Saharan Africa. I became a part of Street Action after working with one of their partner organizations in Durban, South Africa. Tom Hewitt who runs the Durban-based charity supported by Street Action was my former student at the University of San Francisco.

As a Filipino American, these transnational nongovernmental organizations (NGOs) whom I consult for apparently value the experience and perspectives that I bring from having been raised and socialized in a developing country for the early part of my life. After all, I grew up surrounded by an enormous number of Manila street children. We played and ate together. Thus, in between Filipino field observations and interviews inside London churches, at the Philippine Embassy on Trafalgar Square, and crowded migrant flats (a.k.a.

apartments) near Edgeware Road and East London, I was in serious chats at the ultra modern cafes of the Royal Festival Hall, Tate Modern, and Institute for Contemporary Arts for Street Action.

I am not the only Philippine diapora diplomat helping connect the complex divide between developed and developing countries, between the haves and the have-nots. I met many in my travels and fieldwork. In many ways, the Filipino men and women I interacted with in London are treading the same line. Most migrants from developing countries living, working, and worshipping in a powerful developed country are still looked at as ethnic, exotic, and peripheral. However, as my fieldwork narrated in this chapter reveals, the Philippine diaspora diplomats' spiritual, occupational, and association contributions in London are not insignificant—like the lives of the HIV/AIDS exposed migrant Zulu street children that I am trying to assist in South Africa. The religious, work, and organizational soft power of Philippine diaspora diplomats should be recognized in the same way that present-day career Philippine Foreign Service diplomats, like Consul General Tess de Vega, Consul Tess Lazaro, and Attache Edith Malilin, value them.

The religious Filipinization or the *kasamahan* and *bayanihan* influences emanating from their Philippine spirituality and faith are helping save the Queen's church and London Christian and Catholic congregations from certain demise. Clear evidences are the Anglican-Aglipayan alliance and the Catholic Church's encouragement of a Filipino ethnic chaplaincy. With the blessings and encouragement of their Filipino pastors, like Fr. Telen and Fr. Ino, they introduce Philippine religious beliefs, practices, images, and traditions, including the *Simbang Gabi* and Christmas novenas. In turn, a number of Filipino migrant faithful who are members of these churches have benefited from having their prayers answered and their undocumented immigration status insulated. Over the decades, the London faithful have learned to accept Filipino congregations and worshippers as part of their own.

Occupationally, Philippine diaspora diplomats Filipinize London through their *kasamahan* and *bayanihan* influences associated with their labor, skills, education, or training. Most visible are the Filipina nurses, like Myrna M. and Imelda M., who attend to patients at private and National Health Service (NHS) hospitals and clinics, as well as the thousands of Filipino caregivers at senior homes and assisted living facilities. Less visible are the thousands of Filipino chefs, like Chef Randy M. and Chef Felix B., who spruce up menus and spice up recipes at Greater London hotels, restaurants, and department stores. And more invisible are the Filipino domestic helpers and nannies, like Jenny D., Rosel T., Lenlen V., Dona S., and Angie A., who allow London's busy bankers, entrepreneurs, stock brokers, physicians to sustain Britain's commonwealth.

In terms of associational Filipinization, Filipino migrants exercise their *kasamahan* and *bayanihan* influences in forming new or joining existing organizations and going to informal gatherings. Their unique and colorful hometown, homeland, professional and culture associations blend diversity, creed, and charity. This was illustrated by the cultural and civic activities of the Batangas Association UK, the Centre for Filipinos, and the Philippine Centre. Their transnational spiritual, second-generation and school, and progressive organizations mix youthful vigor and curiosity, religious charisma, and political advocacy. This includes the Phil-UK, Pinoy-UK, the Filipino Catholic Community Prayer Group, and the two London-based jury system advocacy groups. Indeed, their establishment and growth both benefit and bridge London and their heritage.

CHAPTER 5

Dubai: Port of Security, Prayers, and Play

Which passport do you think has greater diplomatic acceptability in the Middle East—a blue U.S. passport or a green Philippine passport?

My cousin Galen's 60-day United Arab Emirates tourist visa stamped on the third page of his green Philippine passport was about to expire. This meant he needed to physically leave Dubai and reenter on an employment visa, or pay a hefty fine. Like other migrants in his position, he had three options: one, go on a long bus ride and exit in neighboring Al Buraimi in Oman; two, take a one-hour flight across the Persian Gulf to Kish Island, Iran; or three, go back to the Philippines and apply for a work visa at the UAE Embassy in Manila.

Whatever option my cousin chose, his employer, a South African-owned cigarette factory, assured him an approved work visa issued by the UAE Ministry of Labor that he would show the UAE immigration officer for his reentry. The options seemed straightforward to me. After consulting his brother Guimo, a UAE migrant worker for more than a decade, the brothers decided that Galen should just exit via Kish Island.

This was the most commonly chosen option of Filipino migrants since the round-trip land travel to the UAE-Qatar border was too long while a return trip to the Philippines would take not only more time than the Qatar option but would also be more expensive. As part of my fieldwork, I decided I should tag along to witness this exit process since I would be able to meet and interview Filipinos at the airport, the plane, and during the overnight stay at the hotel frequented by migrant workers. I would also be able to observe other migrant nationalities. I did not see a problem exiting and re-entering since I was a U.S.

citizen and did not need a UAE visa. Little did I know that what I thought was my advantage over others would be my undoing.

We took the long taxi ride from Fujairah to Dubai. When we got to the airport terminal, it was packed with people. We went straight to the airline counter where we were told that all flights that day to Kish was fully booked. I could see from my cousin's eyes that he was nervous and desperate. We frantically asked around and learned from a Filipina Muslim working at the Iran Aseman Airlines counter that there were still available seats to Qeshm, another Iranian island on the Persian Gulf but we needed to purchase them that very moment. We hurriedly bought the Qeshm tickets and thanked our helpful *kababayan*.

The flight only took 40 minutes. When we landed, we were directed to the small airport terminal and lined up for immigration clearance. The lines were long since there were more than 150 passengers and only three open counters. I stood behind my cousin who was holding his Philippine passport. One fourth of the people on the flight were Filipino migrant workers from Dubai, Abu Dhabi, Sharjah—they were accountants, waitresses, cashiers, sales representatives, band members, nurses, and manufacturing workers like my cousin. The rest were construction workers from South Asia, entertainers from Eastern Europe, and hotel workers from East Asia. Everyone went through immigration without a problem. I watched as all the Filipino women started putting on *hijabs* (head scarves). Those that did not have any were given *abayas* (long overgarments). They were also given a separate line to use and sailed through smoothly.

When my turn came at the counter, the stern-looking Iranian immigration officer glanced at my blue U.S. passport and then at my face. "American?" the officer asked. Yes, I said. He immediately called his supervisor who took me to an interrogation room. I felt a chill and was nervous. More than a hundred pairs of eyes were on me as I was escorted to the room by two men in military fatigues. The supervising officer was joined by three other men. They took turns asking me questions in their limited English. Why was I entering Iran? Where do I live? What did I do in Dubai? One of them held my fingers to a deep blue stamp pad ink and fingerprinted both hands. It was then that it dawned on me that they thought I was an American spy. I had a camera, a digital recorder, note pad, etc. One of the heavily armed guards singled out a wooden rosary among my belongings and asked if I was a Christian. I hesitated, then said, "Yes." I waited for a consequence to my response.

I told them I was not an American spy. I was a history teacher at a Philippine school in Dubai. To add more emotion to my drama, I pulled out a picture of my daughter when she was one year old (she was really 18 years old then) and asked the lead interrogator if he had a child. He said "yes" and looked at the picture with sympathy. They peppered me with questions about my background then tested me with this final question to verify if I was really a history teacher: Name an influential leader in Persian history. Without batting an eyelash I answered: "King Darius". Their body language told me that they seemed satisfied.

After a pause that seemed like an eternity, the lead interrogator smiled and blurted in broken English: "You Filipino teacher. You Asian like me." Then he nodded his head and looked at the others who agreed with him. My answer was from standard Asian history lesson from a Philippine high school. They were finally convinced I was really a fellow Asian who "accidentally" became an American. I didn't even know what was written in the "release" paper I signed since it was written presumably in Persian. With dark blue ink still visible on my fingers, I was finally let go. When they were out of sight, I did the sign of the cross and looked to the sky and exclaimed, "*Salamat po!*" (Thanks!).

This experience reminded me that the next time I should not underestimate the soft power influence of a Filipino citizen's green passport. What is more acceptable than my blue U.S. passport in the global hierarchy of nations, according to the Islamic Republic of Iran and many other Middle Eastern states, is my Filipino appearance, deference, and demeanor. Our Western Asian neighbors expect this from their fellow Asian Games compatriots from the East, South, and Southeast. Cousin Galen and other Filipino diaspora diplomats benefit from the sense of Asian brotherhood and acceptability all over the Middle Eastern region. Thus, I entered what the U.S. State Department considers a rogue state as an unwelcome American and was released by the Iranian government because I was to them a Filipino, an Asian brother. Respect is one of the perks of being a Filipino American diaspora diplomat. Lesson learned: I opted for dual citizenship and got a Philippine passport as soon as I got back to San Francisco. I also bought two *keffiyehs* (male Arab scarves) to fend off the cold winters in America and sand storms in the Middle East.

Soft power points made, I proceed in this chapter with my discussion of blossoming and mutually beneficial Filipino and Emirati relations. In the context of a relatively tolerant Islamic state, I also talk about how Philippine diaspora diplomats are able to spread inter-faith respect throughout the Arabian Peninsula while discreetly practicing their own brand of Christian religiosity, from Catholic to evangelical, from Tagalog masses to Filipino-style fellowship. Then, I elaborate on Philippine occupational influences in the strategic ports of Dubai and Fujairah which are teeming with highly efficient Filipino seamen, office staff, divers, and port workers. I also discuss their entrepreneurship and diversification of Emirati food through the introduction of Philippine delicacies and franchises at restaurants, airports, hotels, cafes, and malls all over the UAE. Lastly, I elaborate on Filipino migrants' associational influences in Dubai and the Arab region via their formal and informal organizations, like their Philippine overseas schools, year-round basketball leagues, fraternities and sororities civic and community projects, among others. I end the chapter with a final story and some concluding remarks on their Middle East *bayanihan* and *kasamahan* impact.

Securing a major source of insecurity

Compared to the entry into Iran, my deplaning at the ultra-modern Dubai International Airport was uneventful. After stamping and handing me back my blue U.S. passport, the serious Emirati immigration officer in a long white tunic with a matching Arab headcloth, asked me: "*Filipino?*" When I grinned and nodded, he blurted out smiling: "*Kamusta?*" I answered in half Tagalog and half Arabic, "*Mabuti, shukran!*" Humored, we both ended up laughing loudly. What a difference!

Millions of Philippine diaspora diplomats work on the ground to help uphold the many formal security and political commitments, treaties, and arrangements the U.S. has with the UAE and its neighbors on the Arabian Peninsula and the Persian Gulf. Essentially, they help secure a geographic region of western insecurity. After all, the global war on terrorism has triggered a renewal of geo-strategic alliances, consensus, and coalitions.

Next to Saudi Arabia, the UAE and the other Gulf Cooperation Council (GCC) states are staunch security and economic allies of the U.S. in the Middle East. Essentially, it gives the U.S. a number of proxy voices and votes in the influential Arab League since all GCC states are members of this organization. Its security commitment to the GCC allows the U.S. Navy, Army, and Air Force unrestricted access to military installations in Bahrain, Kuwait, Quatar, Oman, Saudi Arabia, and the UAE, whose port of Mina Jebel Ali is a favorite stop for American carrier battle groups.

Al Dhafra Air Base outside of Abu Dhabi is the home of the U.S. Air Force's 763rd Expeditionary Air Refueling Squadron while the Fujairah International Airport hub logistics site in the NAVCENT AOR is for air cargo coming from Japan and other points in the Pacific theater via Diego Garcia.

Its presence in GCC territories does not automatically mean that everyone on the streets of GCC countries are excited to rub shoulders and give high fives to Americans, especially those in uniform. Extreme caution is practiced. Most U.S. military personnel stay on base or inside the heavily fortified American embassies and consulates. Whenever they are on the street they are not in large groups, nor are they in uniform. They try to blend in with tourists at shops and restaurants; some women even wear head scarves and long dresses with sleeves. Men with short crew cuts bunched together are certainly red flags. Military or civilian Filipino Americans do not have these problems. They are so many people on the streets who look like them.

Prior to my trip I read that the discovery of oil and later, natural gas, brought a new era of wealth and prosperity to what were then tribal sheikdoms sprinkled across the sprawling Arabian Peninsula, along the southern coast of the Persian Gulf and the northwestern coast of the Gulf of Oman. In 1853, the sheikdoms signed a treaty becoming a British protectorate. With huge petroleum profits flowing in, the ruling Arab sheikhs eventually consolidated power and wealth and formed the United Arab Emirates in 1971. The UAE has an official population of 4.6 million (2006) but only around 20 percent are ethnically Emirati, entitled to UAE citizenship and a UAE passport. The rest of the population is composed of short- and long-term Arab, Iranian, South Asian, East Asian, North American, and European migrants. There are more than 300,000 Filipino migrants or the equivalent of 15 percent of the population. A large majority of Filipinos work in Dubai and the neighboring emirates of Sharjah, Ajman, Ras al-Khaimah, Umm al-Quwain, and Fujairah. The UAE has one of the highest Human Development Index in Asia and ranks 31st globally. In 2008, it had a GDP (Purchasing Power Parity) of US$200.5 billion and quite a high per capita GDP of US$39,077, making it the 20th richest country in the world.

Undoubtedly the richest among the seven states that comprise the UAE, Dubai is the land of endless sand, the tallest building in the planet, seven-star hotels, man-made islands, highly efficient ports, and millions of migrant workers. In its previous life, Dubai was a sleepy fishing town with a population of only 1,000 in the 1800s. It survived on a barter economy of pearls and regional sea trade. But by the beginning of the 20th century the city started making a name for itself for having one of the largest and most diverse *souks* (markets) in the Arabian Peninsula. There were specialized *souks* for fabrics, gold, pearls, and spices, which exists until today. Dubai's present revenues are mainly from the booming tourism, trade, real estate and financial services. Compared to the other emirates, oil receipts make up only less than 10 percent of the total. These sectors are the reasons why Dubai draws a wide range of migrant (or expatriate) workers from restaurant servers to investment bankers. From its humble beginnings, Dubai has become the most modern and western city in the Middle East.

All migrant workers and other travelers to Dubai, except for those coming from 34 privileged nations, need a 60-day visit visa stamped by UAE diplomatic posts in various countries. Although the Philippines is not in the list of 34 no-visa-needed countries, this inconvenience has not discouraged the continuous labor relations between the Philippines and the UAE as evidenced by fully booked daily flights from Manila to Dubai. Emirates, the UAE's national carrier, even offer direct flights six days a week which is supplemented by non-direct flights via Qatar Airways, Kuwait, Cathay Pacific, Gulf Air, Philippine Airlines, Thai Airways, and Singapore Airlines.

As a U.S. citizen, I was granted a visa upon arrival at the ultra-modern Dubai International Airport. After standing in a long line for arrivals, I went to the duty-free shop to get some wine and was surprised that the sales staff and check-out cashier were both Filipinos. My fieldwork started right then and I was just at the airport! I got the usual *kababayan* questions from them: *"Taga-saan ka atin?"* ["Where are you from back home?"] *"Baguhan ka ba?"* [Are you new?] *"Bakit ka nandito sa Dubai?"* ["Why are you here in Dubai?"]. When the cashier asked for my passport to verify my duty-free eligibility, he remarked, *"Buti ka pa kayo sir, kano na!"* [Lucky you sir, you're already an American!].

I briskly walked out of the glass doors when I saw my cousins, Guimo, Galen, and Guimo's wife, Maite D at the arrival area. We were excited to see each other in another land since we had not seen each other in years. We were not only part of the Philippine diaspora, we were also part of the Gonzalez diaspora and our hometown, Santa Ana's, exodus abroad. Seeing them made me forget the very tiring 24-hour journey from San Francisco I have just been through.

Filipinos started coming to the UAE in the 1970s and many have now established businesses. Some brought their families and relatives while others have children who studied and set up families here. This is why I met migrants with three generations of family members working there.

Maite is a second-generation migrant worker to the UAE. Her parents were here before her. Guimo and Maite's two children went to elementary and high school at international schools in Fujairah, are now in college in Manila. Guimo facilitated the arrival of a new set of Gonzalezes—his brother Galen, Galen's partner Matet, and nephew Poch. He found Galen and Poch entry level jobs at a cigarette factory and referred Matet to a fellow Filipino association member who owns a Philippine food business and restaurant.

Guimo, Maite, Galen, Matet, and Poch are likewise part of the larger group of Filipino Middle East migrants numbering more than two million strong—and growing. The diaspora diplomats from this region remitted to their Philippine families and hometowns more than US$2 billion in 2007.

Over the past decade, the UAE has grown to become the Philippines' sixth largest source of foreign exchange remittances in the world. The turn-of-the-millennium wave of roughly 300,000 Filipino migrant workers in Dubai are employed in almost every occupation including architecture, construction, cargo shipping, design engineering, ports, energy, information technology, banking and finance, marketing, hotels, health care, real estate, retail, restaurants, telecommunications, tourism, and domestic help.

Besides world-class port workers and seamen, the UAE has become the top destination for new hires in nursing (ranked 2nd), entertainment (ranked 4th), domestic help (ranked 4th), information technology (ranked 6th), teaching (ranked 8th), and caregiving (ranked 9th), from 2001 to 2007. Together with

Filipino workers from other parts of the UAE, they sent back more than half a million dollars for education, health care, investments, and other family and community needs. Given this volume, the Philippine consulate in Dubai processes more than 200 passport renewals a day. Some transact business and seek help at the Philippine Embassy in Abu Dhabi.

Two hundred passports a day!

During my visit in 2008, I met the dynamic Philippine Consul Butch Bandillo, another new-breed FSO, like the ones I met in London and Dhaka. Besides passports, the consulate staff needed to conduct approximately 500-600 civil wedding ceremonies annually, or around 20-30 per week. Ninety-nine percent of the women are pregnant and need to get married to maintain their legal status and their jobs. UAE strictly enforces Islamic (Sharia) laws on adultery, pre-marital sex, and other immoral acts. If caught, the prescribed maximum punishment is death by stoning which could also be reduced on appeal to a prison sentence, flogging, and/or fines. Because of the pregnancies, the number of births average around 500-600 yearly. The number of deaths, on the other hand, is 1-2 persons weekly.

The Philippine Consulate holds monthly community meetings to be in touch with these issues and concerns. Many of the Filipino migrants, like those I met in Dhaka and Singapore, hope that their UAE stay is only a bridge to immigration to the U.S. and UK.

There are those, like my auto mechanic, Cris Mayrena and his family, who have succeeded in this path. Active members of Couples for Christ, Cris and his wife Lucy began their diaspora journey with work contracts in Abu Dhabi, then Dubai, to finally co-managing their own vehicle maintenance and repair shop in San Francisco.

The Philippine Chamber of Commerce and Industry (PCCI) has always had cordial relations with the Federation of UAE Chambers of Commerce and Industry consisting of the seven chambers of commerce of the Emirates. PCCI created the Philippines-UAE Business Council in April 2007 to step-up trade and investment promotion activities. The UAE is ranked 20th among the Philippines' 212 merchandise trading partners. The Emirates are the number one Middle East trading partner of the Philippines, ahead of Saudi Arabia (#35) and the other Gulf Cooperation Council economies. In 2007, the Philippines exported more than US$200,000 worth of electronics, garments, and fresh fruits like bananas and pineapples, to the UAE. It supplies 99 percent of bananas and pineapples in Dubai's markets. However, the Philippines imported more than US$1.2 million of petroleum products from the UAE in the same year, creating a US$1 million trade imbalance.

Interestingly, Dubai has 15 sister cities -- from Detroit, Michigan in the USA to Dundee, Scotland in the UK -- but does not have any sister city in the Philippines, a glaring omission given the size and of the Filipino migrant population. In fact, despite more than three decades of people-to-people relations, none of the UAE states has a sister city in the Philippines. Neither does any Middle Eastern country. There has to be more Filipinos from Cebu in Dubai than Americans from Detroit or Scots from Dundee. Maybe UAE officials feel that they do not need one given the large scale Filipinization of their surroundings?

Religious Filipinization

Everywhere we went in Dubai, I was amazed at the blending of glistening crystal skyscrapers and domed minaret towers, evidence of the successful balance of modernity and tradition. The UAE, somewhat like the Philippines, is still very much a religious state. Ninety six percent of the population is Muslim, and most are Sunnis. There is no separation of mosque and state. The UAE's constitution declares Islam as the official religion for all seven of the constituent Emirates of the federal union. I heard several tour guides say that Dubai is home to 188 mosques. As we passed the sail-shaped Burj Al Arab hotel and the touristy Jumeirah beach, I saw the majestic Jumeirah Mosque, the largest and the most photographed for its modern Islamic architecture and splendor. Not too far behind in unique beauty is the massive Grand Mosque which could accommodate 1,200 worshippers. Each emirate helps maintain mosques in their jurisdiction and employs all the Imams.

Dubai is the most liberal and open-minded among the Emirates about allowing the practice of other faiths. Across the Middle East region, the UAE is reputed to be the most tolerant and respectful [of other religions], though tolerance has its limits. In Dubai and the other Emirates, non-Muslims are prohibited from proselytizing or distributing religious literature beyond the walls of their designated spiritual compounds under penalty of criminal prosecution, imprisonment, or deportation. Muslims are also expressly prohibited from converting to other religions, but conversion by non-Muslims to Islam is viewed favorably. During Ramadan, all Dubai residents and visitors are required to abide by restrictions imposed on all Muslims. Some of the Emirates, like Sharjah, are more conservative at interpreting religious freedom than adjoining Dubai.

Dubai's relatively more liberal religious policy has allowed the construction of Hindu temples, Catholic and Christian churches, Sikh Gurudwara, Indian Orthodox, and Coptic Orthodox spiritual sites in land approved by the Emir. Most non-Muslim worshippers hold their main mass or services on Fridays. The late Pope John Paul II pioneered closer Catholic-Muslim ties and became the first pontiff to enter a mosque. His successor and close adviser, Pope Benedict XVI, has continuously reaffirmed the Catholic Church's "deep respect for Muslims." Thus, the Vatican has carefully nurtured its bilateral relations with the UAE, as an integral part of the Apostolic Vicariate of Arabia which includes Bahrain, Oman, Qatar, and Yemen.

Filipino diaspora diplomats help sustain the Vatican's policy of respect and intercultural dialogue. Geographically, the Vicariate of Arabia covers 1.2 million square miles. More than half of the more than a million Catholic worshippers in this vast Vicariate are from the Philippines. Their weekly financial contributions and volunteer service fuel the faith. They do not complain about the fact that in most of the Catholic churches they go to, there are no crosses that could be seen from the outside, no tall steeples with statues or religious images, no church bells or chimes, and very small sign boards. In my interviews, I heard the power and beauty of the word "respect" for the culture of their host government, employer, and neighbor said over and over.

Tagalog masses are held in almost all the Catholic Churches under the Vicariate. In neighboring Doha, the capital of Qatar, Filipino migrant Tom Veneracion is parish priest of the Our Lady of the Rosary Church, the center of the Catholic faith in the tiny country. He is assisted by international parishioners, the bulk of whom are Filipino men and women who serve as lectors, altar servers, collectors, commentators, choir, etc. Filipino migrants are the core of the Vicariate's "prayer warriors" and "new apostles" who reach out and visit members and non-members in hospitals, jails, prisons, ships, ports, special economic zones, oil rigs, encampments, compounds, and military installations. In the countries of the Vicariate, the key to practicing a non-Muslim religion is discretion and respect. This was how it was done in

2008 when Father Tom opened the doors of the first Christian church structure in Doha with around 5,000 faithful in attendance.

In the UAE, the Filipino Catholics I observed on Fridays and Saturdays (equivalent of Saturday and Sunday in the west) joined Indian, American, Lebanese, and European Catholics at Our Lady of Perpetual Help Church in Fujairah and Saint Mary's Church in Dubai. Baptisms, object blessings, confirmations, first communions, funeral services, marriages, block rosaries, bible study, and catechism, are common weekly Catholic rites and rituals. The Filipinos combine these Catholic staples with traditional venerations and festivities like the Santacruzan. Fr. Michael Cardoz, who I met in Fujairah, said that he has seen this same phenomenon at Saint Joseph's Cathedral in Abu Dhabi, Saint Michael's Church in Sharjah, Saint Anthony's Church in Ras al-Khaimah, Church of Saint Francis of Assisi in Jebel Ali as well as the sub-churches in Kalba, Khorfakkan, and Dibba. Without Filipino migrants, many of these Catholic churches would be half empty.

Philippine diaspora diplomats practice and spread the Catholic faith even in very restrictive foreign regions like the Middle East and South Asia. The late Pope John Paul II called them modern-day evangelizers, praising their spiritual fidelity. For instance, in Saudi Arabia, the public practice of non-Muslim religions is forbidden. The more than a million Filipino migrants spread all over the country do not even have a physical church to go to. Instead they risk persecution by holding home bible studies, welcoming occasional visiting pastors into their secluded compounds, and sneaking into U.S. military installations and diplomatic missions which is the only place where masses are boldly held.

Filipino migrant workers and their families are a significant part of the Catholic membership in the Apostolic Vicariate of Kuwait. Aside from the Holy Family Cathedral in Kuwait City, they pack the Our Lady of Arabia Parish in Ahmadi for the last Friday of the month's 3:30 p.m. Tagalog mass. Filipino families also come in droves to the 2 p.m. second Friday mass at Saint

Therese Church in Salmiya. They even attend non-English services at Tehran's two Cathedrals—Saint Mary's and Saint George's as well as Baghdad's Saint John's Church. In Dubai and the other Emirates, I noticed that they risk public display of faith by discreetly nodding, looking at each other's eyes, holding hands, bowing heads, whispering softly in Tagalog, and smiling together. Filipino Catholic migrants have been the most welcomed in the Middle East.

To get the approval of the ruling Emir in the Persian Gulf Emirate of Fujairah, the church of Our Lady of Perpetual Help was constructed to blend with the homes and mosques in the neighborhood. There is no cross visible from the outside. The mass schedule was typed on a small piece of white paper; the Tagalog mass was at 7:30 p.m. on the second Tuesday of every month. Inside the church is a colorful shrine to the Santo Niño de Cebu, the most popular religious symbol in the Philippines.

Introducing the Santo Niño to Arabia

Not content with just attending masses, Filipino diaspora diplomats in the Fujairah, Abu Dhabi and Dubai have set up local chapters of Couples for Christ, the largest lay faith movement emanating from Asia. According to Fr. Cardoz, the parish priest of Our Lady of Perpetual Help Church in Fujairah, it is one of the most active spiritual groups in the UAE and had started discreetly with meetings at the Philippine Embassy compound in Abu Dhabi. In Fujairah, besides organizing the monthly Tagalog masses, Couple for Christ members promote the renewal and strengthening of Christian family life by evangelizing married couples every Friday at 4:00 p.m. A number of Filipino migrants also join Sri Lankan and Indian Catholics in the Legion of Mary adoration every Friday at 5:00 p.m. Most of the Catholic children, including my cousins' kids, attended Saint Mary's School.

In January 2008, I met the coordinators of Couples for Christ Fujairah, Paul and Louise Manahan, who, it turned out, also lived in Santa Ana, Manila where I grew up. They have been active with Couples for Christ UAE since 1997 and they credit the group for their happiness and contentment. Their five children are with Kids for Christ.

Paul and Louise arrived in then-sleepy, slow-paced Dubai in 1992 and lived there for eight years before moving to Fujairah. Born and raised in Santa Cruz, Laguna Province, Paul M. works as a petroleum surveyor and has a Bachelor's degree in Naval Architecture from Namei University in the Philippines. His company flies him all over the Persian Gulf region to inspect petroleum ships and offshore platforms. Louise is from Bacolod, the capital city of Negros Occidental. Besides their college education, the couple brought their technical and managerial experiences to the Dubai and Fujairah companies they worked for. Paul emphasized that Couples for Christ is not only a spiritual, Eucharistic, or couple support group. Past and present presidents of the United Filipino Association in the Emirates (UFAE-Fujairah), including current President Tess Bautista, go to the group for financial assistance at the UFAE-run halfway house for runaway domestic helpers, Filipino and non-Filipino. Couples for Christ members have never hesitated to pass the hat around to assist them. With more than 100 members, Couples for Christ-Fujairah is also an active supporter of Gawad Kalinga (GK) projects in the Philippines as well as in raising funds for causes, e.g., disasters in Asia, brought to them by Filipino priests.

Shepherding an evangelical flock in Arabia

Filipino migrant Catholics are not the only ones constructing and maintaining the booming UAE economy and contributing to its modernization and westernization. Filipino Protestants and Independents are also very much involved in work, prayer, and shepherding an evangelical flock in the Arabian Peninsula as well. I met some of them all over Dubai and nearby emirates. They came from mainstream Protestant backgrounds—Methodists, Baptists, Presbyterian, Episcopalians, United Church of Christ, and Disciples of Christ. I also bumped into Philippine Independents from the Iglesia ni Cristo and evangelical Pentecostals from the Jesus is Lord Movement.

Envisioned as "a Lighthouse for God in the Middle East," the Dubai Evangelical Christian Centre (DECC) in Jebel Ali is where most Philippine Protestants and locally converted Catholics join other nationalities, including local Arabs, in prayers and worship. Meeting every Friday at eight and ten in the morning at the Maranatha Hall of the DECC is the United Christian Church of Dubai (UCCD) which is an evangelical Christian church comprised of more than 1,000 members representing over 50 nations. The Arabic Evangelical Church of Dubai (AECD) is a non-denominational evangelical church with some 200 members from about 10 Arabic speaking nations. Friday morning worship services begin at 11:00 am.

Other churches that are active in Dubai are the Dubai Holy Trinity Church, Emirates Baptist Church International, Church of Jesus Christ of Latter-day Saints, The Deira Brethren Assembly, Mar Thoma Church, Mar Ignatius Church, Miracle Hands Ministry, New Covenant Church Dubai, The Well of New Life Fellowship, Church of the Living Word, Foursquare Church, and

King's Revival Fellowship. Some Filipino diaspora diplomats are occasional-
to active members of some of these evangelical churches. There were also
a number of Iglesia ni Cristo members, who refused to be interviewed, who
would meet at rented office spaces or members' homes. I also met El Shaddai,
Charismatic, and Jesus Is Lord Movement faithful in Dubai and Fujairah. There
were some Philippine Independent Church members who went to the English
services at the Holy Trinity Anglican Church near the Wafi Centre in Oud
Metha Road. Fifty-five miles north of Dubai are the Filipino Church of Ras
al-Khaimah and the Redeemer and King Filipino Church of Ras Al-Khaimah.
Their pastors are affiliated with the Conservative Baptist Association of the
Philippines.

One very active Philippine-bred evangelical church, meeting every Friday
at 10 am and Sunday at 8 pm at the Dubai Evangelical Christian Centre is
Victory Christian Fellowship (VCF). I learned about it from Cher Jimenez, a
visiting media fellow at the University of San Francisco, who worked for three
years in Dubai and attended VCF. She introduced me via e-mail to its pastor,
Rouel Ascuncion, who arranged to meet me at the massive Dubai Festival
City. Cousin Guimo and I got there early so I decided to window shop and
people-watch. The mall covers an area of 2.1 million square feet with 550
shops, a 12 screen cinema complex and 90 international restaurants, bistros
and cafes including 40 open air dining venues along Canal Walk. I bumped
into many Filipino men and women who were salespersons or as shoppers at
every other shop. They were also food servers and greeters at the restaurants.

Victory Christian Fellowship (VCF) is an evangelical Christian church
which began in the Philippines in 1984. It is a member of the global Every
Nation Churches and Ministries, the Philippine Missions Association,
and the Philippine Council of Evangelical Churches. VCF's international
spiritual mission is "to honor God and advance His kingdom through church
planting, campus ministry, and world missions" or simply to "Honor God.
Make Disciples." It began with Filipino campus ministers and presently has
numerous church planters, like Pastor Rouel, who serve as cross-cultural

missionaries to more than a dozen nations in Asia, Europe, and Africa. VCF currently has 51 churches in the Philippines, 13 in Metro Manila and 38 in various provinces. It has grown from a handful of college students to 34,000 worshippers, including families, by 2008 in the Metro Manila area alone.

During my visit with Pastor Rouel and his wife, I learned that a number of Filipino migrant workers with Catholic or Protestant upbringing, like Cher, have converted in Dubai and joined this Philippine church led by a charismatic and dynamic pastor. They feel that Pastor Rouel is a more accessible person and delivers a more pragmatic and dynamic lesson for them in Dubai.

Among VCF's active members are RK and Joanna, a young couple who left lucrative jobs in call centers in Makati to try their luck in another country. After a very challenging start searching for jobs in Dubai, walking kilometer after kilometer, building-to building, and going floor-to-floor and office-to-office leaving lots of resumes and going through stressful interviews, they found relatively high-paying junior executive jobs in stable multinational companies. Like many evangelical Filipinos, they are happy to find a familiar church to help them through the many tough trials in a foreign land.

Occupational Filipinization

Maintaining the efficient and effective operations of Persian Gulf ports is a major role for Philippine diaspora diplomats. How? The interior topography of the UAE is 32,278 square miles (83,600 square kilometers) of harsh desert land with negligible water sources. But beyond the exterior fringes of the Arabian desert sand the UAE built and manages several world-class ports, including one of the world's largest, Jebel Ali Port. Other important ports in the UAE include Port Zayed, Khalifa Port, Port Rashid, Port Khalid, Hamriyah Port, Port of Ajman, Saqr Port, Um Al Quwain, Khor Fhakan, and Fujairah Port. However, the UAE does not have enough talent to manage and maintain these geo-strategic commercial and military infrastructures.

For instance, the Port of Fujairah, one of the busiest commercial ports in the UAE, is managed by Dubai Ports (DP) World, one of the world's most reputable port administrator, managing more than 40 marine terminals in 22 countries, including the Philippines. Seventy five percent of DP World's highly skilled labor force at Fujairah port is Filipino. Fujairah Port is also known as a favorite refueling stop for the U.S. Navy since the Iran-Iraq war in the mid-1980s. With a bunkering capacity that is ranked third in the world after Singapore and Rotterdam, the port is strategically located approximately 70 nautical miles from the Strait of Hormuz, a major sea lane shared by Gulf nations allied with the U.S. War on Terror. In this critical chokepoint, all ships must pass through the territorial waters of Oman and Iran, a nation with no diplomatic ties with the U.S. The U.S. Navy constantly patrols the area since 40 percent of the world's petroleum needs go through the Strait of Hormuz. Besides Mina Jebel Ali in Dubai, the port of Fujairah is a critical stopover for tankers and carrier battle groups.

This narrow strait has been a frequent flashpoint for the U.S. and Iranian naval forces. During the heat of military confrontation, Iran threatens to block off this very critical passageway to the oil that runs through the veins of globalization. One encounter that long-time DP World Filipino port superintendent Armando T. still vividly remembers is the tragic 1988 downing of an Iranian passenger plane by the guided missile cruiser USS Vincennes. Two hundred ninety innocent civilians perished in that tragedy.

During my visit to his DP World command post overlooking tall cranes and hundreds of steel containers, Ramon C. pointed out a group of U.S. Navy ships preparing to refuel and re-supply from a distance, a normal occurrence at the port. The day before, according to him, they created the secured square area I was seeing using empty steel containers as walls. When I asked him why they had to do this for the U.S. Navy, he said, "*Para daw hindi makita ng publiko ang ginagawa nila* [They said so the public does not see what they are doing]." I see a Navy sniper strategically positioned on one of the steel containers. Ramon C. warned me not to take photos. I comply. No wonder visitors at the gate were warned not to bring in cameras. I was given a special courtesy pass by the Emerati port security officer as a courtesy to my *kababayan* escorts who were well- respected and well-liked port employees.

With more than 200 Filipinos working the three shifts, it is not surprising to see them everywhere in this bustling place. A Filipino forklift operator was rushing to load wooden crates filled with groceries and toiletries for the thousands of U.S. troops based in Iraq. A Filipino diver is helping carry a propeller replacement for one of the Navy ships. Ramon C. told me that aside from the Filipino seamen from the container and commercial ships, he has also met some Filipino American Navy sailors stationed in San Diego, California, the homeport of the Pacific Fleet and the largest navy facility in the U.S. west coast.

From my vantage point, I could also see the other end of the port where I watched one of the more than 100 Filipino dock operators skillfully maneuvering towering metal cranes that were lifting 40-foot steel containers packed with clothes and accessories made in the garments factories located in the United Arab Emirates, Qatar, and Oman that are destined for retail stores in Europe and North America. They were outside the cordoned off and heavily policed area. I also witnessed newly docked ships getting ready to offload merchandise from North America and Europe which will end up in Dubai's more than 50 shopping malls or transshipped to the other major cities in the UAE and the larger GCC. Some of the ships arrived from Bangladesh and other south Asian ports and were destined west to Europe and America's East Coast. Some of the container ships were going further east through the narrow Straits of Malacca to Singapore, Manila, and other parts of the East and Southeast Asia and eventually cross the vast Pacific western and unload products for the busting markets and malls of Canada, the United States, and Latin America.

Inside this highly secured UAE port, Philippine diaspora diplomats have been able to use their charisma on Emirati government officials. During my stay in Fujairah I helped my cousin and Fr. Michael draft a letter to the

Fujairah port authorities to provide a prayer room where workers can meditate and practice their religious rituals. The request was granted, so Filipinos are now able to worship, meditate, and pray individually or as a community together with Emiratis and other migrant workers from various countries at an ecumenical prayer room. Fr. Michael and a Filipino priest based in Dubai occasionally say mass there. The priest and ministers also provide spiritual and psycho-social counseling to both port workers and ship crew members regardless of nationality.

Diversifying Emirati cuisine

Being at a historic trading crossroads in the Persian Gulf, Dubai attracts migrants from the Middle East and North Africa, particularly from Algeria, Djibouti, Egypt, Iran, Iraq, Jordan, Lebanon, Morocco, Tunisia, West Bank and Gaza, and Yemen. They bring with them not only their goods but also their rich and delightful cuisines. With the opening of Dubai as a center of finance, recreation, shopping, and security, global cuisine is now available from an increasing number of restaurants, from popular fast-food chains to luxurious fine-dining cafes.

Filipino migrants have also made their mark on Dubai's busy and complex food scene. Filipino cuisine in fact is easily available in various places, such as the departure area of the Dubai international airport and at the Karama area of downtown Dubai.

Philippine fast food franchises like Chowking and Jollibee are there. Chowking has 10 Dubai food outlets selling Filipino-style noodle soups, dimsum, and rice toppings, while Jollibee has two. Just like in the Philippines, where it has more stores and sells more hamburgers than McDonalds and Burger King, Jollibee in Dubai is more popular than both American chains especially among Philippine migrants.

At the bustling Karama area, Red Ribbon and Goldilocks, two of the biggest bakeshops in the Philippines, are also present, manned and managed by Filipino migrants. Besides working and managing these Philippine franchises and restaurants, Filipino migrants are also popular recruits for western chains including McDonalds and Burger King because of their sharp English skills, caring approach to customer service, and pleasant personalities and disposition. Philippine diaspora diplomats are significant players in the food service industry of Dubai.

Tired of Dubai's Jollibees and Chowkings? Go for some of the thirty other alternative Philippine home-style restaurants especially their "specialties" (Figure 5.1 is a list of the popular ones).

Figure 5.1
Filipino Restaurants in Dubai

Restaurant	Area
365 Restaurant	Satwa
Acoustic Pinoy	Airport
Banana Republic	Bur Dubai
Bulwagan	Karama
Chikka Grill	Sharjah
Chowking	10 locations
Delmon	Karama
Equator	Bur Dubai
Far East Restaurant	Karama
Fiesta Filipino	Karama
Goldilocks Bakeshop	Karama
Goto King Al Attar Shopping Mall	Karama
Hard Court Pinoy Grills	Bur Dubai
Jollibee	2 locations
Kabalen Restaurant	Karama
Magic Fork Restaurant	Bur Dubai
Maharlika Café	Bur Dubai

Restaurant	Area
Manila Garden	Deira
Philippine Restaurant	Sharjah
Pinoy Grill	Deira
Red Ribbon Bakeshop	Karama
Rocky's Café	Bur Dubai
Salfit Restaurant	Bur Dubai
Salu Salu	Deira
Sampaguita	Deira
Sendan Cafeteria	Karama
Smiling Bar-B-Q & Shabu Shabu	Satwa
Spot Café & Cucina	Bur Dubai
Tagpuan	Karama
Tansu Kitchen	Airport

Source: Dubai fieldwork, January 2007.

Each Filipino restaurant has developed its own signature dishes which customers crave and drive long distances for. Kabalen Restaurant, one of the nine in Karama, with its cozy interior that evokes home, serves the best *adobong manok* (chicken in soy and tamarind soup). If one is not satisfied with Bulwagan's *pancit canton*, then one can drive to Rigga Street in Deira for Pinoy Grill's two heavenly house specialties: *bulalo* (beef shank and marrow bone soup) or *lumpiang sariwa* (fresh vegetable roll).

Chikka Grill in Sharjah regularly participates in the internationally acclaimed Dubai Food Festival. The restaurant showcased Philippine food alongside other ethnic dishes prepared by chefs from Curry Leaf, Chopstix, El Rancho, Bombay, Bite Rite, Teppenyaki, Fish n Chips, Jimmy's Killer Prawns, Sidra, Biryani Express, Dashi Dai, and Delifrance. The soft power influence of Philippine restaurants and chefs have been so pervasive in Dubai that the Philippine Consulate General in Dubai, Philippine Business Council, and the Renaissance Dubai Hotel organized a Filipino Food Festival in June 2009. Filipino resident chefs from the Renaissance -- Ofelia Fuentes, Norberto Dagonoon and Rina Tecson -- displayed the best of Philippine regional cuisines. Many of the Filipino chefs whip up dishes from recipes passed on to them by their grandmothers.

Ironically, it seemed easier to find a genuine Filipino restaurant than an authentic Emirati restaurant in Dubai. When I asked my Emirati friends what their favorite restaurant was, they pointed to the five-star hotels and classy malls that served Arab, Persian, Lebanese, or Moroccan cuisine. They claim that Emirati food is a combination of the recipes their ancestors passed down and these regional influences. Hence, it is safe to say that there are more Philippine restaurants in Dubai than Emirati ones.

At my Fujairah city home base, the local community savors Philippine cuisine at the Al Mabrook (Mabuhay) Restaurant. Besides the tasty, authentic Filipino food, it has earned a good reputation even among non-Filipinos for its clean surroundings, simple décor, reasonable prices, and most of all, their courteous and professional Filipino staff which included my cousin Galen's partner, Matet.

During one of my rice and crispy *pata* (deep fried pork leg) meals at the Al Mabrook, I spoke to the owners, Elmer and Eva Pacheco. They said it is not difficult to cook authentic Filipino food since the ingredients could be purchased fresh from the local wet and dry markets. I went to the Central public market of al Ghorfa with cousin Guimo a couple of times and saw first hand where restaurant owners get their fish, vegetables, beef, and even pork supplies. I was intrigued where the meat for my delicious crispy *pata* came from. It has become the signature dish for the restaurant and sought after by Filipinos and non-Filipinos alike.

Not surprisingly, market vendors and shopkeepers knew catchy words and phases in Tagalog, like *"Kamusta ka, kaibigan?"* (How are you, friend?)

and "*mura dito*" (cheap here). True enough, all the ingredients for Filipino dishes were available there. Pork and other *haram* (forbidden) items were readily available at designated groceries and supermarkets. One Emirati store owner added though that they are handled carefully and separately from *halal* (permissible) meat and products. In Dubai alone, there are three licensed grocery stores marketing special Filipino cooking ingredients as well as choice-cut pork and pork meat products—CM Supermarket in Karama, Dubai, Philippine Grocery in Satwa, and De Belchore in Karama. No wonder Al Mabrook had 18 types of pork dishes. Aside from my favorite dish, they also served savory *batchoy* (noodle soup), breaded pork chop, pork *nilaga* (stew), pork *sinigang* (sour soup), *dinuguan* (pig blood stew), *lechon kawali* (pan fried pork), among others.

Associational Filipinization
Educating the Next Generation

Philippine international private schools in Dubai and other parts of the UAE magnify the soft power influence of Filipino and Filipina diaspora diplomats. They are also the largest visible annual gathering which brings significant segments of the Philippine community together with other ethnicities and nationalities, including Emirati. Graduation, parent-teacher conferences, sports competitions, cultural shows, and other preschool, elementary school, and high school functions gather together students, faculty, administrators, parents, staff, Philippine and UAE officials, and their friends in the hundreds and sometimes thousands. Figure 5.2 is a list of Filipino pre-school, elementary, and high schools recognized by the UAE Ministry of Education (MOEYA) and the Philippine Department of Education (DepEd).

Figure 5.2
Philippine schools in the UAE

School name	Location	Curriculum	Year	Students
Pioneers International Private School	Abu Dhabi	Philippine K-10	1990	1000
Philippine National School	Abu Dhabi	Philippine K-10	1998	1200
PISCO Private School	Abu Dhabi	Philippine K-10	1995	781
United International Private School	Dubai	Philippine K-10	1992	1340
The Philippine School	Dubai	Philippine K-10	2008	816
Far Eastern Private School	Sharjah	Philippine K-10	2001	503
Pioneers Modern School	Sharjah	Philippine K-10	1993	150
The New Filipino Private School	Sharjah	Philippine K-10	1996	874

Source: Philippine Schools Overseas (PSO), 2008.

The increase in the number of diaspora diplomats leaving with their families or building families overseas has created a strong demand for Philippine schools. Most of the educational institutions whose curricula are accredited by or are in the process of being accredited by the Philippine Department of Education (DepEd) are encouraged to become members of the consortium, Philippine Schools Overseas (PSO).

As of 2008, there are 44 Philippine international schools in nine countries – Bahrain, China, Greece, Kuwait, Libya, Oman, Qatar, Kingdom of Saudi Arabia, and United Arab Emirates. The Gulf region, which includes the UAE, is home to 38 Philippine international private schools. According to the PSO website, 41 have been accredited by DepEd, while the rest are in various stages of applying for accreditation. There are more than 23,000 students presently enrolled in Philippine international schools at various levels, ranging from pre-elementary, elementary, and high school. According to the Philippine Overseas Employment Agency, the presence of these schools makes the UAE one of the top 10 destinations of Philippine-trained elementary and secondary school teachers since 2001. Not surprisingly, Oman, Saudi Arabia, Bahrain, and Qatar are also in the top ten over the same period.

The Inter-agency Committee on Philippine Schools Overseas (IACPSO), comprised of the Department of Education (DepEd), Department of Foreign Affairs (DFA), Department of Labor and Employment (DOLE), Overseas Workers Welfare Administration (OWWA), and the Commission on Filipinos Overseas (CFO), in cooperation with PSO members, facilitate the easy reintegration of Filipino migrant children in the Philippine public and private school system by reviewing the curriculum of the PSO members and certifying subjects they are taking. All of the Philippine schools in Dubai also accept expatriate children from India, China, the U.S. Canada, among others. All the Philippine overseas schools in the UAE have kindergarten to grade 10 or fourth year high school curriculum by Philippine public school standards. The oldest and one of the largest schools is the Pioneers International Private School in Abu Dhabi while the newest is the Philippine School in Dubai. In 2008, more than 6,000 students went to the eight UAE Philippine schools.

In January 2009, the Al Shaab Club in Sharjah was the venue for the sixth annual sports fest of Dubai Philippine international schools. Teams from PISCO Private School in Abu Dhabi, Far Eastern Private School (FEPS) in Sharjah, The New Filipino Private School (NFPS) in Sharjah, and The Philippine School (TPS) in Dubai competed in basketball, volleyball, and dance promoting camaraderie and cultural diversity among Filipino youth and their classmates. Just like their parents, these next-generation diaspora diplomats have initiated a number of civic and outreach projects benefiting Dubai and their Philippine hometowns.

In San Francisco, London, Singapore, Dubai, and many other cities I visited, I encountered members of familiar Philippine fraternities and sororities like Alphi Phi Omega, Tau Gamma Phi, Upsilon Sigma Phi, Alpha Kappa Rho, Zeta Phi Sigma, and Beta Sigma, among others. There are also military and paramilitary brotherhoods like Guardians Brotherhood and Scout Royale Brotherhood. I learned that some were parents of the children who attended the Philippine Overseas Schools in Dubai and Sharjah.

Founded in June 1999 by a group of diaspora diplomat brothers in Dubai, Alpha Phi Omega, Philippine Alumni in UAE has expanded to directorates in Al Ain, Abu Dhabi, Sharjah, and Dubai. Over the past years, the Dubai AΦΩ alumni chapter had organized successful paintball and basketball tournaments as well as raffle draws to raise funds for brothers and sisters who are in Philippine prisons. I learned this from Mickey Santos whose son, Damon, was going to the Pioneers Modern School in Dubai.

Dribbling basketballs on the sand

Move over Premier Football League and camel racing! Filipino expatriate communities are forming basketball leagues in parks, gyms, playgrounds, and recreation centers of London, San Francisco, Dubai, Singapore, and Dhaka. They play ball year-round.

The Filipino Basketball Centre in Sharjah organizes the largest Filipino men's and women's leagues in the world with more than 70 teams participating in their summer and winter competitions. Teams come from all over the Emirates. The Dubai teams are some of the most competitive among the Filipino communities in the Middle East. Competitions are normally open to any team, Filipino or non-Filipino, who wish to join the league. The American expatriates who participate in the games love it even if they do not have enough numbers to create a U.S. league. However, they must learn to adjust to Philippine-style play and Philippine Basketball Association rules. Filipinos are masters of man-to-man defense. Most players make up for their lack of size and athleticism with agility, speed, stamina, wit, and focus. The games are usually very intense. The on-court refereeing and off-court officiating are quite professional and of high caliber. Coaches and supporters get pumped up and emotional on the sidelines. Some former professional, amateur, college varsity (NCAA and UAAP) players get involved as coaches or players.

At the Fujairah and Dubai games I watched, the majority of the players were Filipino migrants, including many of mixed-race. The team representation come from a colorful blend of hometowns, church groups, alumni associations, cities where they now live, companies where they work, or just a group of friends who came together to play. Most of the games I witnessed were very seriously competitive and highly organized. The players come from far distances bringing large groups of families and supporters. The opening ceremony includes pretty muses and remarks from community leaders including Philippine ambassadors and consul generals and high ranking local officials. Filipino pastors provide ecumenical invocations at opening ceremonies.

At the city of Fujairah in the UAE, my nephew Poch G. and I were walking on Corniche Road when a loudspeaker from a nearby mosque started blaring out that evenings' call to prayers in Arabic. We paused. I took advantage of this breather and savored the fresh salty breeze from the Gulf of Oman. When the chanting ended, we continued our stroll to the Fujairah International Marina Club. On one side was a brightly lit basketball court with teams in colorful uniforms warming up while their families and supporters socialized in the sidelines. The referee blew his whistle and the fourth UFAE Winter Basketball league (2007-08) was well on the way. Poch, a cigarette factory worker during the day, was going to be the scorekeeper for that night's game. My two cousins, Galen G., who works with Poch at the same factory, was going to be the lead official while Guimo G., a professional diver at the Port of Fujairah was league chairman. This was the second round of games at an annual league sponsored by UFAE.

That cool January evening I watched Vopak in green go head-to-head with Asteras in red. Vopak was an all-Filipino team while Asteras was an international group comprised of Emiratis, Iranians, South Asians, and Arabs. Guimo knew most of the Asteras players since they went to elementary and high school with his son, Luigi, and daughter, Gabby, at the local international school. There were six teams playing in this particular Fujairah league. Some of the teams drove in from as far away as Sharjah and Dubai. Many players compete year round in basketball leagues organized by Philippine associations in all seven emirates of the UAE. There were 12 participating teams in this winter league, namely Sarah Saloon, Mac Marine, Fujairah Sharks, Asteras, Port of Fujairah-Marine Department, Vopak Horizons, Rock Wool Barako, Al Dana, Mega Saloon, AR-Roeya, Athena and Fujairah Surveyors.

Pinoy basketball action in Fujairah

During half-time, Galen told me that on opening night Athena won narrowly, 67-65, over Fujairah Surveyors while Sarah Saloon outplayed Fujairah Sharks with a come from behind 88-60 victory. That night, Jennifer B. of team Sarah Saloon received Best Muse honors while the Rock Wool Barako team won for Best Team Uniform. "This tournament will go on for three months and games will be played every Thursday and Friday from 6pm-10pm," nephew Poch added with a smile. The Filipino associations in the UAE coordinate with each other to minimize overlapping schedules.

In Abu Dhabi, the capital of UAE, 24 teams registered for the 2008 Pinoy Ekspat Inter-Faith Basketball League. It also included two ball clubs—an all UAE squad and a team of Kenyans and Americans. At Dubai's Filipino Basketball Center, on the other hand, 41 teams played ball in four different categories which keep commissioner Ric Roces, a former PBA cager, busy all year round. The leagues lasted 22 consecutive weeks and ended in September.

At Sharjah in 2009, the Filipino Basketball Centre (FBC) hosted the first-ever Filipino Women's Basketball tournament at the Al Shaab Sports Club, Al Hazana, Sharjah. It played for 22 Fridays. All games started at 8pm. The men's 2009 tournament was participated in by more than 30 teams and competed for the coveted Sixth Winter Basketball Tournament trophy and cash awards.

Back in Fujairah, at the newly painted basketball court of the Marina Club, where private luxury yachts were docked, my cousins and I stumbled upon Lucio and his brother BJ. To find cousins and nephews in Dubai was already unbelievable but to discover that our Santa Ana childhood friends were also in Fujairah was certainly surreal. BJ was on one of the basketball teams competing.

We reminisced about our past over barbeque at Guimo's house. Life was much simpler then—go to school in the morning and then play basketball in our driveway in the afternoon. Now we were thousands of miles from our hometown, married with children to support. Lucio and BJ are among the millions of Filipino seamen remitting their earnings back to their hometowns. But unlike the majority of Filipino seamen who work on container and transport ships or military vessels, these two worked for the private pleasure boats of a rich Kuwaiti family with business interests all over the Persian Gulf. Basketball brought us together as kids in the Philippines and basketball once again brought us together but, this time, as Filipino diaspora diplomats.

Summary and Conclusion

I observed Filipino diaspora diplomats not only helping their own but also at-risk and needy migrants from other countries—the classic definition of *bayanihan* applied to humanity. After my Qeshm airport clearance, Iranian authorities put me and my cousin Galen on a taxi. We were driven for miles and miles in total darkness before finally arriving at Tolla Inn Hotel. This was where all the other passengers were taken. The place was packed. Everyone was tense since we were not expecting to stay overnight. Many were led to believe that it was an airport-to-airport arrangement. A lone Filipina front desk staff with a rose colored *hijab* placed Philippine nationals together in one dingy room. We were with two nervous Filipino construction engineers, Jonathan and Raul. They confessed that they had no money or extra clothes. The Filipina checked them in and waived the cost of the room. My cousin and I offered to share whatever money we had even though we did not know how long we were going to be trapped in Qeshm.

All the other passengers were curious about what happened at the airport but I was too exhausted to answer questions. I was also too tired to "complain" about the dirty toilet, cockroaches on the floor, and stinky bed sheets. I just crawled into one of the four steel beds and crashed. When I woke up the following morning, I still did not feel safe. I wanted to leave immediately but could not. Our anxiety and stress levels increased when we were told that all flights out were fully booked. They did not know when we could leave and so they took our passports.

Migrants from all over the world were constantly checking a makeshift board where faxed employment offers from Dubai were posted. While exploring the quiet spacious grounds, Galen and I discovered two Filipino restaurants: Kuya Omar Restaurant Café Videoke and Alimasagan Restaurant. It was surreal. There were no other restaurants in the area. Kuya Omar served Philippine breakfast food, including fried chicken joy ala Jollibee over white rice. It was the most popular item on the menu among the non-Filipinos.

Galen and I ordered chicken and rice, and sang Tagalog and English songs with a group of Filipina migrant workers and their Romanian co-worker. Other migrants joined us and looked less depressed. Migrants of the world temporarily forgot about our dire situation. Kuya Omar lent money to those who did not have any. He also gave them food. During my last evening, a group of us sat around in the courtyard and smoked *shisha* (water-pipe) together to suppress bowel movement, the bitter cold, and as an anti-depressant. But most of all, Kuya Omar's hospitality, soul food, and generosity helped.

Among government officials from both nation-states, the tone and tenor of diplomatic relations between the Philippines and the UAE in the past decade could be summed up by two blockbuster Filipino movie hits: the sad 1997 film "The Sarah Balabagan Story" on the attempted rape and incarceration of a Filipina domestic helper in Abu Dhabi, and the bilateral issues that followed; and the light-hearted 2005 film "Dubai," about the dreams and loves of three young migrant friends.

The Filipino community in Dubai is the main driver of the slow but smooth recovery. They have learned to take care of their own, and on occasion, other needy migrants. They have also learned not to wait for UAE or Philippine government authorities to act, as the leaders and organizers of this chapter has revealed.

In Fujairah, the United Filipino Association in the Emirates (UFAE-Fujairah) opened up a halfway house for run-away domestic helpers. When I visited the halfway house, there were Sri Lankan and Indonesian migrants too. It is the largest Filipino organization in Eastern UAE with more than 200 active members. UFAE has become the de facto Philippine Consulate in Fujairah. Not surprisingly, UFAE members who are also members of the Couples for Christ group make up the bulk of the English and Tagalog readers, ushers, and altar servers at the Our Lady of Perpetual Help Catholic Church. Coming from all over the Philippines, they are Fujairah's entrepreneurs, bankers, port employees, administrative staff, nurses, hotel staff, and factory workers, among others.

In sum, the spiritual, occupational, and association influences from my Gonzalez relatives, cousins Guimo, Maite, Galen, Matet, nephew Poch, and their children, along with hundreds of thousands of Philippine diaspora diplomats in Dubai, Sharjah, Fujairah, and surrounding areas are certainly significant. This is notable given the complicated social, cultural, economic, and political context of the UAE.

In terms of religious impact, the multitude of Philippine diaspora diplomats through their churches and spiritual services have been spreading inter-faith respect in the Middle East and are helping shepherd an evangelical flock in Arabia. They are doing it in the most discreet and sensitive way possible. Through their formal and informal *kasamahan* gatherings at Catholic and Protestant churches, Filipino migrants and their families and friends are able to keep the Philippine faith and culture alive and growing. In response to their very respectful requests, the ruling UAE royal families who control the various Emirates have been quite gracious and accommodating. The Emirs of Dubai, Abu Dhabi, and Fujairah have granted them special permission to practice their Christian religions and even donated land for their churches. Philippine Christian migrants and their friends have been very careful not to abuse this kindness and generosity. They know their proper place and function in Dubai's blossoming religious landscape. The focus of their *bayanihan* church-giving has been for the maintenance of their faith, the less fortunate in other countries, and their families back in their Philippine homeland.

Occupationally, their jobs and businesses allow Philippine diaspora diplomats to remit thousands of dollars annually back to their families and churches in their hometowns. Through the grace of God, they have become the *bayanihan* catalysts for much-awaited miracles. Their English skills, labor, education, and training are critical in assisting Dubai achieve world-class success. The Gulf states need them as part of their team and they bring with them their Philippine *kasamahan* socialization and professional attitudes. As divers, engineers, mechanics, clerks, sales persons, crane operators, seamen, managers, supervisors, and U.S. Navy sailors, their operational support role in securing and maintaining the strategic commercial and military value of the UAE's Persian Gulf ports has been outstanding and noteworthy. Further inland, Filipino and Filipina diaspora diplomats facilitate the diversification and internationalization of Emirati cuisine, cooking, and food by sharing and mainstreaming family recipes, regional flavors, and home cooked meals through their multitudes of Dubai franchises, restaurants, and hotel chefs.

In terms of their associational Filipinization, or the *bayanihan* and *kasamahan* influences from their participation in existing or formation of formal organizations and informal gatherings. Filipino diaspora diplomats deepen their *kasamahan* impact and involvement in Dubai society through their Philippine overseas schools and their thousands of enrollees, their introduction of year-round Philippine men and women's basketball leagues, their Philippine alumni fraternities, sororities, and brotherhoods, and their *bayanihan* efforts to protect the welfare of their at-risk counterparts, regardless of nationality, particularly those who work as domestic helpers.

CHAPTER 6

Dhaka: Garbs, Games, and Globalization

The sweltering July heat felt like 100 degrees Fahrenheit (or 38 degrees Celsius) with extremely high humidity. It did not bother me very much at first since this weather was no different from the summers in Manila, but since I just came from the foggy cold summer of San Francisco where it was a nippy 60 degrees Fahrenheit, I was sweating and burning. Nonetheless, this was the perfect time to witness a world-class merchandise inspection in Dhaka, when the factory manager thinks no inspector in his right mind would dare go out.

The heat did not seem to bother Jun Pastrana, 42, a Filipino migrant who, like me, has roots in Bulacan province. A former textile industry employee in Manila, he is the "Senior Quality Assurance Inspector for The Children's Place (TCP)," according to his business card. I joined Jun on his unannounced weekend visit to a Dhaka garments factory producing TCP's name brand, "Place Jeans" for their retail stores in the U.S., Canada, and Puerto Rico. His job is to ensure that TCP's job order is in strict compliance with the production standards and labor laws of the U.S. before San Francisco Filipino migrant Jasmine M. sells the kids' jeans at TCP's store in Daly City's Serramonte Center.

Bilal, the driver, opens his boss' car door and we are greeted by a security guard in camouflaged khaki attire who then stomps a boot hard on the cement floor. BOOM! And then he smartly salutes us. It reminded me of the poker-faced sentries in front of Buckingham Palace in London. I am very glad we entered the building. Inside it's a little better — just around 90 degrees.

The moment we enter the brightly lit shop floor, hundreds of Bangladeshi men and women hunched over seemingly endless lines of sewing and cutting machines get jittery. It is as if Darth Vader entered the ventilated room. The Bangladeshi manager rushes to greet Jun cheerfully, but the Filipino inspector doesn't smile back. With the manager following nervously, Jun heads straight to a pile of size eight Place jeans and randomly pulls out at a pair from the middle. He examines it carefully, tugs hard at the front button, pulls down the zipper, and then throws the jeans back into the pile. Jun P. grabs another pair and asks me to look at the back pocket stitching closely. "*Tingnan mo ang tahi nito, pare, hindi pantay* [Take a look at the sewing of this one, brother, it's not aligned]," he pointed out, shaking his head.

Tape measure in hand, he shows this to the quality controller, who, with his head half bowed, apologizes profusely in English—"sorry boss, sorry boss, sorry boss...." Jun sternly says something to him in Bangla and tells me, "*Pare, malaki yung responsibilidad namin dito* [We have a huge responsibility here]." Though visibly not happy with the discovery, the Bangladeshi manager turns to me and blurts out in broken Tagalog, "*magaling* [good] boss Philippine!" and gives a thumbs up sign. I just witnessed firsthand why The Children's Place has a good reputation among brand shoppers in San Francisco.

When I saw Jun again at Banani Church's Saturday evening English mass, it seems like I am with a different man. Wearing khaki shorts and a cotton shirt, he was grinning and joking with fellow Filipino parishioners, most of them active members of the Philippine Society of Bangladesh, the only homeland association in Dhaka. One guy notices his new haircut and teases him about it, "*Pare, bagay sa iyo ang kalbong gupit! Kailan uli ang pa-basketball ng PSB*? [You look good with your bald look! When is the next PSB basketball game?]." A young girl is running circles around him and he is making faces at her. "*Namimiss ko tuloy, yung anak ko sa Pilipinas* [I miss my child in the Philippines]," he said to me. Jun is one of the Filipino migrants performing diaspora diplomacy in Bangladesh while connecting Dhaka to San Francisco and the rest of the global garments supply chain not only via the clothes he inspects but via his prayers and his associations.

In this chapter, I discuss the ongoing efforts of Filipinos and Bangladeshis to nurture historic ties—trading experiences from a developing state in Southeast Asia to another developing nation in South Asia. A deeper analysis of the influence of Filipino migrants in Dhaka will illustrate that there is more to Philippines-Bangladesh relations than just a Global South-to-Global South link. I illustrate the importance of small but significant pockets of Philippine religious influences in Dhaka, which like Dubai, is overwhelmingly Muslim. I also discuss the occupational influences of Filipino men and women as fashion merchandisers, designers, technicians, nurses, educators, and as development consultants. I highlight the possibilities of soft power from influential Filipina personalities and entrepreneurs in a culture still largely dominated by men. Finally, I close with Filipino associational influences through their formal and informal gatherings, from forming expatriate bands, watching Philippine musicians at Dhaka's five-star hotels, to networking via shopping, sending, and shipping, and their support for the Philippine Society of Bangladesh's philanthropic and civic projects. As in the previous chapters, I end with a final vignette and some concluding thoughts on soft power through *kasamahan* and *bayanihan*.

Interceding for global non-state actors

Before leaving for my Bangladesh fieldwork, one of my students asked, "Why would Filipinos who come from a poor developing country want to work in a poorer developing country like Bangladesh?" I answered, "The same reason they go to a rich country. It's about the money they would never be able to earn in the Philippines, to create a better life for their family". Besides, Filipinos are the chosen go-betweens for emerging global businesses, churches, and societies. They intercede in a very respectful but tactful way.

Unlike San Francisco, London, Dubai and Singapore, Dhaka is still a budding global city, part of the larger developing economy of Bangladesh, with an estimated per capita GDP of only US$1,500 in 2008, ranked 197th out of 220 countries in the world. Comparatively, Manila is much more cosmopolitan and westernized, integral to a Philippine economy that is twice the per capita GDP as Bangladesh's. But this South Asian economy seems poised to do some catching up, powered by a booming garments industry that left the Philippine's relative cheap labor market for an even cheaper workforce in Bangladesh.

Dhaka, the capital city, is slowly becoming a metropolis of contrasts with evidences of both underdevelopment and modernization. It evoked the sights and sounds of the Manila I left in the 1980s: brownouts four times a day, beggars at every street corner, mothers carrying naked babies, rickshaws moving against the traffic flow, heavy choking pollution from vehicles and industrial plants, roads quickly flooding with the slightest downpour, open sewers with green and blue toxic chemical from nearby factories, flies and maggots hovering over garbage piles, unpaved side roads, daily headlines on corruption and overseas migrant issues, and military checkpoints on major thoroughfares. When I arrived in the summer of 2008 a caretaker government was in place, and there was increased military and police presence at the airport, the ports, and critical government offices, but it was relatively peaceful.

Mixed in with these bleak scenes, seldom touched on by the media, are signs of an emerging modern South Asian metropolis: private universities charging thousands of dollars a semester in tuition fees; western fast food franchises like KFC, A&W, and Pizza Hut; new high rise condominiums and office constructions; pricey malls; classy restaurants; grocery stores stocked with products from all over the world; international schools and clubs for the growing expatriate community; Japanese and American SUVs and sports cars; and brand-name garments manufacturing all over Dhaka and its bustling suburbs. As it is in Manila, Dubai and Singapore, the inflow of foreign capital and business has created a great divide in Dhaka. In the garments industry alone, there are those who can afford to live in the high rise condominiums in Gulshan and those who come from the slum settlements near Narayanganj.

Having grown up in Manila, it did not surprise me to see some of the rich locals and foreign expatriates in Dhaka -- supposedly one of the world's poorest cities -- wearing the trendiest fashion, ala London and San Francisco. In fact, some were actually wearing next season's name brand clothes, yet to hit shopping malls in Western Europe and North America, with the dirt-strewn pavements of the city as backdrop. Not to be outdone, Filipino migrants were just as trendy, on the job, in church, and especially at parties. One was even wearing a Jack Ashore shirt and matching neck tie which retails for hundreds of euros! They must have very high paying jobs, able to buy them dirt cheap, or wear very authentic looking fake items, I thought.

In terms of formal diplomatic ties, Bangladesh has an embassy in Manila and the Philippines has an embassy in Dhaka. It is worth noting that the Philippines was the first country in the world to recognize the newly independent People's Republic of Bangladesh in 1972. Since the opening of diplomatic relations between the two Asian states, eight treaties have been signed, covering trade, cultural, and technical cooperation. Government officials on both sides feel that there is a lot of potential to increasing the relatively small US$28 million trade volume (2007) between Dhaka and Manila. In that period, the Philippines imported roughly $5 million worth of garments, fertilizers, semi-conductors and exported $22 million of electronic products, computer hardware, and software, a $17 million trade surplus favoring the Philippines. Bangladesh has a more significant people and trade flow with the Philippines' ASEAN neighbors, particularly Singapore and Malaysia. They also host more than a million Bangladeshi temporary and permanent migrants. The Philippines and Bangladesh share political influences from policies and resolutions handed down by the Organisation of the Islamic Conference (OIC).

Although there are no direct flights between Manila and Dhaka, there is a noticeable amount of human movement. This temporary and permanent migration is the understudied aspect of bilateral ties, consequently linked to globalization which I uncovered. There are close to 500 Bangladeshi professionals working in the Philippines, mostly at the Asian Development

Bank (ADB), United Nations agencies, the World Health Organization, and the International Rice Research Institute (IRRI) as well as students at various Manila universities. The Philippines is also a destination for Bangladeshi's seeking higher education, particularly for Catholic studies.

Comparatively, Figure 6.1 shows that there are 977 Filipino temporary and permanent migrants in Bangladesh based on Philippine Embassy in Dhaka 2008 estimates.

Figure 6.1
Occupations of Philippine diaspora diplomats in Bangladesh

	Number	Percent
Garments professionals	471	48
IT technicians	269	28
Engineers	51	5
Business owners	26	3
Domestic helpers	20	2
Beauticians	13	1
Students	37	4
Nurses	9	1
Others: accountants, educators, drivers, etc.	81	8
Total	977	100

Source: Philippine Embassy in Dhaka, "Report to Congress", June 2008.

Thinking of Bangladesh as a country of destination for international migrants seems illogical. It seems to be capable of fulfilling its own labor needs with a rich and talented population of more than 150 million. This is half the population of the U.S. and more than twice the size of the United Kingdom's.

Like Jun P., close to half of Filipino migrants work for the garments industry, particularly upholding western regulations on merchandising quality assurance and corporate social responsibility. More than a quarter of them work for the fast-growing telecommunications sector. Philippine-trained engineers and IT technicians work for global contractors like Ericsson (Sweden), SingTel (Singapore), WorldTel (USA), Alcatel (France), NEC (Japan). They maintain fiber optic lines, build transmission towers, set-up switching, radio, microwave links, and create IT enterprise software. During my 2008 fieldwork, I met Cebuano-born and educated Paulino E. who worked as the Service Delivery Manager for Ericsson. He was there with his wife and two children. The other 25 percent of Philippine diaspora diplomats in Bangladesh worked as domestic helpers, beauticians, students, nurses, accountants, teachers, drivers, UN agency staff, as well as business owners.

The countries in this region of the world are not usually migrant destinations, at least before the garments and textile boom. Rather, like the Philippines, fellow Asian states like India, Pakistan, Sri Lanka, Maldives, and Bangladesh are major countries of origin for both temporary and permanent migrants. So discovering Filipinos in populous South Asia, particularly a small but influential group based in Dhaka, is an interesting sociological and international relations phenomenon. But I found out from interviews with the Dhaka inspectors that some of them formerly worked elsewhere in the South Asia region doing the same job. A large majority of the Filipino migrants in India, Pakistan, and Maldives were also garments professionals like Jun P. As a matter of fact, there are more Filipino migrants in India than in Bangladesh.

Religious Filipinization

How would it be possible for Philippine diaspora diplomats to influence a city which, by sheer numbers alone, is predominantly Islamic? This is an account of Filipino and Filipina migrant religious *kasamahan* and *bayanihan* influences at the margins of Bangladesh but at the heart of Dhaka's spirituality and faith.

According to the Bangladesh Bureau of Statistics, a large majority of Bangladeshis are Muslim, around 90 percent, mostly Sunnis. Nine percent are Hindus, and the remaining one percent are Buddhists, Christians, and others. The Constitution of the People's Republic of Bangladesh establishes Islam as the state religion but also provides for the right to practice of other religions. The Filipino migrants I met in Bangladesh, just like their *kababayans* in the United Arab Emirate, are used to celebrating Christmas day and Holy Week with minaret towers blaring out Islamic prayers. Similarly, they help to discreetly maintain and grow Christianity in a predominantly Muslim state where local authorities disdain efforts to convert persons from Islam and where the main preferred social identifier of people is religion. Unlike in the U.S. or the United Kingdom, it is not unusual for a person to declare in informal or formal conversation that he is "Muslim."

The majority of Philippine diaspora diplomats in Bangladesh lives, works, and worships in the vast Catholic Archdiocese of Dhaka. Around 800 Filipino migrant Catholics unite in faith with more than 78,000 Bangladeshi Catholics from the Archdiocese, particularly at churches with English masses. I saw Jun P., Carmen L., Charles V., and Paulino E. at the Saturday masses at Banani Church and met more informants for my study including Filipino migrants who worked at United Nations agencies and the World Bank. Seeing many members of their families at worship was also refreshing. Besides the archdiocese, there are some Filipino migrants sprinkled among the dioceses of Chittagong, Dinajpur, Khulna, Mymensingh, and Rajshahi.

One Saturday in the middle of August, I decided to do community service with Estela Ilagan, a Filipina merchandise manager employed for the last eight years at a French-owned buying house for Slazenger promotional sports apparel. She is one of the firm's most valued employees. There are nine other Filipino professionals at her firm. Bangladesh firms like Filipino faithful like Estela since she is not Bangladeshi and therefore could be sent to negotiate with buyers and suppliers in countries where Bangladesh is not supposed to have political and economic ties. Unlike her Bangladeshi colleagues, Estela is comfortable meeting Israeli clients. A business trip to Israel, in fact, is a welcome pilgrimage to the Holy Land for her. Bangladeshi firms have earned millions of dollars through Filipino migrant workers like her.

That day was Estela's scheduled bi-monthly sortie to "Mother Teresa's house," officially the Nirmal Hriday Home of Compassion. We rode her chauffer-driven company car from Gulshan across very crowded streets to Holy Cross Road in the Uttara district of Dhaka. The gated compound was run by nuns from the Missionaries of Charity, a Catholic order of women established by the legendary Mother Teresa of Calcutta, India.

When we got there, hundreds of small children were amassed outside the white concrete walls. They got excited when they saw Estela and surrounded our vehicle. The guard opened the compound gate for us but did not allow the children to go inside. I helped her driver unload several large brown boxes of clothes and candies which Estela had gathered from other Filipino merchandisers. These were disposable samples, slightly damaged, or deformed name brand shorts, shirts, pants, and other clothes which did not pass quality control inspection. Sometimes the other Filipino merchandisers, like Jun P., and those from her office would go with her. But that day, it was just the two of us.

Inside, Estela introduced me to the nuns running the place. We stopped at a room filled with abandoned women who were sick and did not have any place to go. The place was bustling with activity since it was the day of the weekly feeding of the children we saw outside who live in the nearby slum settlements. Leading our small group of volunteers was Sister Eleanor Estrella, a Filipina from Davao City in southern Philippines. We were just starting our conversation when a swarm of noisy children descended on the walkway we were standing in and hurriedly seated themselves at long brown tables. There was a lot of pushing and jockeying for places. Those who were not able to fit lined themselves on the wall and sat down. Some kids were even carrying their baby sister or brother. Others appeared sick and malnourished. They all looked so hungry and eager to eat but still managed to smile back at me. One impish boy drummed on the brown table and the rest followed his lead. They stopped when the food came.

I first assisted Sr. Eleanor prepare plastic plates with a scoop of white rice, a hardboiled egg, and some curry dahl. Then I moved on to helping Estela distribute the plates and cups. Using their hands, the children quickly gobbled down the food as if they had not eaten in days. After the first 50 kids were fed, the guards herded them out and then ushered in another batch of kids. They kept coming and, at one point, I thought we would not have enough.

On one side of the outdoor makeshift feeding area there were two Bangladeshi women volunteers squatting around a large tub of water speedily washing used plates and cups. Many of the children were asking me for more

Sister Eleanor, a Filipino nun, is a dedicated member of the Sisters of Charity spreading her faith and its work in Dhaka.

food. It was heart wrenching looking at their faces. "Dahl! Dahl! Dahl!" they screamed at me. I was sweating and tearing up at the same time as I dished out second servings. I noticed one girl slip the hardboiled egg in her dress pocket. "*Para sa nanay o tatay nila*, [For their mother or father]," Estela whispered to me. We fed more than 300 hungry children that day. It was exhausting but so gratifying. No wonder Estela liked to come regularly and Sr. Eleanor had taken this on as her lifelong vocation.

I finally got a chance to visit with Sr. Eleanor when all the hustle and bustle in the compound subsided and we were all able to catch our breaths. Because of her accounting training from the Philippines, she is their religious community's finance person. I learned from her that there are hundreds of Filipinas among the more than 4,500 sisters from all over the world working in 133 countries. The Missionaries of Charity, which began their work in Bangladesh in 1972, is one of 13 congregations of Catholic nuns in the country. The others are the RDNM Sisters, Holy Cross Sisters, Maria Bambina Sisters, PIME Sisters, Maryknoll Sisters, Marist Missionary Sisters, Toomiliah Sisters, Lady of Sorrows Sisters, Luigine Sisters, Shanti Rani Sisters, Salesian Sisters, and Blue Sisters. Sr. Eleanor got her calling six years ago. As my last question, I asked her how much clothes she had. She answered, "Three". Sr. Eleanor said this was all part of the Mother Teresa sisters' vows of chastity, poverty, obedience, and commitment to help the poorest of the poor.

Expanding the spiritual base at Banani

Filipino and Filipina migrant faithful revitalize Christianity in predominantly Islamic areas of South Asia by giving money and time to support religious projects and activities. Both Our Lady of Perpetual Help Catholic Church in the United Arab Emirates and Banani Catholic (or Holy Spirit) Church in Bangladesh were built with the help of growing Filipino migrant communities. At the latter, I observed Filipino migrants contributing to the English mass collections—three times a week. They also act as ushers, lectors, and choir singers as well as musicians. Their support and active worship helped expand the small chapel for 50 persons into a full-blown church which could presently accommodate more than 300 people.

The church is tucked inside the sprawling compound of the Holy Spirit Major Seminary in Banani, right beside a Muslim cemetery. I took one of the colorful rickshaws from Gulshan, where I was based, across the dense traffic. After watching my "driver" weave in and out of people and cars and at times going against the traffic flow, I was convinced I made the right decision. I made it to the 6:30 pm mass that day with time to spare and I was able to socialize with Taposh and some of the Bangladeshi seminarians and Korean nuns.

Every Saturday at 6:30 pm, there were simultaneous masses – one in English and another one in Korean. I clearly recall the atmosphere in one mass among the many I attended because of its personal significance. After Father Rex Kulas' introductory remarks, I did the bible reading to an attentive congregation clearly suffering from the sweltering heat and humidity that Saturday evening but eager to hear the word of God. They were thankful for the dozens of electric fans blowing air into their sweating faces. The humidity reminded me very much of my hometown's church in Manila and Novena Church in Singapore. Coincidentally, that Saturday service at Banani Church in Dhaka was on the feast day of my namesake, San Joaquin, and the feast day of my hometown patron, Santa Ana. I only found out during the opening prayer by Fr. Rex, "Today, we celebrate the feasts of San Joaquin and Santa Ana who are Mother Mary's parents and therefore the grandparents of Jesus Christ….."

Before the mass, I was invited to sing with the choir organized by Filipino nurses, merchandisers, accountants, and engineers and joined by Bangladeshi from the attached seminary. In the beginning the melody sounded familiar but I did not recognize the lyrics. I smiled when I realized that the Filipino choir leader had simply translated Tagalog church songs to English. Our Filipino accented intonations, loud voices, and distinct melody led the singing. There were 150 attendees, 54 were Filipino. A Sri Lankan migrant himself, Father Rex K., told me during my visit to his residence that he was an avid musician so he encouraged the Filipino parishioners to form a choir. He, like me, went to an elementary school run by La Salle Christian Brothers. They did not have a hard time finding guitarists and a pianist as well as willing singers. Their group expanded when Bangladeshi seminarians joined them. Eventually, the choir grew to 12 singers and musicians. That night, before the mass, I jammed with them—seven Filipinas and four Filipino migrants, and three Bangladeshi seminarians. Jed, the guitarist, also played for the choir during the Bangla masses at Saint Christina's Catholic Church.

Fr. Rex introduced me to Fr. Ajit Costa, rector of the Holy Spirit Major Seminary, as well as Fr. Joyty Costa the parish priest of Saint Mary's Cathedral. During our conversation, I found out that a number of Bangladeshi priests had gone to graduate school in the Philippines. For instance, like Fr. Ajit, Fr. Joyty Costa had just returned from graduate studies in theology at the Ateneo de Manila, a Catholic Jesuit University like the University of San Francisco where I teach. Holy Cross Father Liton Gomes who was stationed at the University College of Notre Dame on the other side of Dhaka also did graduate school in accounting at the University of Santo Tomas, the oldest Catholic university in Asia. They were all happy to have Filipino Catholics help fill up their masses, take the lead in building up the choir, and are helping develop the musical dimension of future Bangladeshi priests at the Holy Spirit seminary. Fr. Joyty said that the Archdiocese welcomed Filipino migrant priests like Fr. Rex and Fr. Alex, who is with the Holy Cross Fathers, since there is a lot of work to do spreading the word of God in a country of more than 150 million. Philippine diaspora diplomats help them in accomplishing this gargantuan task.

Occupational Filipinization

Just like in San Francisco, London, Dubai, and Singapore, Philippine diaspora diplomats have deeply influenced many global occupations in Dhaka with their innovative skills, solid education, caring service, and advanced technical training.

The gigantic appetite for name-brand clothes in San Francisco, London, Dubai, and Singapore has created a highly competitive mass manufacturing job market in countries like Taiwan, Dominican Republic, Honduras, Vietnam, Sri Lanka, China, India, and Bangladesh. In Dhaka, I found quite a number of Filipinos, like Jun P., not on the factory production line but as highly skilled quality control, design, engineering, and merchandising professionals. These quality assurance professionals ensure that shoppers in Nordstrom's, Harrods, Festival Mall, and Takashimaya get the best quality clothes for the most reasonable price possible.

To provide the greatest value to consumers and still secure maximum profits, name-brand clothing companies locate to a country with the lowest overhead cost, particularly labor. Cheaper labor in other parts of the world precipitated a serious decline in the once vibrant garments and textile industries of the Philippines, where the 2007 minimum wage was US$8.00 per day while in Bangladesh it was just around US$1.00 per day.

By the late 1980s, name brand manufacturers from Europe and the U.S. closed many of their Philippine factory operations and moved to cheaper Asian labor markets like China, Thailand, Sri Lanka, India, Cambodia, Vietnam, Indonesia, and Bangladesh. But while many of the factories in these countries could provide the skilled line workers and supervisors, western brands still needed a layer of independent, resourceful, and creative professionals in the highly specialized product merchandising, vendor sourcing and negotiation, social and environmental inspections, and quality assurance functions. This is where Jun P. and his peers come in.

Quality assurance (QA) and compliance (QC) attained heightened concern at the turn of the millennium when corporate social responsibility (CSR) became the industry buzzword. Businesses had to abide by strict international labor, environmental, and ethical standards. They essentially needed to re-examine the impact of their supply chain activities from customers, suppliers, employees, shareholders, communities, to other stakeholders.

From Bangladesh in South Asia to China in East Asia, heavier emphases were placed by scholars and practitioners on global and regional-level CSR issues such as human rights, environmental and health concerns, worker welfare, corruption, and social safety nets. On the corporate level, the CSR issues were board governance, ethical fund management, shareholder accountability, corporate restructuring, corporate citizenship and factory level quality assurance. Why hire Filipinos? Because, for years, the QA and QC applications and practices of most Philippine firms have been heralded by American and European companies as aligned to western standards.

On the frontlines of the manufacturing process are hundreds of thousands of Bangladeshi line workers, many laboring more than eight hours a day, 26 days per month for a mere 2,000-3,000 Taka (US$28-US$43). They sew, cut, stitch, measure, iron, patch, pile, price, wash, tack, fold, and package. But a highly trained and experienced person representing the international brand company placing the order still needed to ensure that ventilation and lighting systems were adequate, scissors were tied to tables, no children were hired, buttons do not fall off easily, chemicals used in the washing process were disposed of properly, first aid kits were available, exit signs were visible, proper spacing between workers were followed, among others. Violations led to hefty fines on the factory owners. For example, a $15,000 fine would be imposed if a sewing needle was found on clothing being shipped out to distribution warehouses in North America or Western Europe.

Thus, reliable and highly qualified CSR enforcers – or quality assurance inspectors, merchandisers, technicians, and administrators — became the niche job filled by many veteran garments workers from the Philippines. The Philippine Embassy in Dhaka estimate that half of the more than 1,000 Filipinos in Bangladesh work in the garments industry. Multinational apparel and accessories corporations know that hiring a Filipino from the Philippines meant they do not need to send a highly paid executive from their Western European or North American home offices. The overall compensation package for Filipinos would be less and they will still get quality inspections. After all, how many home office employees and their families would agree to brave the searing heat, pollution, poverty, and the inconvenience of living in Bangladesh?

The good reputation of Filipinos grew and it did not take long for brand manufacturers such as Old Navy, Gap, Slazenger, Terranova, H&M, Marks and Spencer, Hanes, Mango, Puma, Nike, and retail giants Carrefour, K-mart and Walmart, to look forward to seeing Filipino quality assurance inspectors and merchandisers in the buying houses they hired to contract out the work to local factories. Some, like The Children's Place, preferred a more direct route and thus offered Jun P., who was then working for a buying house, the job as its exclusive quality assurance inspector. TCP established a retail store office in Dhaka, similar to those of the Gap, Walmart, and JC Penney. Other multinational firms hired Philippine-based merchandisers and quality assurance inspectors to go to the various Asian countries where they had factories. Many of these clothing companies are happy knowing that Filipinos, like Jun P., are monitoring the day-to-day operations of the factories, making scheduled and unscheduled visits. Hence, they pressure the buying houses to renew the contracts of the Filipinos.

Figure 6.2
Companies with Filipino Merchandisers and
QA Inspectors

Company	Country
Adidas	Germany
American Eagle	USA
Ann Taylor	USA
Banana Republic	USA
Benetton	Italy
Bloomingdales	USA
Carrefour	France
Chart Mondiale	UK
Dockers	USA
George	UK
Hanes	USA
JC Penny	USA
John Deere	USA
Kmart	USA
Levis	USA
Lumiere	Australia
Mango	Spain
Marks and Spencer	UK
Mervyns	USA
Mossimo	Australia
Nickelodeon	USA
Nike	USA
Old Navy	USA
Puma	Germany
Slazenger	Australia
Terranova	Italy
The Children's Place	USA
The Gap	USA
Walmart	USA
Zara	Spain

Source: Philippine Embassy, Dhaka, 2008.

Jun P. and I traveled through highways, floods, and dirt roads to a remote manufacturing plant in Ashulia, in the fringes of Dhaka. We were greeted at the IDS Washing Factory administrative building by a young, smart-looking Filipina in her chocolate brown Esprit jean dress. Jennifer M., a 31-year old migrant from Dau City in Pampanga province is the "Washing Queen" (formally Director) in the supposedly man's world of the garments industry— jeans production. She seemed very much respected and in control of the washing plant where name brand jeans get their final color and effects. She is assisted by another Filipino, Technical Manager Jess A. from Iloilo province, in supervising the local factory workers' machine-driven sand blasting as well as manual sand papering, spraying and rubbing. The end-product was the creased, whiskered, damaged, destroyed, or scraped look that U.S. and European fashion designers are selling as the latest trends. It is also where European brand jeans for H&M, Mondiale, George, and Zara, and U.S. brand jeans for Levi's, Gap, TCP, Walmart, and Mervyns are price tagged, ironed and folded, bar tacked, plastic bagged, and boxed ready for shipment directly to North American and European warehouses. Every person working in the washing process was male—600 in all! Because Jennifer M. was such an valuable and indispensable asset to them the Bangladeshi factory owners had a special women's toilet custom-made for her. With her and Jess A. at the helm, they need not be at the factory daily. They trust that Jennifer M. and Jess A. know what they are doing.

Administering world-class education

During my sorties, I met many scholars and researchers like Dr. Rollie Buendia at the School of Oriental and African Studies in London, Dr. Bobby Mariano, Dr. Mars Ang, Dr. Rey Ileto, and Rod Severino at Singapore Management University, the National University of Singapore, and the Institute of Southeast Asian Studies as well as numerous eminent professors at San Francisco's finest universities and colleges. Although there was no Filipino professor at the only university in Dubai, Zayed University, it still was not a surprise to meet eminent Filipino educators in Dhaka, particularly in the highly competitive private business and technology education market.

What came as a surprise was meeting Dr. Carmen Z. Lamagna, the only woman university Vice-Chancellor in Bangladesh higher education. For centuries, the higher rungs of educational administration in Bangladesh have been very much a male-dominated occupation but this did not deter this mild-mannered Filipina from shattering what many consider a tradition. Vice-Chancellor Lamagna also pioneered a world-class business, arts, and technology curriculum within the context and limitations of a tough developing economy setting. This made Bangladesh President and University Chancellor Muhammad Jamiruddin Sircar say the following in nominating her for one of the Philippines highest honors, "Due to her able leadership and strong determination, the American International University-Bangladesh has earned fame and good reputation both nationally and internationally... Her devotion and contribution is very much honored and useful for our socio-economic development particularly in the field of higher education in Bangladesh."

On the basis of President Sircar's endorsement and her many accomplishments, Vice-Chancellor Lamagna was awarded the Philippine Presidential Award for Overseas Filipinos in 2006. Her effectiveness as a diaspora diplomat is anchored on her Philippine educational training and experiences.

Dr. Carmen Lamagna came to Dhaka in the early 1990s as a technical consultant from one of the top computer schools in the Philippines' AMA Computer University. Born and raised in Manila, she received her Bachelor of Science in Chemical Engineering from Adamson University in 1978 and passed the licensure examination for Chemical Engineers on the same year. She subsequently obtained her masters degrees from the Philippines and a doctoral degree from the U.S.

Dr. Lamagna went to Dhaka upon the insistence of one of her former AMA students, a Bangladeshi. From the transfer of technology from Manila came

the idea and opportunity to establish the American International University —
Bangladesh (AIUB) in 1995. Under her guidance, AIUB has earned its place
in higher education in Bangladesh and abroad within a short period of time.

The Vice-Chancellor is also an active officer of many Bangladesh, South
Asian, and global educational and welfare bodies. She is a sought-after
presenter on the importance of educational administration and information
technology in Bangladesh and the Philippines. She has a large number of
articles of outstanding interest on national and international topics published in
various journals and dailies. This Filipina migrant's stellar rise in the academe
and continuing dedication to the development of higher education has earned
her a remarkable niche in Asia, particularly in Bangladesh. I also noted that
her Bangladeshi staff adored and respected her tremendously. Assisting her
are two Filipino senior educational managers, Dr. Charles Villanueva and
Assistant Professor Danny Morgia.

A veteran educational administration, teacher, and international
consultant, Dr. Villanueva is dean of both the Faculty of Arts and Social
Sciences and the Faculty of Business. He is also in charge of making sure
that AIUB is measured and assessed vis-à-vis world-class educational and
training standards. Dr. Villanueva is the best person for this task since he
was a teacher before becoming a career civil servant with the Philippine
Department of Education, Culture and Sports. A native of Aklan province in
the Visayan region of the Philippines, he has done decades of consulting on
educational concerns for the Asian Development Bank and UNESCO. Dr.
Villanueva also ensures that AIUB's business and technology graduates are
also well rounded in their general education with core arts, humanities, and
social sciences courses.

Computer Science Assistant Professor Morgia has been AIUB's Director
of the Information Technology Department since 2003. He replaced another
Filipino IT specialist who moved to Dubai. Born in Sorsogon Province and
raised in Metro Manila, Prof. Morgia manages the university's IT infrastructure

which is reputed to have the highest bandwidth capacity in all of Bangladesh. He is in Dhaka with his wife and their four sons.

Carmen, Charles, and Danny are not the only diaspora educator diplomats in Bangladesh. During one of my lunch meetings at a roadside Italian restaurant at the sprawling suburbs of Dhaka, I bumped into engineering lecturer Jenefer Carlos who teaches at the International University of Business, Agriculture and Technology (IUBAT) located at the Uttara Model Town. She specializes in Digital Logic Design, Circuit Analysis and Electronics Analyses and Design courses for future Bangladeshi engineers, technicians, and scientists. Jenefer got her undergraduate degree in engineering from the prestigious *Pamantasan ng Lungsod ng Maynila* (University of the City of Manila) and was a lecturer at STI Colleges of Metro Manila and AMA Computer Learning Center prior to migrating with her husband to Dhaka.

Filipino migrants have certainly made their imprint on the Bangladesh tertiary education system, allowing them to transfer valuable technical knowledge that will help make a fellow developing country more advanced and competitive in the highly globalized market.

I've met a lot of University of San Francisco (USF) alumni in the U.S. and the Philippines but meeting one in Dhaka who was also Filipino was certainly unexpected. I was introduced by World Bank consultant and violinist Sabrina to Mars Ugarte, managing director of CEMEX, a multi-billion dollar Mexico cement company, who stayed in the same service condominium as her. He was sent to run CEMEX operations in Dhaka by CEMEX Philippines. We were joined by another Filipino CEMEX senior manager. After our talk, which ended around 11 pm, they left for a surprise visit to one of the CEMEX cement plants in the fringes of Dhaka.

Associational Filipinization

Filipino musicians and vocalists in Dhaka could be heard not only in Banani Church but in hotels and restaurants. When I was there in the summer 2008, all the five-star hotels in Dhaka—including the Radisson, the Westin, and the Sheraton—had Filipino bands. This would not be a surprise to any expatriate or seaman who travel the world since Filipino bands are all over Asia and the Middle East: Seaview Hotel in Dubai, Hard Rock Café in Seoul, Pan Pacific Hotel in Bangkok, Roppongi Mall in Tokyo, Goodwood Park Hotel in Singapore, Shilin Night Market in Taipei, and even the Tonga Room at the classy Fairmont Hotel in San Francisco. I've even jammed with some in Tokyo, Singapore, and San Francisco.

But Bangladesh is not a usual destination for Filipino bands. According to the Philippine Overseas Employment Agency compendium of statistics, they normally work in the hotels and entertainment districts of Japan, South Korea, Hong Kong, or the United Arab Emirates. In 2007, more than 4,500 performing artists left for Japan, while more than 1,000 went to South Korea. More than a hundred went to the Hong Kong and the UAE.

The air-conditioned lobby of the 272-room five-star Sheraton Hotel in Dhaka was definitely a welcome escape from the hot and muggy weather outside that July evening. It was almost nine o'clock in the evening but I noticed that the comfortable cushioned sofa chairs were still bustling with men and women in nice business attire. Hard at work, representatives of American, Asian, and European companies were face-to-face with owners of Bangladeshi garments factories and buying houses. They were exchanging documents, typing on their laptops, punching keys on their calculator and deep in discussion. Business cards were laid out in front of some on the coffee tables. After the serious exchanges, some bid farewell to their Bangladeshi counterparts while others went with them to the nearby restaurant bar.

Outside the bar was a large glass-enclosed poster with the header: On the Spot Band at The Bar, 8pm – 11:45pm everyday, except Friday. There was a glossy picture of three young Filipinas with an older gentleman. The bar was packed. I joined a couple of Philippine Embassy staff members and some garments merchandisers at a table in the outside patio area. The band was playing old and new pop songs. Some people were clapping along, others were dancing.

After their first set, the band went straight to our table and I was introduced to them: vocalists 19-year old Sandra, 21-year old Eunice, and 24-year old Jiselle, and keyboard player and band manager 52-year old Kuya Jun Perez. I complimented their gig. "*Maraming salamat po* [thank you very much]," they said. We were joined by Rashid B., the Bangladeshi Bar and Lounge manager. I asked him why he hired Filipino bands over local bands. He said it is because of the clarity of their American English, their wide repertoire of American pop songs and their lively stage presence which entices patrons to clap, sing, and even dance. Rapport with the audience is critical. "It makes our customers forget the stress they had during the day........ and when they are happy they eat and drink more," Rashid B. added. Besides, hotels, restaurants, and expatriate clubs with liquor licenses are the only places allowed to sell alcohol. These were critical ingredients for bringing Bangladeshis and the expatriate community together. On the surface, the Filipino band helps make Dhaka appear more modern and cosmopolitan.

Rashid confided that local Bangladeshi businessmen have told him that the Filipino bands at Dhaka's five-star hotels help them create the comfortable ambience that is familiar to their western principals and a relaxed space away from heated and stressful boardroom discussions. "Bands from Europe may be good in instrumentals but cannot sing American songs very well and they lack creative choreography and performance.... Bangladeshis and foreigners like to request Shakira, Beyonce, Michael Jackson, Madonna, and Ricky Martin songs..... A Russian band cannot sing them," explained Rashid.

True enough, Jun, Jiselle, and Eunice could perform songs ranging from my '80s music to my daughter's '90s music. Some of the other Filipino bands even accommodated requests for songs in languages other than English and Tagalog. When a Japanese group asked for a Japanese song, they sang the Southern All Stars 2000 hit song "Tsunami". And when a Taiwanese businesswoman requested a Chinese song, one band belted out an F4 medley. Sometimes, Latino visitors would request a Spanish song, and as a Filipino, I am not surprised when the keyboard player did "Besame Mucho."

After their break from their first set, band leader Jun started with the intro chords for Boys Town Gang's "Can't Take My Eyes of You," Jiselle and Eunice followed with a dance and then with, "You're just too good to be true......." I was pulled to the dance floor for a fast cha-cha by one of the energetic Filipina grandmas. With the two girls singing, clapping, and prodding, more people—American tourists, European merchandisers, Bangladeshi locals, Japanese investors—who were looking to unwind joined us in the fun. This is exactly what Rashid meant.

There a lot of Filipino migrants who are international civil servants. In Dhaka, I met some who work for the Philippine Embassy, UN agencies, the World Bank, the Asian Development Bank, as well as the United Kingdom's Volunteer Service Overseas (VSO) program. Most of the foreign expatriates in Bangladesh work for international development agencies, relief organizations, or embassies.

Based in Dhaka, the UN country team (UNCT), consists of 10 UN agencies, including the World Bank, which funds and coordinate their work through the UN Resident Coordinator (RC). Their sound advice, technical assistance, and project financing has helped the country maintain a slow but sure macroeconomic growth. Over the last 10 years, Bangladesh has also had impressive gains in key poverty and quality of life indicators. In the 1990s, the economy grew by only an average of 4.75 percent per year. Gross Domestic Product (GDP) per capita has jumped from US$273 in 1990-91 to US$1,400 by 2008. I met many of these foreign consultants at hotel lobbies and international members-only clubs. I discovered that they do not always use their hard power institutional positions to influence the host society. Many of them were also capable of soft power diplomacy as musicians.

Dr. Jose Edgardo "Ed" Campos, my former boss at the World Bank, was one of these Filipino international civil servants. Ed is the World Bank's Governance Adviser to Bangladesh. He took me to a meeting one afternoon to meet his multinational "development team." The meeting turned out to be a gathering of music lovers in their ranks. Ed introduced them to a genre of music he picked up in the Philippines—Latin and modern jazz as well '80s R&B and pop.

At band rehearsal, I met Indonesian American Larry Maramis, a UNDP staff member, who played a number of musical instruments including the drums and the guitar. Band leader Ed played the keyboards, and Filipino management consultant Kent S. played the bass guitar. They were joined by sax player Sasha a German textile buying house owner; violinist Sabrina, a Chinese American lawyer consulting for the World Bank; cellist Honor F. an Irishwoman from the British Department for International Development; and cellist/harmonica player Hilary S. the First Secretary of the Canadian High Commission.

The vocals were provided by Ramon V., a ponytailed University of the Philippines fine arts graduate designing Banana Republic apparel; Bangladeshi husband and wife, Saif (the lead guitarist) and Simin, as well as Bangladeshi Leo. Simin sang a Brazilian "Mas Que Nada" in Portuguese by rock band Maroon 5. She was convinced by Ed to sing his arrangements of Carol King's "Its Too Late" and "So Far Away" as well as Deborah Cox's "Call Me". Leo was at first not comfortable with The Doors' "Light My Fire" but then picked it up after some coaxing and coaching. A young Bangladeshi performed Filipinized melodic arrangements of Carlos Santana's "Smooth", "Oye Como Va", and "She's Not There". During my visit, the band was preparing for their sold-out concert at the Heritage, a restaurant serving delicious Bangladesh cuisine. The show was a grand follow-up to their successful gigs at the Le Saigon restaurant and the Nordic club.

Even I got to do an impromptu performance. At his flat one evening, Ed, on keyboards and Sabrina, on violin, encouraged me to sing the popular Filipino ballad "Bakit Ngayon Ka Lang [Why did you arrive only now?]," to help entertain the weary Swiss and American consultants of the World Bank. Along with bottles of duty-free wine, we were able to help them relax after an intense anti-corruption workshop with high ranking Bangladeshi military and government officials.

Networking via shopping, shipping, remitting, and *padala*

There is only one Filipino association in Bangladesh—the Philippine Society of Bangladesh (PSB). Through its socials and the church, Filipinos are able to network with each other. The Philippine Independence Day celebration in Dhaka, like in Singapore, London, San Francisco, Dubai, and everywhere

Filipino garments inspectors in action at a Dhaka clothes manufacturer.

else in the world, showcases Filipino food and culture for the host country and diplomatic corps to experience. PSB also sponsors a basketball league and a scholarship fund for poor Bangladeshi elementary school children and street families. Filipinas married to Bangladeshi provide the sustained grunt work and energy to the PSB since they are permanently there, as opposed to the temporary migrants in the garments or telecommunications industry.

I met families socializing with locals and foreign workers

at the Fantasy Kingdom and Nandan waterparks. Their children, the next generation diaspora diplomats, seemed better at interacting than their parents. They were so polite to me and some even felt comfortable at calling me "Tito [uncle]." The children were a delight to hang out with. Many of them poked fun at my American accent as we huddled to watch Filipino shows on cable TV. Some of the children I spent time with were from mixed marriages. Many of the Filipina migrants who have permanently settled in Dhaka met their Bangladeshi husbands as migrant workers in Saudi Arabia, London, Hong Kong, or as long-distance penpals. They have wonderful Filipino Bangladeshi mixed-race children, lucky to be carrying both cultures and heritages. The kids also spoke the language of hip-hop, Facebook, MTV, and Nintendo DS and Wii. They thought I was a "cool uncle" to know all this hip stuff. I observed that they spoke Bangla and English as well as understood the Tagalog or Philippine dialect of their mothers. Their parents made family the center of their associational lives. Some migrant families have brought extended kin, including grandparents and aunts and uncles.

A major associational preoccupation of PSB members is shopping. "*Kasi wala namang masyadong magawa dito, pwede pang pagkakitaan* [there's nothing to do here....and you could earn extra money from it]" was the "excuse" given to me by one of the PSB members. It turns out that Dhaka is a shopping haven for name-brand clothes.

Inside their shopping malls, i.e., Bashundhara City, Rifles Square, Eastern Plaza, Navana Tower, the ambience and experience are still not quite Union Square in San Francisco, Oxford Street in London, Orchard Road in Singapore, Mall of the Emirates in Dubai, or even Greenbelt in Manila. But I found products that would compare to name-brand bargain finds in these cities when I went with Arvee Policar and Deli, her Indonesian shopping buddy, to Bongo Bazaar. The two were typical migrant housewives, in charge of the home, children, and social entertaining while their husbands work.

There are so many Filipinos who shop in Bongo Bazaar that stall owners and package handlers know phrases in Tagalog. I was greeted with, "*Kamusta ka*? [How are you?]," "*Mura lang*! [Cheap!]," "*Magkano gusto mo*? [How much do you want to pay for this?]," and "*Salamat* [Thank you]." Some of them worked in Saudi Arabia and other parts of the Middle East and learned basic Tagalog from their Filipino co-workers and friends.

Clothes and apparel that are deemed "rejects" by PSB members like Jun P. and the other quality assurance inspectors normally end up in two places: in the dirt-cheap bargain stalls of Bongo Bazaar or inside balikbayan boxes destined for the Philippines. These boxes then go to containers stacked in Chittagong and Narayanganj, port cities in proximity of the Bay of Bengal, before being transported by ship to various destinations. Not surprisingly, according to Fr. Ajit Costa and Fr. Rex K. who also visit the ports, most of these vessels had Filipino crew members and the first thing they would ask the administrators is, "Where is the church here?" Interestingly, the balikbayan boxes destined for Filipinos in Manila have the same name-brand products that will be sold at the shops of multinational retailers in various big cities.

Many of what Estela, Jun, and other quality assurance inspectors and merchandisers call stock lot rejects end up in Metro Manila--at well-known shopping haven called Greenhills. Stores in Greenhills teem with "rejected" clothes sent home in balikbayan boxes by Filipino garment workers from Sri Lanka, China, India, Vietnam, Indonesia, as well as Bangladesh. Because they are rejects, it is legal to sell them in Greenhills, despite the name brands. My daughter once bought a pink Abercrombie and Fitch mini skirt for 200 pesos (US$4.00) while I got a trendy Aeropostale hoodie for 250 pesos (US$5 bucks!).

Globally, it seemed to me that Filipino women migrants are more entrepreneurial than their male counterparts. Even their assuming the lead breadwinner role by going overseas as service sector workers takes a lot of entrepreneurial spirit and financial risks. At PSB, I met a number of Filipina entrepreneurs who were married to Bangladeshi. They got together often and even became business partners. Some have become successful entrepreneurs. I observed and talked to three spirited ladies with children on tow at a contemporary western restaurant on Road #101 in Gulshan Two. They were the co-owners of Coachroach Magic Solutions (CMS), which takes the first letters of their first names, Carol N. from Pangasinan province, Marilou J. from Samar province, Sarah K. from Negros Occidental province.

Money changers are plentiful since Bangladesh is a large migrant country of origin. I did not have any difficulty exchanging my US dollars to taka. The government has a liberal, deregulated policy when it comes to receiving foreign worker remittance from outside Bangladesh and exchanging these currencies locally. But sending remittances out is heavily regulated. Local and foreign banks have to abide by strict controls. This creates a big dilemma for PSB members. They therefore use creative means to send their precious earnings back home.

One arrangement is for their companies to remit all or a portion of their salaries directly to their beneficiaries in the Philippines. Another is through a PSB member who charges a transaction fee for sending through them. They e-mail, text, or call a family member in the Philippines to transfer funds to whoever they designate. Then there is the *paki* (please or kindly) approach or more specifically the phrase *"pakidala naman sa Pilipinas"* (kindly bring home to the Philippines). During home leave, fellow members do help out other PSB members by agreeing to bring home much-needed cash and gift items for their families and friends especially if they come from the same hometown. They take turns returning favors.

Compared to the other cities in this book where there are multiple ways to send care boxes (balikbayan boxes), in Dhaka there is only one, a small freight forwarding business owned by PSB President Lilia Aquino, who works full-time as a garments merchandiser for several western brands. Her entrepreneurial spirit reminded me very much of Eva the woman behind the business and culinary success of Mabuhay Filipino Restaurant in Fujairah,

UAE. I met many Lilias and Evas during my fieldwork. They defy the stereotype that Filipina diaspora diplomats are only capable of being domestic helpers, entertainers, and nurses.

When I met another PSB member, Filipina nurse Charito Sideno Parvez, the Assistant Chief of Infection Control Department for Square Hospital located in Dhaka's West Panthapath, I concluded that Philippine-trained nurses indeed influence health care settings all over the world. In my global travels, I've met the products of nursing programs from the northern-most schools in Luzon, to the Visayan universities, all the way down to the southern-most colleges in Mindanao. Charito told me that there are a handful of them working for Dhaka's private hospitals. All of them are married to Bangladeshis they met while working as nurses in the Middle East. They see each other at PSB, the Philippine Embassy functions, or would run into each other in the shopping malls and parks.

Summary and Conclusion

During another one of our many surprise factory visits, Jun P. intimated that TCP wanted him to visit the U.S. *"Gusto ko rin makita yung mga iniinspect ko dito kung saan at papaano tinitinda* [I also want to see where and how they are selling the clothes I inspect here in the U.S.]. Unfortunately, even with a letter of invitation from the TCP corporate head quarters in New York he was denied a U.S. visa. I offered to accompany him to the U.S. Embassy and vouch for him in my capacity as a U.S. citizen and an Immigrant Rights Commissioner for the City and County of San Francisco. But first, I examined his documents. Jun P. was earning a US$5,000 monthly salary, tax-free, plus allowances. His home was subsidized by TCP, he had a company car with a driver and his gas paid for, and representation expenses—meals with clients and suppliers – were covered. Would he exchange his comfortable lifestyle in Dhaka for the trials and tribulations of new immigrant life in the U.S.? I don't think so. Actually, I know a lot of Americans who would love to trade places with him.

On the searing hot morning of the visa interview, Jun P. picked me up from my apartment. We were both wearing business suits. Thank goodness for the car's strong air conditioning! At the fortified U.S. Embassy, I flashed my San Francisco city hall ID and U.S. passport to the guards and was led to a separate entrance for American citizens. We were able to grab a seat in the standing- room-only waiting room. I could see that Jun was nervous but was also feeling confident since I was there.

After a long wait, his name was called and we entered a small interview room. The consul on the other side of the glass panel was wondering who I was. I presented my Commissioner's ID, U.S. passport, and gave him my city hall business card with the seal of the City and County of San Francisco. The consul smiled and said, "Yes sir, what can do for you?" "I vouch for Mr. Pastrana and would like to host him at my home in San Francisco," I

Quality assurance inspector, Jun P., shows of his many
inspirations back in the Philippines.

responded. The young Caucasian consul looked at me and then my official credentials. He then asked me to leave the interview room so he could talk to Jun alone. After a few minutes, he came out with the widest grin. *"Nakuha ko na, pare* [I got it, bro!]!" I knocked on the door, then peeked into the room and said to the consul, "I appreciate it. Have a great day!" He smiled, "You're welcome."

The following day we celebrated. Jun P. cooked a hearty feast of *kutsinta* [pink rice cake], fragrant white rice, and giant red crabs for lunch. We were surrounded by his closest friends and, as backdrop, a collage of family pictures, mostly of his wife and kids, who were back in his Bulacan hometown. *"Salamat uli* [Thanks again]" he said to me and then he look up, *"Salamat din po* [Thanks too]."

In many ways, this story illustrates the influences of a transnational diaspora diplomat. As a Filipino American public official and professor, I carry multiple influences in multiple country settings and situations. Many Philippine diaspora diplomats do too. We help each other since we are sewn together in a gigantic patchwork of social capital. I did not just see but also felt that faith, work, and gatherings are key ingredients that bond the Philippine diaspora diplomats together. They may take this for granted in cities where there are so many Filipinos, such as San Francisco, Singapore, Dubai, and London, but not in Dhaka where they number less than a thousand in a metropolis of close to seven million residents. Filipinos in Dhaka gravitated towards each other at church, at the factory, and at Philippine Society of Bangladesh parties.

The extent of religious Filipinization (both *kasamahan* and *bahayanihan* influences) in Dhaka may not compare in scale and magnitude with San Francisco or London but the Filipino men and women I met there have certainly made their mark on the practice of Catholicism where they live and work. Banani Church and the Catholic Archdiocese of Dhaka are very much alive in spirit and action because of their active involvement. They join the hundreds of other foreign expatriate Catholics from Europe, Latin America,

Middle East, and other parts of Asia along with the thousands of local Dhaka Catholics. The stories of garments merchandiser Estela Ilagan from Manila and Sister of Charity Eleanor Estrella from Davao City who not only attend mass services but also do service and action amongst Dhaka's most impoverished and vulnerable residents exemplify the human rights and social justice influence of Philippine diaspora diplomats in a South Asian Muslim metropolis. They are joined by other Filipino men and women on their Fridays or Saturdays days off who expand not only the spiritual base of Christianity by *kasamahan* gatherings but the Christian *bayanihan* spirit in action.

Philippine diapora diplomats have deeply influenced many occupations in Dhaka with their innovative skills, solid education, caring service, and advanced technical training. They are well liked and valued by western companies for their fluency in English, knowledge of western practices, loyalty, creativity, adaptability, and their can-do attitude. Hence, name-brand firms and buying houses do not mind moving Jun P., Estela, and many others from the Philippines and paying them higher salaries. Companies know that a skilled Filipino migrant worker would still be more cost-effective than transplanting an expensive, demanding European or American employee and his or her family.

Filipino men and women migrants are an integral part of the growth engine that is moving Bangladesh to competitiveness and leadership in certain industries like garments and textiles. Filipino garments industry inspectors, merchandisers, engineers, technicians, and designers are enssuring the quality of "Made in Bangladesh" labeled products. They act as a bridge between Bangladeshi factory owners and Western brands, making sure that the former understands and implements the highest standards of corporate social responsibility and product quality control anchored on human rights, environmental rights, gender rights, and labor rights. Filipino accountants, engineers and managers also enable the efficient and effective operations of energy and power contractors, cement companies, and IT infrastructures. They have also made a significant impact in higher education as teachers, staff, and administrators. Philippine diaspora diplomats are taking Bangladesh to a world-class education level, particularly in the technology field, which is comparable to, if not better, than what they got in the Philippines.

In terms of associational Filipinization, their *kasamahan* influences go beyond Philippine Embassy-initiated Philippine Independence Day commemorations and Ambassador-sponsored social and cultural events. It actually begins at Banani church where members of the Philippine Society of Bangladesh (PSB) are the core musicians and singers of the choir and readers of the bible. PSB members do not just gather during birthdays, anniversaries, and basketball tournaments. Compassionate diaspora diplomats also transform their *kasamahan* into *bayanihan* influences by raising funds and donations for Dhaka street children and families as well as for their Philippine hometowns. They socialize and network at the handful of glamorous shopping malls, western restaurant franchises, groceries, beauty salons, and theme parks. They also see each other when shipping *balikbayan* boxes (care packages), *padala* (send something through a departing townmate), and remitting money to their families. Filipino and Filipina expatriates cum band members jazz up the Bangla entertainment scene with classic and modern Philippine and western tunes.

CHAPTER 7

Singapore: In Service of God, Country and Growth

How could ASEAN bilateral relations go from tragedy to triumph?

"Just maid, *lah*! Why *ha*?" asked the puzzled Dave Foo. Mr. Foo was evidently extremely disappointed when his very important business trip to Manila was cancelled on the advice of his travel agent. He expressed his frustration while we were dining on *lumpia* and *sinigang* at GP Asian Restaurant in Lucky Plaza. Like many Singaporeans, it was difficult for Mr. Foo to comprehend the international political hoopla over the scheduled execution of what he considered an insignificant Filipina diaspora diplomat.

What created a serious tiff between two staunch Southeast Asian neighbors was the March 17, 1995 hanging of Filipina domestic helper, Flor Contemplacion, for the death of her fellow "maid" and the Singaporean child she was caring for. The Singapore justice system had handed down the guilty verdict and punishment years before. Nevertheless, questions doubting her culpability were circulated by the Philippine media days before her death sentence was to be carried out at Changi Prison. The stories created public doubt which rippled across the South China Sea through the emotional protest rallies that gripped the streets of Manila.

Then the climax: images seen across the Philippines of a tearful candlelight vigil in front of the Singapore Embassy becoming unruly after her death was announced on the radio. The most liberal press in the region, along with opposition politicians hungry for lethal ammunition against the ruling administration during a crucial election year and migrant rights groups eager to have a martyr for their cause, fanned the hot flames which sparked a protracted "word war" between the two governments.

The Singapore government defended its justice system and its honor, and hit back through the *Straits Times*. Fears of reprisals against its citizens grew. Government travel warnings were issued. Travel to and from the two countries was reduced to a trickle. Many fearful domestic helpers decided to leave Singapore aboard Philippine government-sponsored rescue flights. Both countries recalled their ambassadors. The Singapore Prime Minister's official visit to the Philippines and scheduled military exercises were postponed. Unprecedented in Philippine history were the resignations of two top-ranked, Cabinet-level department heads—the Secretary of Foreign Affairs and the Secretary of Labor and Employment.

Nobody would have been able to predict the political tsunami and destruction that followed since trade between the two countries was flourishing and the security front was calm. It was barely five months after the Philippine-Singapore Business Council was launched in Singapore by then-Philippine President Fidel V. Ramos and then- Singapore Prime Minister Goh Chok Tong. Additionally, weeks prior to the furor, defense ministry representatives from both ASEAN (Association of Southeast Asian Nations) countries were discussing joint naval operations through the U.S. sponsored Cooperation Afloat Readiness and Training (CARAT). Trade and military cooperation were at their peak. This led Singapore's major daily, *The Straits Times*, to even portray the two countries as a loving couple in their February 14 1995 Valentine's Day cartoon.

The Straits Times 1995 Valentine's Day Cartoon

Lesson learned about hard power versus soft power: Strong and vibrant trade and security bonds are no longer the only pillars of ASEAN diplomacy. People-to-people ties are as crucial to regional harmony. This entails the respect and preservation of Singapore-Philippine diaspora ties whoever the migrant sojourners may be—whether maids or ministers. There is little distinction in this new diasporic world. No matter their station, they are all citizens of ASEAN, citizens of the world.

Results? The international community watched as a long-overdue *magna carta* providing safety nets and protecting the welfare of diaspora diplomats was passed by the Philippines Congress not long after Contemplacion's death. On the Singapore side, government, business, and civil society supported the creation of spaces for migrant worker gatherings and activities, not just for Filipinos but all foreign workers. Similar migrant safety nets were put in place at other ASEAN countries. Flor Contemplacion was not "just a maid." She became a rallying point for family, country, ASEAN migrants, and the millions of Filipino diaspora diplomats who shared her migration story, particularly the difficulties and the tribulations.

These are my recollections and reflections. Singapore was my second country "posting" as a Philippine diaspora diplomat after the U.S. Since living and working there for five years, Singapore had also become my country, my home, my beef *kway teow*, my National University of Singapore, my Filipino Association of Singapore, and my Novena Church. It affected me. This sad incident, which happened a year after my arrival and a few months prior to the Sarah Balabagan case in the United Arab Emirates, helped heighten international migrant labor vigilance and concern for Sarah's.

Significant events in Filipino and Singaporean people-to-people cooperation rekindling mutual influences are discussed in this chapter. Additionally, I elaborate on the Philippine diaspora's religious influences which are felt strongly in Singapore's old and new Catholic churches and the growing number of Filipino Christian Protestant ministries and fellowships. I also discuss Filipino occupational influences as migrants power Singaporean families and firms towards double-income capacity and double-digit growth rates.

Included in this chapter are the regional and international media influences of award winning cartoonist Deng Miel of Singapore's *Straits Times*, BBC World News broadcaster Rico Hizon, as well as Filipino professors and researchers educating the next-generation Singaporean and ASEAN leaders at the city-states' premier universities, research institutes and policy think-tanks.

Finally, I elaborate on Filipino associational influences in Singaporean and Philippine homes. I also highlight the individual influences of domestic helpers like veteran Manang Encar and the members of the more than 10,000-strong Filipino Overseas Workers of Singapore, our Bayanihan Centre, and our skills training programs. I narrate how the Filipino community in Singapore organizes the longest Philippine Independence Day commemoration in the world. I end the chapter with a final story and some concluding comments on their *bayanihan* and *kasamahan* influences.

Transforming Bilateral to Transnational

How did the two ASEAN partners transcend tragedy, moving from tepid bilateral relations to vigorous transnational collaborations? What was the role of civil society organizations, faith-based groups, and influential individuals to this transformation?

In the years following the incident, people-to-people relations evolved to become a focal point of bilateral cooperation alongside economic ties. It has also become more transnational with the involvement of multiple state- and non-state diplomats. The Philippines and Singapore, after all, unlike the other countries discussed in this book, are Southeast Asian neighbors and geo-strategic allies.

Their spat is not unprecedented. There have been other neighborly rows in the region: Malaysia and Thailand's over land border issues, Singapore and Malaysia's over water and many other concerns, the Philippines and Malaysia over North Borneo, Indonesia and its close *konfrontasi* (confrontation) with Singapore and Malaysia, among others. It is common for ASEAN members to grate against each other. But because of their common interests, they also learn to live with each other.

Moreover, the Philippines and Singapore are both founding members of ASEAN which they started with three other Southeast Asian countries (Indonesia, Malaysia, and Thailand). ASEAN now has ten members (with the addition of Brunei, Vietnam, Laos, Cambodia, and Burma). In ASEAN meetings, the Philippines and Singapore have adapted characteristics of their organization's decision-making style anchored on *mushawarah* (consultation) and *mufakat* (consensus). Through ASEAN, the Philippines and Singapore are aligned and in harmony with the largest Islamic nation in the world—Indonesia—as well as one of the world's most economically advanced non-OPEC Islamic state, Malaysia.

Besides ASEAN, the Philippines and Singapore are together at many other traditional hard power and soft power meetings. For instance, they are also founding members of Asia Pacific Economic Cooperation Council (APEC) which brings together countries from North America and Latin America to North and Southeast Asia to enhance economic growth and prosperity for the Pacific Rim region. The Secretariat of APEC is located in Singapore. They also participate in the Asia-Europe Meeting (ASEM) bridging Southeast Asia with Europe. In 1997, the Philippine and Singapore representatives joined others in creating ASEM's precursor, the Asia-Europe Foundation (ASEF), which "seeks to promote mutual understanding, deeper engagement and continuing collaboration among the people of Asia and Europe through greater intellectual, cultural, and people-to-people exchanges between the two regions." In 2005, the first Asia-Middle East Dialogue (AMED) that gathered countries from North and Southeast Asia, South and Central Asia, West Asia, to North Africa, was held in Singapore.

Signed in Hanoi, Vietnam in December 2008, the Philippines-Singapore Action Plan provides the blueprint for rebuilding bilateral economic cooperation in the post-Contemplacion era. As a result, growing transnational ties which will be elaborated on in this chapter has translated into a notable expansion in bilateral trade which averaged more than 25 percent growth in the past five years.

Singapore is one of the wealthiest countries in the world in terms of Gross Domestic Product (GDP) per capita (US$51,649 per capita GDP in 2008).

Its sustained economic prosperity is anchored on its human resources since it has little natural resources. Its highly skilled human capital base powers its export-oriented development program. Much has been said about the economic capital and product flows, with the Philippines contributing to this growth. But little has been reported on the massive human capital imported from the Philippines which is also critical to the gross domestic production of Singapore.

The Philippine Department of Trade and Industry, reported total merchandise trade between the two countries at US$9.3 billion, around nine percent of total trade, in 2007. Singapore is the Philippines' number one ASEAN export market and was ranked sixth in its total merchandise trade with 212 economies in the same year. The trade balance, however, favors Singapore, with exports amounting to US$ 3.1 billion and imports at US$6.2 billion, a trade deficit of US$3 billion.

What does the Philippines need from Singapore? It imports mineral fuels, lubricants, and electronic products to help it achieve the manufacturing performance of its ASEAN sibling. Meanwhile, the Philippines exports the much-needed electronic valves, refined petroleum products, office and data processing machines and parts, and electrical circuit apparatus needed to sustain Singapore's robust GDP. The Philippines is Singapore's 13th largest trading partner. Singaporean companies in the Philippines include Keppel Bank and Keppel Properties. They are active members of the Singapore-Philippines Association (SPA) a networking organization whose key aim is to promote understanding and friendship between Singaporeans and their Filipino counterparts.

With a population of 4.5 million people, Singapore's strong economic growth has led to the creation of more jobs in the first quarter of 2008. There are always specialized jobs in the fast-moving technology sector and domestic service work which local Singaporeans are unable to fill. Comparatively, the Philippine has a population 20 times more than Singapore, 33.7 million of which were employed in the same quarter, and an unemployment rate of 7.4 percent. Thus, there is a surplus of skilled technical talents that are attracted to jobs in neighboring ASEAN states.

Since Singapore and the Philippines do not share a common land, air or sea border, the main bases for military interface are through their ASEAN security partnerships. Since 1971, along with Indonesia, Malaysia, and Thailand, both countries have pledged to keep the Southeast Asian region a Zone of Peace, Freedom and Neutrality (ZOPFAN) or a nuclear-free area. Established two decades later, the ASEAN Regional Forum (ARF) has now become the venue for preventive political and security diplomacy and confidence-building between ASEAN and the rest of the world. Both the Philippines and Singapore are founding participants of ARF. Both also participate in CARAT military operations, mentioned earlier, which are exercises between the U.S. Navy and the naval forces of Brunei, Malaysia, Philippines, Singapore, and Thailand. CARAT exercises are meant to increase participating ASEAN navies' interoperability through maritime interdiction, information sharing, and tactical collaboration with the U.S.

In terms of diaspora diplomacy, there are two times more Filipino migrants globally than the total population of this 640-square-kilometer city-state, sandwiched between Indonesia and Malaysia. The ASEAN region is a mix of migrant countries of destination and countries of origin. For instance, like the Philippines, Indonesia and Thailand also deploy a large number of temporary migrant workers to neighboring East Asian countries and the Middle East (Southwestern Asia) region.

In 2007, the Philippine Overseas Employment Agency estimated that there were more than 150,000 Filipino migrants in Singapore. Approximately 30,000 are permanent residents while the rest are temporary and irregular migrant workers. When I was working in Singapore in the 1990s, the number of domestic helpers in Singapore was less than 90,000 while in Hong Kong it was close to 110,000. Upon my return in 2009, I was surprised to find out that the Singapore figure had overtaken Hong Kong's over the years. With this number in 2007, Singapore plays host and home to the third largest Philippine diaspora community in Asia, after Japan with 202,557 Filipino migrants and Malaysia with 244,967. No wonder close to one fifth of the total remittances from Asia in the same period originated from the Lion City.

Globally, Singapore is the eighth largest source of foreign exchange wire transfers flowing into the Philippines. Officially, about 240,000 Filipinos "visit" the country annually, making them one of the biggest foreign tourist arrivals at Changi International Airport. Conversely, more than 80,000 Singaporean tourists and business visitors came to the Philippines in 2007. These arrivals are facilitated by discounted direct flights offered by multiple regional airlines not just originating from Manila but departing from Davao, Cebu and Angeles City.

There is a dark side to this increased volume of human movement. The lure of high paying service sector jobs, more flights, budget airfares and visa-free travel created the ideal conditions that increased the illegal trafficking of Filipinas into Singapore annually. The Philippine Embassy reported 212 cases in 2007, a significant increase from the 125 in 2006 and 59 in 2005. In its *2007 Human Trafficking Report*, the U.S. State Department highlighted a general increase of Asian women, particularly from China, Indonesia, Thailand, Malaysia, the Philippines, and Vietnam, who have been deceived or coerced into sexual servitude in Singapore. This led the State Department to downgrade Singapore from a Tier One compliance category in 2006 to a lesser Tier Two in 2007.

Singapore and the Philippines have since introduced regulations to correct the situation including the arrest of human traffickers and the filing of criminal cases against them. More stringent requirements have also been imposed on departing minors and young women. Nevertheless, it is still common to meet dozens of Filipinas working the red light entertainment places on Orchard Road, People's Park, Paramount Mall in Katong, and Duxton Road in Tanjong Pagar.

Religious Filipinization

Off ka ba sa Linggo? Saan ka magsisimba? (Are you off this Sunday? Where are you going to church?)

These are the most common conversation starters I heard from the many Filipina domestic helpers working at the flats near my own at Gilman Heights on Depot Road, especially when it was nearing Sunday.

All of the 30 churches comprising the Catholic Archdiocese of Singapore has a Philippine diaspora diplomat parishioner. Aside from HDB (Housing Development Board) flats and Lucky Plaza, a Catholic church is probably the most visibly Filipinized institution in Singapore society. This social phenomenon is magnified immensely because of the smallness of Singapore, in terms of geography and population. You could identify migrant Catholic Filipino men and women among the hundreds of thousands of churchgoers of various ethnicities. Filipinos were active as ushers and collectors, bible readers, lectors and commentators, Eucharistic ministers giving communion, as well as choir singers and instrumentalists. Some tidied up the pews after masses while others taught Sunday school. Choir practices were always lively occasions. Those with children would participate in church activities while their kids attended Sunday school. I also did my part by occasionally doing the readings at my parish, the Blessed Sacrament Catholic Church, which was a quick bus ride from my university flat.

Christians constitute approximately less than 15 percent of Singapore's population, around five percent (32.9 percent of Christians) are Catholics and the remaining less than ten percent (67.1 percent of Christians) of other mostly Protestant denominations. In the Philippines, it is the inverse of these figures—approximately 90 percent of the total population is Christian, 84 percent of them are Catholics.

In Singapore, the largest Catholic ethno-linguistic group is the bilingual Tagalog-English speaking Filipino community, followed by French, German, Hong Kong Chinese, Indonesian, Japanese, Burmese, Korean,

North American, Latin American, Australian, Middle Eastern, European, and African groups. To accommodate this wide diversity of cultures and languages, the Archdiocese's churches offers services in Mandarin, Hokkien, Teochew, Tamil, Burmese, Malayalam, Tagalog, Sri Lankan, and Korean, in addition to English and Tagalog.

Because of the growth in the number of temporary and permanent migrant Catholics from India, the Philippines, Europe, and the Americas, the Archdiocesan Commission for the Pastoral Care of Migrants and Itinerant People was formed by the Archdiocese with the encouragement and blessing of the Vatican. Under the guidance of the Catholic Archbishop of Singapore, the Commission provides "migrants a sense of belonging and security through acts of compassion such as befriending, hospital visits, providing food and shelter, skills training, legal aid, information and referrals." These include migrant construction workers, domestic helpers, students, spouses and local employers, regardless of religious affiliation.

In Singapore, there was a Tagalog mass at 10:15 am every fourth Sunday at Novena Church on Thomson Road. If one got there at 9:45 am, there were no more seats. Hundreds of Filipino migrants and their families just end up standing at the patio, the adjoining building, and the gardens. Because of their days off, either on the first and third Sunday or second and fourth Sunday, Filipino Catholics would often do "Bisita Iglesia" (attend mass at a different Singapore Catholic church every Sunday), even if it is not Holy Week.

The Archdiocese of Singapore through its website assures Filipino diaspora diplomats that there will be a Tagalog mass that will fit virtually any busy schedule. There is a Tagalog service available in all four major districts of the city-state's relatively small 640 square kilometer (247 square mile) area, roughly the size of Metro Manila and just a third of its population.

In 1999, I was already leaving Singapore to return to California when Father Angel Luciano, a Filipino priest, was transferred by his religious organization, the Congregation of the Immaculate Heart of Mary, from Manila to the Church of Saint Michael. His transfer was specially requested to the Vatican by the Archdiocese of Singapore. Father Angel had done pastoral work in Africa for decades and I was pleased to see someone provide culturally appropriate spiritual guidance to the Filipino flock.

He immediately worked with the leaders of the various Filipino organizations to establish the observance of *Simbang Gabi*, Christmas novena masses, in Singapore. The Archdiocese of Singapore and local and expatriate Catholic parishioners welcomed the introduction of this new tradition. Like the London practice, the Singapore version of Simbang Gabi is held at ten participating Catholic churches. Novena masses are held at 8:00 p.m. But unlike the London, San Francisco, and other global city versions, the Singapore ones have themes.

In 2008, the focus of Simbang Gabi was "The Ten Commandments" and began at the Church of Saint Anthony of Padua on December 15th based on the theme "Thou shall have no other Gods before me" and concluded at the Church of Saints Peter and Paul on December 24th with the theme "Thou shall not covet." All the masses were well-attended by a diversity of ethnicities. As in the Philippines, Filipino food and fellowship flowed after each mass.

With the blessing and guidance of the Archdiocesan Commission for the Pastoral Care of Migrants and Itinerant People, through Fr. Angel, Filipino community groups in Singapore have also started weaving in other Philippine religious practices to the fabric of the country's diverse ethno-spiritual landscape. Together with locals and expatriate Catholics, Filipino diaspora diplomats initiate and organize the Flores de Mayo and Santracruzan in May and June as well as Visita Iglesia, Stations of the Cross, and *Siete Palabras* (Seven Last Words of Christ) during Holy Week in March or April. They are also on the second year of the Peñafrancia participated in by nine churches in August to September. To complement Simbang Gabi, they hold a Christmas lantern display and contest and lots of Christmas gatherings in December.

The Philippine El Shaddai group in Singapore is the largest chapter in

Southeast Asia. Boasting more than 5,000 active members, it has become one of the largest and most energetic Catholic charismatic organizations in Singapore. Coordinated by Vince Leong, a Singaporean lay person, they meet every Sunday from 1:00-5:00 pm. I have attended El Shaddai services under the pouring rain at the town plaza in Santa Ana and at the basement of Saint Mary's Cathedral in San Francisco's chilly winter. In mid-July 2009, my wife and I joined them in the cozy (now) air-conditioned confines of my old parish church, Blessed Sacrament Church on Commonwealth Drive. We were greeted by a huge glossy blue banner with bold yellow printing: "El Shaddai Singapore Chapter, Where Jesus Christ is Lord." The spacious church was almost packed so I was glad we found a seat. Given the demographics of the Philippine diaspora population in Singapore, I was not surprised to see that most of the attendees were women.

The Singapore El Shaddai services were the same as those in Manila, San Francisco, London, and other parts of the world. The women wore veils, were conservatively dressed in plain basic hues, and some had the traditional El Shaddai white cloth with psalms written in Tagalog on their right shoulder. As is in every El Shaddai service, the attendees loudly participated, singing and clapping vigorously. You could really feel the charismatic spirit engulfing everyone in the church. At this one, there were very emotionally gripping moments but also lots of laughter at the priest's jokes. I always enjoy attending their services.

Formed in 1984, El Shaddai DWXI Prayers Partners Foundation International is one of the largest Catholic Charismatic Renewal Movement in the world, claiming to have eight million members throughout the Philippines and in other chapters in more than 100 countries across four continents.

Like in San Francisco, one of the most active Catholic youth groups is Singles for Christ (SFC). SFC-Singapore began in 1993, six years after the founding of Couples for Christ (CFC) Singapore at the Nativity Church of the Blessed Virgin Mary in Upper Serangoon Road. The SFC is a ministry of CFC intended for single men and women who are at least twenty-one years old and not more than forty years old. The heart and soul of SFC is the "household" with five to eight men or women who meet weekly for mutual support and encouragement in their Christian life. A household's purpose is to build an environment that supports the Christian life of the individual - a venue for encouraging and hastening spiritual growth.

Aligning itself with CFC's thrust of "Building the Church of the Poor," SFC has taken on the SAGIP program of adoption, education and support of street children, starting off with Bagong Silang, the biggest relocation area which is the center of CFC's "Work with the Poor." In 2006, SFC Singapore hosted the "Second Global Leaders Forum: Shine Out!" at Holy Trinity Church on Hamilton Road. Its mother spiritual organization, Couples for Christ, began in 1981 and together with allied ministries, i.e., Kids for Christ, Youth for Christ, Handmaids of the Lord, and Servants of the Lord, has grown into a global movement for the renewal and strengthening of Christian family life. There are CFC and SFC chapters in 160 countries, with more than 300,000 members. CFC is so influential globally that the Vatican, through its Pontifical Council for the Laity, recognized Couples for Christ as a Private International Association of the Faithful according to Canons 298-311 and 321-329 of the Code of Canon Law.

Investing in Miracles at the Lion City

Just like their Filipino Catholic brothers and sisters, Filipino Christian migrant faithful have also been making an impact on the membership growth and spiritual practices of Singapore's Protestant community and Singapore civil society as a whole. Figure 7.1 lists the 32 Filipino Protestant Christian ministries, fellowships, and groups registered with the Philippine Embassy, more than the 21 registered Filipino Catholic organizations. Combined, Filipino religious gatherings make up the largest Philippine association in Singapore, more than all the other groups—i.e., cultural, sports, alumni, fraternity, professional, hometown—combined. Many of their church pastors and leaders coordinate through an umbrella group called Network of Filipino Churches in Singapore (NetFil).

Figure 7.1
Filipino Protestant Christian Groups in Singapore

1	Bartley Christian Church
2	Bethesda Pasir Ris Christian Church
3	Christian Neighborhood Church
4	Church of Singapore
5	Club4thee
6	Community of Praise Baptist Church
7	Cornerstone Community Church
8	Faith Community Baptist Church
9	Filipino Joy Fellowship
10	Filipino Ministry
11	Foursquare Church
12	Full Gospel Assembly
13	Grace Assembly of God
14	His Sanctuary
15	Horizon Church and Ministries International
16	Iglesia ni Cristo
17	International Baptist Christian Church
18	Inter-Varsity Christian Fellowship
19	Jesus is Lord Church
20	Jesus Reigns Ministries
21	Living Word Ministries
22	Marine Parade Christian Center
23	Seventh Day Adventist Church

24	Shalom Baptist Church
25	Take the Nations for Jesus
26	The Kingdom of Jesus Christ
27	The Living Word Fellowship
28	Trinity Christian Center
29	Victory Family Centre
30	Wesley Filipino Fellowship
31	Word International Ministry
32	Yishuan Christian Church

Source: Registered with Philippine Embassy, 2009.

This Filipino spiritual pervasiveness is acknowledged and highly valued by the faith-based organizational counterpart of the Catholic Archdiocese of Singapore—the National Council of Churches of Singapore (NCCS) which is the network coordinating the activities of the major Christian Protestant and Evangelical denominations and churches in the Lion City. They include the Anglican Diocese of Singapore, Assemblies of God of Singapore, Lutheran Church in Singapore, Methodist Church in Singapore, Presbyterian Church in Singapore, The Salvation Army, Mar Thomas Syrian Church, Saint Thomas Orthodox Syrian Cathedral, Church of Singapore, Evangelical Free Church, and many other independent churches and Christian groups.

As it is in San Francisco, London, Dubai, and Dhaka, many of the Filipino Protestants in Singapore were originally Catholics. Other Filipino migrants established independent churches in the city-state and then opened up new ones in the Philippines and other parts of the world. There are also the independent Filipino Christians like the Iglesias from the Iglesia ni Cristo Church who attend Wednesday, Thursday, Saturday, and Sunday bible studies or worship services at a home on Gaylang Road or rented hotel function rooms in the Orchard Road area. Aglipayans from the Philippine Independent

Church attend Sunday Anglican services at the grand Saint Andrew's Cathedral which is conveniently located in the high-traffic and densely populated central business district. In recent years, independent non-denominational mega-churches, like City Harvest Church, Faith Community Baptist Church, New Creation Church, Grace Assembly, and Hope Church, have attracted some Filipino migrant faithful.

Over the past decade, the number of Christian churches with Filipino groups or ministries has grown to 25. Hence, there are also more than a dozen Filipino pastors and lay leaders representing Protestant and Independent congregations attending NCCS meetings. The Christian Protestant denomination in Singapore with the largest number of Filipinos is the World Assemblies of God Fellowship and its affiliates. Globally, it has 300,000 churches with about 60 million adherents and thousands of missionaries worldwide, including the Philippines. One of these sovereign affiliates is The Living World Fellowship (TLWF). Founded in 1989, it is the first Filipino religious congregation to be registered with the government of Singapore. TLWF has been worshipping at the Singapore Power Auditorium in 2007 to accommodate its expanding membership and have begun two extension churches in Cubao and Olongapo, Philippines. There are more than 300 members who are a mix of domestic helpers and professionals.

Sandwiched between the Singapore Power Corporation building and Gulford Gardens on Upper East Coast Road is the Emmanuel Assembly of God Church. Like TLWF, it is aligned with the World Assemblies of God. The Filipino fellowship began with a small group of domestic helpers who were waiting in an adjoining room while their employers attended the service. They have grown to more than 30 dedicated members. With approximately 4,000 active members including around 100 Filipinos, Grace Assembly of God is certainly one of Singapore's largest Christian megachurches worshipping at a modern 1,200-seat auditorium and 400-seat chapel. Reverend Dr. David Lim leads a multi-lingual, multi-ethnic church with a total of ten weekend worship services in English, Cantonese, Hokkien, Mandarin, and Filipino. Prior to coming to Singapore, Pastor Lim spent many memorable years as a professor and administrator at Asia Pacific Theological Seminary in Baguio City, which is 150 miles north of Manila.

A Philippine-born Christian church is Word for the World Christian Fellowship (WWCF) which meets at the Lian Soon Building on Horne Road. WWCF began as an independent Christian church in the heart of the Philippines' financial district, Makati. From the garage of Church of God missionaries in 1980 emerged larger meetings at the Intercontinental Hotel function room and eventually other WWCF churches in major cities of the Philippines, such as Greenhills, Quezon City, Manila, Cebu, and Zamboanga. WWCF has since gone international. Besides Singapore, it has expanded its mission field to Hong Kong, Australia, Dubai, South Korea, the U.S., Canada, Nepal, Burma, and Sri Lanka. WWCF Singapore has more than 300 Filipino members who are mostly professionals.

During my summer 2009 fieldwork in Singapore, I met with an old friend, Pastor Rey Navarro, the highly energetic spiritual leader of the Filipino ministry of the International Baptist Church of Singapore (IBCS). Pastor Rey and I used to work directly with outreach and skills training programs for Filipina domestic helpers. IBCS is located on King's Road across from Saint Ignatius Catholic Church.

Upon the invitation of Pastor Rey, I joined the IBCS men's fellowship during their fourth Saturday bible discussion in July 2009. It started with an upbeat introductory Tagalog spiritual song, entitled "Salamat, Salamat" (Thank you, thank you) and then went into a more serious exchange on "Developing a Devotional Material."

Established in 1985 before Pastor Rey arrived in Singapore, the Filipino Ministry is an integral part of IBCS' Christ-centered, bible-believing fellowship of Protestant Christians with roots in the American Southern Baptist tradition. More than 50 different nationalities from Asia, North America, and Europe participate in IBCS services. Among the top three largest ethnicities represented are Singaporeans, Americans, and Filipinos. IBCS is allied with the Conservative Baptist Association of the Philippines and the Greenhills Christian Fellowship in Metro Manila. The Filipino Ministry's concern is "to provide spiritual nourishment to our fellow Filipinos in Singapore. Regardless of their status in life, dialect, and religious affiliation, we want to serve them." More than ten years ago when I first met Pastor Rey, most of his attendees were domestic helpers. More professionals have joined since then.

Hope Filipino is an integral congregational subset of the fast growing Hope Church Singapore. The Filipino evangelical service in Singapore has the largest number of Christian professionals, i.e., engineers, architects, nurses, accountants, etc., attending their 3:00 and 6:00 pm Sunday services among all the other NCCS churches. Hope Filipino began with just 32 Filipino members in 1997. Its membership has since grown from 550 in 2005 to 750 a year later, filling up the expansive worship space at the Nexus Auditorium. A Filipino band provides the musical backdrop with special solo renditions from contemporary musicians. It is not uncommon to hear trendy and melodic Kenny G saxophone music instead of "boring" gospel choir songs.

A senior team member connects Bible exposition with lessons and experiences from daily living. They celebrate Holy Communion weekly at their services in various rented spaces in Singapore. I encountered them at the Regional English Language Centre Hotel where I usually stayed.

During the 2003 SARS epidemic that hit Singapore, Hope Filipino nurses volunteered at the frontlines, caring for patients without regard for the personal risk of contamination. Hope Church Singapore, and by association, Hope Filipino is part of the Hope of Nations (also known as Hope of God International), an evangelical Christian movement which currently spans 35 countries across six continents.

Geno, one of the members, blogged in July 2009 about the importance of his faith to his migrant life: "I'm a Filipino staying in Singapore for six yrs now currently working in StarHub as Technical Support Analyst. I am married with a two-year old son. I like to play tennis and badminton. I'm into internet surfing and finding missing friends all over the world. I used to live a self-centered life that focused on the worldly things. God has made me a meaningful person by using me to serve in the Filipino Children Ministry. Giving me the opportunity to share my life to the children and helped me to improve my character in terms of my patience, humility and creativity."

Occupational Filipinization

After church, the next questions are usually: *Saan tayo kakain? Saan tayo magpapasyal?* (Where are we going to eat? Where are we going to hangout?) This is where Lucky Plaza and other shopping centers and recreational areas come into the picture.

Lucky Plaza Shopping Center is undoubtedly "Little Manila" in Singapore, its most familiar Philippine diasporic landmark. This multi-story building in the heart of Orchard Road is where you are able to buy almost anything you will find in any Shoemart or Robinson's in the Philippines, from Eskinol facial cleanser to Chippy corn chips. It was where my fellow diaspora diplomats and I went to eat Filipino food, remitted money, got a haircut, exchanged US dollars for Singapore dollars or Singapore dollars for Philippine pesos, sent balikbayan boxes, sang karaoke, and bought cheap airline tickets. The rest, recreation, shopping, and services at Lucky Plaza is what sustains the passion and energy of the hundreds of thousands of Filipino migrant workers and residents who are helping Singapore achieve productivity from double-income households and consequently, double-digit economic growth rates.

Lucky Plaza's fourth to the sixth floors are filled with more than two hundred establishments, from recruitment and employment agencies to mini-marts selling Philippine products like native snacks, magazines, DVDs, CDs, drinks, cosmetic products, and food.

Figure 7.2
Philippine-oriented establishments in Lucky Plaza

Type	Number
Remittance center	16
Employment agency	30
Money changer	17
Mini-mart	36
Travel agency	12
Box forwarding	23
Beauty salon	24
Restaurant & café	25
Others	18
	201

Source: www.luckyplazashopping.com, supplemented by interviews and observation.

Lucky Plaza is also a draw because of its diverse food offerings including, of course, Filipino restaurants like Barrio Fiesta, Batangas Varsitarian, GP Asian, Kabayan, and Jologs which serve authentic hometown dishes, like laing, sinigang, adobo, crispy pata and relyenong bangus that you could wash down with San Miguel beer or calamansi juice.

There is also a wide variety of international cuisines at Lucky Plaza, from East Asian, Middle Eastern, South Asian, to European. Even without a mainstream Philippine food franchise presence in Singapore, like Jollibee or Goldilocks which are present in London, San Francisco, and Dubai, Filipino migrants still have access to quality Filipino restaurants where they take their Singaporean and other foreign friends.

The favorites among migrants and locals outside of the Lucky Plaza staples are Mack's Chicken Inasal, Panyeros, Bonifacio, Ka Roger, Take Out, and Happy V's fried chicken and rice which is just as good if not better than Jollibee. Then there is Mang Kiko's Lechon Stall which opened in April 2009 at the popular Lau Pa Sat Festival Market on Raffles Quay. Open from 10 am to 10 pm every day of the week, this is the first lechon stall in Singapore and the first in an ASEAN country offering a wide variety of *lechon,* from the classic *lechon baboy* (roasted pig), to the *lechon manok* (roasted chicken), and the mouth-watering *lechon liempo* (roasted pork belly).

Helping Singapore Households

How do Philippine diaspora diplomats help create productive Singapore households? In 2008, Singapore had a per capita GDP of US$52,000 making it the ninth richest country in the world, even ahead of the U.S., which ranked 10th, and the United Kingdom, which was ranked 30th, out of 220 countries. Just over forty years old, Singapore has surpassed the per capita growth of neighboring Asian dragon economies like Japan, South Korea, Taiwan, and China.

This sustained high economic performance in all sectors of the Singaporean economy is only possible with corresponding multi-income productivity at the family or household level. The economic demands and pressure on families is high given the high cost of living. Thus, there is a dire need for someone to help alleviate the Singaporean family's domestic household chores as well as elderly and childcare responsibilities. This is where migrants from the Philippines, Indonesia, Nepal, Thailand, India, Burma, and Sri Lanka make their influences felt, right inside hundreds of thousands of HDB flats and bungalows. Their live-in domestic worker contracts require most of them not only to cook and play with the children but also to wash cars, water gardens, launder and iron clothes, tidy rooms, wash dishes, clean toilets, care for aging parents, pick up children from school, prepare their snacks, as well as serve the family breakfast, lunch, and dinner.

Some domestic helpers work more than double the eight hours their husband-wife employers put in a day. Most of them are supposed have two days off a month. But the employer could buy each day off for US$20. Hundreds of thousands of Singaporean families feel the US$250-$350 monthly pay, plus the US$200 monthly government levy, non-pregnancy bond, medical insurance, and exorbitant non-refundable agency fees are well worth the benefits of this labor arrangement. Consequently, maid agencies at Lucky Plaza, Katong Mall, People's Park, and Peninsula Plaza have become very profitable business operations. The levy is a significant domestic revenue generator for the Singapore nation-state.

Between 1997 and 2007, the Philippine Overseas Employment Agency processed an annual average of more than 20,000 Filipino men and women workers, both new hires and rehires, destined for Singapore. In 2007, the figure more than doubled to 50,000. Singapore is the second largest Asian destination of new hires overall after Hong Kong and the fourth largest globally. For over two decades, domestic helpers continue to be the largest chunk of Philippine diaspora diplomats in the tiny but wealthy city-state.

Over the same period, Singapore was also the largest Asian destination of newly recruited domestic helpers, after Hong Kong. In the succeeding years, the city-state has slipped down in ranking to eighth globally with increased demand in Europe (particularly Italy and Spain) as well as the Middle East (particularly Kuwait, UAE, Saudi Arabia, Qatar, Jordan, and Cyprus). However, the figures may be understated since most Filipino migrant workers arrive in Singapore without going through the POEA and the Embassy of Singapore for a visa. They are tourist workers – leaving Manila, Cebu, Davao, or Angeles as a tourist and entering Changi Airport on a courtesy ASEAN two-week tourist visa which the Lucky Plaza maid agency converts into a work visa through the Singapore Ministry of Manpower.

On a Philippine Airlines flight from Manila to Singapore that summer, I was sitting beside two new domestic helper hires for 2009—Rovelyn T., 35 years old, from Cagayan province and Rica M., 26 years old from Negros Occidental province Both of them were nervous and worried but focused on the dreams they had for each of their three children. They know that they will be working for free during the next six months to pay the processing fee advanced by the Philippine recruiter. After this contractual obligation is taken cared off, then they will be able to start sending money home.

Before the plane taxied off the runway, I had to help Rica with her seatbelt while Rovelyn watched. Like many first-time migrants, it was their first plane ride. I helped allay their adjustment fears and reassured them that all would be fine and that they would enjoy the sights and sounds of Singapore. I told them before we parted ways that on their first day off, they should go to the Philippine Embassy on Nassim Road and look for Manang Encar and register with OWWA.

Manang Encar was one of the longest serving domestic helpers in Singapore who now works for the labor office of the Philippine Embassy. Like Pastor Rey, I knew her from my five-year stint in the 1990s. A native of Ilocos Norte, Manang Encar has a Bachelor's of Science in Medical Technology from the University of Santo Tomas. She came as a domestic helper in 1986 to support her five children. In 1992, she, along with a group of domestic helpers, founded the Filipino Overseas Workers in Singapore (FOWS) and the Filipino Group at Novena Church. We met shortly after she helped form these pioneering *kasamahan* and *bayanihan* migrant worker organizations.

At the halfway house for battered domestic helpers, we conceptualized the courses that would be taught at the FOWS Skills Training Program. I became a computer skills teacher for them.

Manang Encar is a past president of Novena Filipino Community and started the Filipino Novena and Mass in 1990. Aside from the FOWS-Skills Training Program (STP), she helped organize the Palarong Pilipino, Awit Patimpalak, among many other activities. Manang Encar has been recognized as a 'model migrant worker' and was chosen to deliver speeches during the state visits of Presidents Corazon Aquino and Joseph Estrada in Singapore. She was a member of the Singapore delegation that presented a PhP2.5 million donation to President Corazon Aquino.

Manang Encar not only worked for the welfare and protection of Filipinos but other nationalities as well. She, along with Rovelyn and Rica, represent the tens of thousands of dedicated Filipina domestic helpers who make it possible for Singaporeans to work hard and stay late in their offices and factories. Their flat-level productivity directly contributes to the wealthy country's robust Gross National Product (GNP).

Since my departure from Singapore in 1999, there has been a demographic shift in new-hire arrivals. From the previous large number of female domestic helpers, it has evolved into the more visible male and female professionals and technicians. Lucky Plaza is my main barometer on this issue since I saw more *kababayans* and their families there from Mondays through Saturdays.

Gender-wise, a Filipino woman was usually profiled as a domestic helper. In recent years, however, there have been close to 18,000 Filipinas in Singapore who are not domestic helpers. As in London and San Francisco, Filipinas have become familiar health care workers at Singapore's medical centers and clinics.

Singapore has become the alternative for female nurses, medical technicians, and caregivers seeking greener pastures overseas but are unable to hurdle the stringent examinations in North America and Europe or are turned off by what they heard about the working conditions in hospitals in the Middle East. They work at Singapore General Hospital, Mount Elizabeth Hospital, Alexandra Hospital, National University Hospital, Raffles Hospital, among others. Ninety percent of senior homes and up to 40 percent of some hospitals are staffed with Filipino health care professionals.

Singapore's booming retail and service sectors have been hiring Filipinos en masse as well. I was surprised to encounter Filipino women at the Changi Terminal duty-free shops and at the Woodlands airport shuttle counter. They are visible as waiters, sales persons, front desk clerks, and bartenders at Watsons on the ground floor of Funan IT Center, Shangri-la Hotel in Sentosa, bars in Boat Quay, restaurants in Clarke Quay, Coffee Bean at the Forum, or Hard Rock Cafe near Orchard Road. The Filipino's natural friendliness, warmth, and charm helps sell expensive name-brand apparel at glamorous shops in Isetann, Wisma Atria, Ion, Plaza Singapura, Forum, Tanglin Shopping, Takashimaya, Tang's, Wheelock Place, Vivo City, Marina Square, Suntec City, among others.

More than 5,000 female migrants join more than 24,000 Filipino male migrants applying their engineering education and technical skills towards enhancing Singapore's flagship information, computer, and communications technology industries. They have made their mark as technicians, programmers, analysts, and engineers at Singapore tech giants including Asia Mobile, Singapore Technologies Telemedia, SingTel (Singapore Telecom), Creative Technology, and Flextronics. Some of them work for the Singapore field offices of even larger multinational tech companies like Nokia, Microsoft, Qualcomm, Sprint, IBM, Dell, and AT&T. Thousands of Philippine diaspora diplomats are also sought-after architects, designers, cruise vessel stewards/stewardesses, entertainers/musicians, trainees, managers, bankers, as well as aircraft mechanics. Whether they are maids or engineers, they do their part in sustaining Lucky Plaza's profitability as well as Singapore's overall competitive edge, boosting corporate and community productivity, and of course, like many Singaporean families, they are helping push its economy towards blistering double digit GNP growth rates.

But why do firms and families hire Filipino migrants? Among the responses I got from the employers I interviewed: "their English is good", "the way they explain a product or service is clear", "the way they smile attracts customers", "you could tell that they are sincere in helping", "happy", "service from the heart", "not obnoxious", "patient with customer", "always smiling", "caring", "learn quickly", "good with children", "knowledgeable", and "service with a smile". Besides, some of the employers I talked to were raised by Filipina domestic helpers. They remember.

In Singapore's Media

Filipino diaspora diplomats are likewise exerting their influence in Singapore media and the academe. The TV and the classroom are the two of the most effective multipliers of soft power influence. They do not just reach Singaporean audiences and students locally but also regionally and globally. Filipino migrants are doing this as world-class broadcast journalists, cartoonists, professors, researchers, and international civil servants. Their educational and experiential credentials are quite impressive and highly respected. They are considered the best in their crafts. Sharp and eloquent in their Filipino-accentuated English, they provide readers, viewers, students, policy-makers, and investors with their candid but incisive thoughts and analysis from business, investments, engineering, economics, to security concerns. When they appear on TV or stand in front of a class, you know they are giving you sound advice or knowledgeable lectures.

Whether I am in a hotel room in London or at the airport in Hong Kong, when I watch the BBC World News there is Rico Hizon. Rico is the Pinoy accent on TV news. From a BBC studio at Shaw Tower on Beach Road, Rico's BBC business reports are transmitted to more than 200 countries and territories across the globe, reaching 276 million homes, 1.5 million hotel rooms, 57 cruise ships, 42 airlines, and 34 mobile phone platforms. This is much more than its archrival, CNN.

Since 2002, Rico has anchored BBC's Asia Business Report and World Business Report. From Monday to Friday, his regional business news and analysis is watched and taken seriously by millions of television viewers from Asia and the world. Based in Singapore since 1998, he is the first-ever Filipino news anchor to work for two of the world's most prestigious television news networks - CNBC Business News and BBC World News.

When I was based in Singapore, a number of my university colleagues and I were often interviewed by Rico, Twink Macaraeg, and Coco Quisumbing for Asia Business News and CNBC. Hizon started his broadcast career with Manila's GMA Television Network covering capital markets, banking and finance, real estate, investment and corporate developments. He anchored the daily business program, Business Today, GMA News Live and Stock Market Live from the trading floor of the Philippine Stock Exchange. Hizon then joined CNBC Asia in April 1995, based in Hong Kong and later in Singapore, where he was the main anchor of the morning edition of CNBC Today, Squawk Box, Market Watch and Power Lunch. He has a degree in Communication Arts and Business from De La Salle University in Manila. His regional and global influence has earned him numerous awards from industry and government, including the highest presidential award for overseas Filipinos.

Rico Hizon, the Pinoy accent on BBC World News

Aside from the BBC, other local, regional, and global news programs also have Filipino anchors or reporters. Channel NewsAsia (CNA)'s Timothy Go presents "World Today," "Asia Today," "Singapore Business Tonight," and hosts "That's IT," a weekly digital lifestyle program. Meanwhile, Jennifer Alejandro is the anchor of the business segment of CNA's "Primetime Morning," where she does up-to-the minute market reports and in-depth interviews with CEOs, financial analysts, fund managers, and economists. Other familiar Filipino faces to news junkies are veteran broadcaster Veronica Pedrosa, formerly of the BBC and currently with Al Jazeera English in Kuala Lumpur, Malaysia, and Hong Kong-based Kathy Yang who hosts Bloomberg News' "Bloomberg Live." Like Rico, they impact millions of television viewers worldwide.

Influencing international print media from Singapore since 1992 is *The Straits Times'* veteran cartoonist, artist, and illustrator Prudencio "Deng" Miel or the man behind "Mielbox". When I was living in Singapore, my colleagues and I always enjoyed the humor in Deng's daily cartoon commentaries. *The Straits Times* is Singapore's highest-selling paper in any language, with a daily circulation of 388,500 and an estimated readership of 1.23 million.

In 2001, the newspaper flew Deng to New York to receive the National Cartoonist Society Newspaper Illustration Award from the U.S.-based National Cartoonists Society (NCS) which is the world's most prestigious association of cartoonists. He joined the ranks of Charles Schulz, the creator of "Peanuts" and Mort Walker of "Beetle Bailey," among others.

Deng began his newspaper career as an editorial cartoonist for the *Philippines Daily Express* and subsequently became chief editorial cartoonist of *The Philippine Star*. His world-famous illustrations have been syndicated by the United Feature Syndicate/Witty World, The New York Times Syndicate, and Writers Syndicate. His cartoons have also been published in *The International Herald Tribune*, *Newsweek*, *Asiaweek*, *World and I*, *Japan Times*, *The New York Times*, *The Washington Post*, *The South China Morning Post*, and *World Press Review*. Deng was educated in the University of the Philippines and the University of New South Wales.

Joining the Academic Community

Working in Singapore's universities and research institutes are some of the most influential minds in engineering, economics, history, and politics. Singapore's undisputed "Mr. Robotics" is Dr. Marcelo "Mars" Ang who conceptualized the Singapore Robotics Games at the regional Olympiad of Robots in December 1993. For the last two decades, Dr. Ang's lectures and tutorials in robotics, mechatronics, automation, and intelligent systems at the National University of Singapore (NUS) have influenced thousands of engineering students at the school's prestigious Department of Mechanical Engineering. He helped propel Singapore's technical and engineering innovations that have given NUS international recognition for its research capacity and output.

Often interviewed and quoted by major Singapore media outlets, including Channel NewsAsia, Dr. Ang began as a lecturer in 1989 and has risen to associate professor. His academic credentials are stellar: a Bachelor's degree in Mechanical Engineering and Industrial Management Engineering from the De La Salle University in Manila, a Masters degree in Mechanical Engineering from the University of Hawaii at Manoa, and Masters and Ph.D. degrees in Electrical Engineering from the University of Rochester in New York. He has dovetailed these university degrees with hand-on industry exposure— technical head of the Technical Training Division of Intel's Assembly and Test Facility in the Philippines and research engineer at the East West Center in Hawaii and at the Massachusetts Institute of Technology.

If Dr. Ang is the expert on engineering issues, Dr. Roberto "Bobby" Mariano is interviewed for regional economic concerns. I met Dr. Mariano at the University of Pennsylvania and after an extensive talk, he "shipped" me off to the World Bank to be mentored by another Filipino, Dr. Jose Edgardo "Ed" Campos. Currently, Dr. Mariano is the Dean of the School of Economics and Director of the Sim Kee Boon Institute of Financial Economics at Singapore Management University (SMU). He has helped bring prestige and credibility to SMU by mentoring its faculty, staff, and students on world-class, Ivy League-standard teaching and research. Prior to moving to Singapore in 2002, Dr. Mariano was a distinguished professor of economics and statistics at the School of Arts and Sciences and the Wharton School of Business at the University of Pennsylvania. He joined the Penn faculty in 1971 and has held visiting positions in U.S., European, and Asian academic institutions. He has a wealth of experience in the corporate and public sectors as well as in academia. Dr. Mariano has authored numerous scholarly papers and books on econometric methodology and applications and has served on the editorial board of several international professional journals. He was the principal investigator in research projects funded by the United Nations, U.S. National Science Foundation, the Rockefeller Foundation, the U.S. Departments of Commerce and Agriculture, to name a few. With a focus on econometric modeling for forecasting and policy analysis, he has been a consultant to various central banks, government ministries, and stock exchanges in Asia as well as private companies in Asia and the U.S.

Illustrious Filipino historian Reynaldo "Rey" Ileto has taught thousands of students in the classrooms of top universities in the Philippines, Australia, Japan, United States, and Singapore. Rico Hizon and I were some of Dr. Ileto's enamored history students at De La Salle University during the martial law years of the early 1980s. He is currently professor of history and Southeast Asian Studies at the National University of Singapore. For more than three decades, Dr. Ileto has influenced the thinking of not just students but also serious researchers worldwide through his many scholarly writings including two prize-winning books: *Filipinos and their Revolution: Event, Discourse, Historiography* and *Pasyon and Revolution: Popular Movements in the Philippines*, 1840-1910. In 2009, *Pasyon and Revolution* was named one of the ten most influential books of Southeast Asian Studies by the Institute of Southeast Asian Studies (ISEAS) in Singapore. He was the only non-Western scholar in the list. Dr. Ileto's books have been recognized with the internationally-renowned Benda Prize, Ohira Prize, Philippine National Book Award, and Fukuoka Asian Culture Prize.

When it comes to Southeast Asian and Philippine political and security issues the go-to guy is retired Filipino career foreign service officer cum Singapore-based scholar, Ambassador Rodolfo "Rod" Severino. I have heard about the legendary Philippine ambassador, top-ranked ASEAN diplomat, and international civil servant from people who have served under him as well as from my family and friends who have met him.

Presently, Ambassador Severino is Visiting Senior Research Fellow and Head of the ASEAN Studies Centre at the Institute of Southeast Asian Studies. His last Philippine foreign service assignment was Secretary-General of the influential ASEAN Secretariat in Jakarta, Indonesia. Before assuming the tough and challenging position of ASEAN Secretary-General, Ambassador Severino was Philippine Undersecretary of Foreign Affairs. He and Singapore President S. R. Nathan got acquainted while they were both Ambassadors to Malaysia. Filled with a mix of intrigue and insight is his recently completed a book, *Southeast Asia in Search of an ASEAN Community*.

There are many more outstanding Filipino and Filipina professionals and personalities living and working in Singapore who have left their mark in areas other than the media and the academy. They have woven themselves into Singapore society as artists, singers, actors, entrepreneurs, bankers, doctors, models, consultants, composers, designers, pastors, publishers, managers, dancers, domestic helpers, among others. In 2009, during one of the festivities commemorating the fortieth anniversary of bilateral relations between the Philippines and Singapore, a photographic exhibit recognizing an illustrious group of forty diaspora diplomats—23 women and 17 men—was unveiled at Flavours 7107 Restaurant in classy Marina Square. The stories of their lives, at play and at work, are at the core of mutually beneficial, harmonious, and sustained Philippine soft power influences in Singapore.

Associational Filipinization

There are more than 80 civil society organizations registered with the Philippine Embassy. Each one of them has varied pursuits, from religious to sports. The number of non-state actors promoting Philippine soft power interests in the Lion City goes over a hundred when business organizations such as media (i.e., newspapers and magazines) and other services (i.e., banks, remittance centers, travel, retirement, insurance, etc.) are added. In spite of this diversity, the one annual event that brings together their activities is the commemoration of Philippine independence in June. June 12th is the date in 1898 when General Emilio Aguinaldo declared the independence of the Philippines from more than three centuries of Spanish rule. The Philippine national flag was raised and the Philippine national anthem, *Lupang Hinirang*, was played for the first time.

Singapore's Philippine Independence Day celebration has earned the reputation of being the world's longest commemoration. It is organized and coordinated by a Philippine Independence Day Committee (PIDC) comprised of a core group of representatives from government, business, and non-governmental organizations. Given its size, it is also probably the world's most organized. Except for the host country, no other nation-state dares put up an extended public display of national culture. In Singapore, June 12 will not outdo the massive National Day celebrations but it definitely out performs America's July 4th festivities in the Lion City.

Figure 7.3
Singapore's 111th Philippine
Independence Commemoration

Date	Event	Venue
June 5-July 7	"Free Spirits at Play": An Exhibition of the Philippines' Top Illustrators	Art Space, Royal Plaza
June 6	Filipino Community Part 1111th Philippine Independence Day Celebration	Hong Lim Park
June 7	Filipino Community Part 2 111th Philippine Independence Day Celebration	Hong Lim Park
June 11-17	7107 Gourmet:Philippine Food Festival by Chef Laudico with performances by Bayanihan Dance Company	7107 Flavours Restaurant at Marina Square
June 12	Flag Raising Ceremony 111th Philippine Independence Day Celebration	Philippine Embassy
June 12	**Philippine Embassy's Diplomatic Corps Reception**	Shangri-la Hotel
June 12-14	**Philippine Country Fair** Philippine Tourism Office	Plaza Singapura
June 13	Philippine Fashion Show By Cora Jacobs	Singapore Cricket Club
June 13	"SULYAP PILIPINAS" Bayanihan National Dance Company	NTUC Auditorium at Marina Square

June 13	Mutya ng Pilipinas Singapore Beauty Pageant	Plaza Singapura
June 14	**Free Legal Aid Clinic at** Philippine Country Fair	Plaza Singapura
June 14	Kantahan, Yugyugan at Flores de Mayo	Chijmes
June 16	**The Bayanihan Experience By Bayanihan National Dance Company** Embracing Ties That Bind	Esplanade Concert Hall
June 21	**National Kidney Foundation Health Screening**	Bayanihan Centre
June 27	**Pamela Wildheart's "Wild and Wicked" Album Launching**	El Toro Restro Bar
June 28	**Thanksgiving Mass, Dinner, and Santacruzan**	Marymount Convent, Good Shepherd Chapel
June 29 – July 30	**"40 years, 40 lives"** Photo exhibit - celebration of Pinoy lifestyle in Singapore by Ms. Elvie Lins	7107 Flavours Restaurant at Marina Square

Source: Philippine Independence Day Celebration Committee, Singapore, 2009.

Because of the Filipino diaspora's extensive geographic dispersion, Philippine Independence Day or "June 12th" is now celebrated in more than a hundred countries all over the world. It used to be that the highlight of a June

12 commemoration was the by-invitation-only cocktail reception hosted by the Philippine Ambassador or Consul General at some five-star hotel or at their diplomatic residence. Not anymore.

In the era of diaspora diplomacy, the culmination of Philippine Independence Day celebrations is the open-to-the-public variety show held at a large open space, usually a public park. It is a major transnational community production. Large corporations from the Philippines and the host country invest in the event as sponsors, donors, and advertisers. Major big-name TV personalities from Manila are flown in and perform alongside Singapore's Filipino talents.

The ones I've gone to culminated in lively variety shows at Suntec City, Haw Par Villa, Fort Canning Park, and Sentosa. They are as large and crowded as the ones I've seen in San Francisco and New York. In 2009, the 111th Philippine Independence Day celebration actually began with a stunning and color-filled art exhibition entitled: "Free Spirits at Play: An Exhibition of the Philippines' Top Illustrators." It was organized at the Art Space of the Royal Plaza on Scotts Road by BBC News anchor Rico Hizon and his wife, Melanie, who are avid art collectors. Viewed by hundreds of locals, expatriates, and tourists, the exhibit continued well into early July.

Then it was a Saturday and a Sunday packed with two-part Filipino community-spearheaded events at the sprawling Hong Lim Park Green between South Bridge and New Bridge Roads. The park is also nicknamed "Speaker's Corner" since it is the official place to hold political gatherings, from election rallies to gay rights protests. On both days, thousands of Filipino men and women availed of democratic space in Singapore under the watchful CCTV coverage of the police. I don't think anybody had to worry about political correctness that day since the line-up of musical performances was led by the legendary Singapore Police Force Band. Major sponsors SingTel, StarHub, Western Union, among others, had booths and gigantic banners hung all around the park.

In 2008, as part of the Philippine Independence Day commemorations Philippine and Singapore government officials, led by no less than President S.R. Nathan honored Filipino national hero, Dr. Jose Rizal, a diaspora diplomat himself, with a bronze bust relief at the Asian Civilization Museum Green.

The 2009 Philippine Independence Day Celebration was well publicized and advertised in various Singapore media outlets as well as inside the high-traffic MRT trains. Award-winning performing artists from Manila and Singapore were top-billed. Part one, Saturday, featured more opening exhibits this time from Singaporean artists and Pinoygraphers, the Filipino photographers group. This was followed by a recognition ceremony for the "Outstanding Filipino and Filipinas Award." The evening was capped by a special June 12th dinner with local talent shows.

Part two, Sunday, saw close to 10,000 people gather at Hong Lim Park Green again but this time to watch famous Philippine TV and movie personalities. Locally bred artists, like Asher, Philippine idol winner and Singapore idol finalist, as well as the wild and the wicked Pamela Wildheart, a popular Filipina Singaporean performing artist. The morning started with the "Fun Walk by the Singapore River," followed by a parade displaying the ethnic costumes and cultures of the Philippines and a "Palarong Pinoy," a sportsfest of traditional games.

With these kick-off events, the month continued to unfold with a food festival at Marina Square, a country fair at Plaza Singapura, a fashion show at the Singapore cricket club, a Flores de Mayo parade at Chijmes, and a UPAAS-sponsored Mutya ng Pilipinas-Singapore beauty pageant. One of the highlights was the performance of the world-renowned Philippine Bayanihan National Dance Company at National Trade Union Congress Auditorium and at the Esplanade Concert Hall. They raised more than US$150,000 benefiting the Singapore Community Chest and the Filipino community's Bayanihan Centre.

At the 2009 event too, the second-generation Filipino migrants made themselves visible   via the Filipino Dance Crew (FDC)/Filipino Dance Club. FDC Siblings (Gino, Gico & Carel) were given the Most Outstanding Filipinos in Singapore award for being the champion of "Beyond Your Style" dance contest in Singapore. This is the Singapore equivalent of the popular MTV show, "America's Best Dance Crew" or ABDC for short.

The PIDC was chaired by Ronnie Albeus, the president of the Filipino Association of Singapore (FAS). Founded in 1937 and older than the Republic of Singapore, FAS is one of the oldest civil society organizations in the Lion City and the oldest Filipino association. It promotes and strengthens the spirit of unity and camaraderie among its members, from all ethnicities. Every year, hundreds of volunteers give time and money towards the success of each commemoration. Tasks and responsibilities are assigned to the working committee's sub-committees who turn to members of their organizations for volunteers.

One of the co-organizers of June 12 events since 2003 is the University of the Philippines Alumni Association Singapore (UPAAS). Its membership consists of UP graduates who are professionals, executives, entrepreneurs, artists and graduate students residing in Singapore. The association's main goal is to support the University of the Philippines' vital role in the development of the Philippine community and the Filipino nation while serving as a facility for interaction and exchange between members of the society and other organizations in Singapore including Singaporeans and non-Singaporeans alike. In the 2009 celebration, UPAAS was joined by the alumni of Mapua Institute of Technology along with fraternity alumni associations of Alpha Phi Omega, Tau Gamma Phi, and Alpha Kappa Rho.

Members of hometown associations from Bicol, Pangasinan, Abra, Batangas, and Aklan provinces are always some of the most actively involved in the Independence celebrations. There were also a number of professional and women's groups represented in the grunt work including the Filipino Association of Bookkeepers, Filipino Ladies Group, Filipino Expat Wives,

Marymount Ladies, Espesyal Pinoy, and PinoyGraphers.

Coincidentally, in the same 2009 Philippine Independence month, one of the newest Filipino sports group in Singapore quietly made waves at the Singapore International Water Festival 500m Dragon Boat Race at Marina Barrage, Singapore. The Filipino Dragons Singapore struck Gold in the Men's Open Division, Gold in the Women's Division, Silver in the Mix Division, and Bronze in the Men's Open Division. The highly competitive group is affiliated with the Singapore Dragon Boat Association and has recruited more than 50 members. This year-old group was overshadowed in their Philippine Independence Day participation by the older multi-ethnic sports groups like Filipino Bowlers Club, Pinoy Golfers Singapore, Kilat Senjata, Pinoy Sports and Recreation Club, Pinoy Badminton Club, and United Arnis Kali Escrima.

Physically present at the June 12 festivities were members of a number of popular, virtual "Filipinos in Singapore" associations—PinoySG.com, flsg. com, and Barangay Singapore. Supported by local business advertisements, PinoySG.com has blog spaces for Couples for Christ, Singles for Christ, Nurses Group, Engineers and Architects Group, Batangueños, Bulakenyos, Ilocanos, and Kapampangans. Similarly, at filsg.com, the following groups share photos and exchange greetings, pleasantries, support, tips, contact numbers, and advice at PinoyGraphers, Filipino Dance Club, Philippine Football Club, University of the Philippines Alumni Association (UPAAS), Singapore Association of Mapua Alumni (SAMA), BikerBoyz Sg and PadyakPinoy Sg, Filipino Billiard Club, and Groove Unlimited.

Forming skills enhancement programs for migrants

"Sigue ha, me klase pa ako sa Bayanihan Centre....Pasir Panjang... sa may Vivo City. Text nalang." [Bye, I still have a class at the Bayanihan Centre...Pasir Panjang...close to Vivo City. Just send me a text.]

This was the parting exchange I overheard from two Filipinos at a restaurant one Sunday. One of them was referring to the world-class migrant worker weekend skills enhancement and reintegration classes established by Philippine governmental and non-governmental organizations. Like Lucky Plaza and churches, these classes bring together Filipino and non-Filipino members of various organizations. Community members volunteer as weekend teachers, mentors, support staff, counselors, coaches, or sign up as students.

The success of these Filipino community-organized weekend courses influenced some Singapore civil society organizations and businesses to form their own classes or encourage employers to let their domestic helpers attend them. Other countries with nationals in Singapore would also either refer their workers to attend these classes or develop their own skills training classes based on the Philippine model.

Both the Singapore and Philippine governments support and endorse these classes, most of which are organized and administered by civil society groups. The major providers are the Filipino Overseas Workers of Singapore, the Franciscan Missionaries of Mary, International Baptist Church of Singapore, Archdiocesan Commission for Migrant and Itinerant People, and Global Pinoy, an association of Filipino entrepreneurs in Singapore.

The largest and most influential is the Filipino Overseas Workers of Singapore (FOWS) – Skills Training Program (STP). FOWS-STP has been replicated as a best practice in government-civil society partnership in Malaysia, Hong Kong and countries all over Asia. More than 8,000 female domestic helpers from the Philippines, India, and Sri Lanka have benefited from FOWS-STP courses. More than a hundred Filipinos and Singaporeans have volunteered thousands of hours to make the program a success. Some graduates have kept in touch and are entrepreneurs back in their home provinces in the Philippines while others are applying the skills they gained from the courses in Dubai, London, Vancouver, and San Francisco. Their FOWS-STP certificates have become part of their employment portfolios and proudly listed on their bio-data or curriculum vitae.

With a membership of more than 10,000, the Filipino Overseas Workers of Singapore is the largest Filipino group and organized by domestic helpers themselves. FOWS-STP is where many church-based and regional associations of Filipinos in Singapore refer their members during their days off, especially after Sunday services.

A core group of dedicated elected FOWS officers manages the hectic Sunday-to-Sunday operations of the FOWS-STP since what began as three courses in 1994 expanded to 22.

The courses are: Aromatherapy, Arts and Craft, Baking (Basic and Advanced), Basic English, Basic Guitar Playing, Bookkeeping and Accounting 1 and 2, Computer Fundamentals, Computer Electives, Computer Technician and Networking, Cosmetology, Dancing, Dressmaking (Basic and Advanced), Entrepreneur and Wealth Management, Filipino Language and Culture Course, Food Production/Preservation, Hotel Restaurant Management and Catering, International Cuisine, Nursing Aide, Tailoring, Taekwondo, and Voice (Vocal) lessons.

The STP courses have both short-term and long-term benefits. They help strengthen the psychological and social well-being of the domestic helpers. Moreover, the modules offered at the OWWA School provide them opportunities to enhance their skills, career, and language development for more effective social and economic reintegration. This is a critical component of the programme since a majority of domestic helpers based in Singapore are underutilizing the education they received from colleges and universities in the Philippines.

From the half-way house cum makeshift STP school, the program moved to a 28-room multi-purpose four-story building on Pasir Ris, near Vivo City. The Bayanihan Centre enables all Filipinos and their many organizations to gather under one roof. I remember the days when we were asking for a proper school site during the administrations of former Philippine President Ramos and Prime Minister Goh. We finally got the approval from the Singapore government through the persistent efforts of former Philippine President Joseph Estrada. The Bayanihan Centre was inaugurated in 2001 during the state visit of Philippine President Gloria Macapagal Arroyo.

I have fond memories of FOWS-STP. On a window sill in my current office in San Francisco sits a shining gold plaque that reads, "Presented to Professor Jay Gonzalez in appreciation of your sincere dedication and great concern for the OFWs in Singapore. Farewell and good luck. Many thanks. From FOWS-STP. September 5th 1999. Singapore." I received it from Manang Encar, FOWS officers, STP staff, and my beloved students on my last day in Singapore and my last day of teaching for them. I earned this citation after five years of volunteer teaching every Sunday when the FOWS Skills Training Program began at a three-bedroom bungalow at 243 Holland Road. This is one of the most gratifying recognitions I have ever received in my life. When my youngest brother, King, graduated with his bachelor's degree, I invited him to stay with me in Singapore to work and also volunteer at STP. King stayed on and continued my computer skills classes.

The Franciscan Missionaries of Mary's Filipino On-going Development Programme (FILODEP) operates at the FMM House of Prayer and Formation at 49 Holland Road. The programme was started in 1986 as a project of former Philippine Ambassador to Singapore Francisco Benedicto and Sister Andy Casuso of the Franciscan Missionaries of Mary (FMM), an international religious order of women. FILODEP has grown tremendously. In 1987, it offered skills development modules on computers, typing, personality development, hair science, guitar, sewing, plant propagation, flower arrangement, paper sculpture and table setting. These courses are offered in two school terms.

From 1990 to 1991, the school had a total enrolment of 400 students with new modules in cooking, cosmetology, accounting and drama. By 1994, the enrolment had doubled to 800. Language classes in English and Mandarin were added to its list of courses. In 1995, FILODEP's student population reached a high of 1,100. However, despite the demand, the FMM sisters decided to limit the enrolment to 900 for 1996 due to the increasing amount of "wear and tear" on their physical facilities, which were not really designed to handle such large numbers.

FILODEP has developed significantly since then to include certificate courses in hair-dressing, tailoring, cooking and baking, among others. These certificate programmes were introduced for workers to develop certain skills for their future when they return to their own countries. FILODEP had opened its doors to workers from Indonesia, Sri Lanka, India, and Burma and aims to attend to their psychological, emotional, intellectual and spiritual needs.

Summary and Conclusion

As a Philippine diaspora diplomat in Singapore, I became heavily involved in helping to improve people-to-people relations. I did my part in opening the hearts and minds of hundreds of young Singaporeans who attended my lectures and tutorials. I was very touched when administrators and students nominated me and I received the National University of Singapore's distinguished teaching award in 1996. So far, I have been the only Filipino faculty member in the school's history to receive one.

In 1997, two years after the Philippine-Singapore spat, I was asked by a local Singapore publisher if I was interested in authoring a children's book for a global country series called *Countries of the World*. The Singaporean representative who visited me at my Gilman Heights flat told me, "It would help make children from other countries in the world, including Singapore and the United States, aware of the Philippines' rich history, culture, and society".

I told him that I had never written a children's book so I will think about it. After he left, my eight-year old daughter who overheard our conversation approached me and said, "Dad, you always do right for big people but what about small people like me?" It took me two years to fully understand this rationale and connect the dots: the book will help the international community of nations better understand the Philippines and hopefully prevent further sibling rivalries, but the target audience would be diaspora diplomats and their next generation. I wrote the "big people" book first, *Philippine Labour Migration* which came out in 1998. Then I finished the children's book, *Countries of the World: Philippines*, which came out in 2001 after my daughter, who was by then eleven years old, read and edited the final manuscript.

After the tough time I had writing for my daughter's peers, I switched back to my own age group and tried to exert soft power influence within the larger academic world by writing for English journals, magazines, and newspapers in Singapore, the U.S., India, Hong Kong, Malaysia, Thailand, Indonesia, Korea, and the UK. I have also presented in European, North American, and Asian conferences. To reach out and share knowledge beyond the English-speaking world about Filipinos and the way we do corporate social responsibility and civic engagement, politics and government, as well as Philippine business culture, I agreed to have several of my works translated in Korean, Chinese, and Spanish. Because of these translations, Filipinos are able to influence practitioners and scholars of international and comparative studies through training programs at the Inter-American Development Bank, the Institute of Southeast Asian Studies, Korea Development Institute, Beijing Normal University, among many other places.

I was not the only researcher intent on going beyond the traditional diplomatic channels to help rekindle the Valentine's flame between the Philippines and Singapore that was snuffed out by Flor Contemplacion's execution. In January 2001, a group of young Singaporean poets and writers decided to reach out. The Singapore International Foundation promised them a financial grant. Nine months later, the Philippine National Commission on Culture and the Arts supported a visit of Filipino writers and poets. Singaporean and Filipino artists met eye-to-eye and heart-to-heart at a Singapore writer's festival. The result of their union was more than what governments could create through diplomatic channels: exchange visits, e-mails, meetings, eating, drinking, beginnings of life-long friendship and collaboration. To seal their renewed bond, an anthology was born, co-produced by publishing houses from both countries aptly entitled, *Love Gathers All* (2002).

In sum, people-to-people religious, occupational, and associational influences were instrumental in molding the healthy and vibrant Philippine and Singapore bilateral relations we see today. Diplomacy is anchored on more solid people-to-people links as opposed to simply tepid government-to-government ties. Singapore prides itself as a country of cultural, ethnic, and spiritual diversity. Thus, the Philippine diaspora diplomats' religious Filipinization or the *kasamahan* and *bayanihan* influences emanating from their church and faith have blossomed and flourished. After all, churches introduce and reinforce values and behaviors into its members which governments cannot legislate, including respectfulness, kindness, and graciousness.

As it is in San Francisco, London, and Dhaka, Filipino Catholic migrant faithful help fill up the pews and collection boxes at Singapore churches every Sunday. Similarly, their Filipino Protestant and evangelical counterparts invest in miracles both locally and internationally at their Lion City churches. Filipino Catholics and Protestants help Singaporean churches nurture inter-faith dialogue and collaboration. They have become global missionaries for them too.

Occupationally, the labor, skills, education, and training influences of hundreds of thousands of Philippine diaspora diplomats are felt inside hundreds of thousands of Singapore homes. They are joined by thousands of migrant nurses, IT technicians, and other professionals. Together, they power economic growth in the Lion City not only as migrant workers but also as consumers, through Lucky Plaza's remittance centers, employment agencies, money changers, mini-marts, travel agencies, box forwarders, beauty salons, restaurants and cafés, and other businesses. As professionals, some Philippine diaspora diplomats have influenced the media, computer and technical education, as well as social science research in Singapore.

In terms of their associational Filipinization or the *kasamahan* and *bayanihan* influences from their participation in existing or new formal organizations and informal gatherings, Philippine diaspora diplomats have been as generous and determined in promoting their culture and helping others as their counterparts in London, San Francisco, Dhaka, and Dubai. The world-class skills enhancement and reintegration programs developed by Filipino non-governmental associations is a model of self-help and assistance to migrants not just for ASEAN countries but also other migrant sending and receiving countries. Unified by role models, such as FOWS founder Manang Encar, FAS President Ronnie Albeus, BBC News Anchor Rico Hizon, Philippine diaspora diplomats in Singapore have been very serious at commemorating Philippine Independence Day and have earned the undisputed reputation of hosting the longest and one of the liveliest.

CHAPTER 8

Conclusion: Philippine Soft Power Lessons

Mahatma Ghandi once said, "In a gentle way, you can shake the world." This is essentially how Philippine migrants have been exerting their influence on cities and states where they work, live, play and worship. They are showing the world that soft power is effective.

Every other year since 1984, after a long international search process, the Philippine president presents "Bagong Bayani" (New Hero) awards to outstanding Filipino movers and shakers and the overseas associations they have formed. It is a fitting tribute that all diaspora nations in the world would do well to emulate, to encourage and support their migrant ambassadors.

A "Bagong Bayani" is a person or organization who has used Filipino soft power to influence minds, spirits and hearts in the countries they now live in. These new heroes have distinguished themselves in their occupations and have been selfless in working for the welfare of their country, their countrymen, their church and humanity as a whole.

With the award accorded them by the Philippine government, these diaspora diplomats are recognized for their exemplary efforts in fostering goodwill among countries and people; enhancing the image of Filipinos as competent and responsible workers; contributing to the nation's foreign exchange earnings; and spreading Filipino values and culture.

A number of recipients are mentioned in the book, including San Francisco Silicon Valley engineer Diosdado Banatao, Dhaka-based education administrator Carmen Lamagda, Singapore domestic helper Encarnacion Montales and news presenter Rico Hizon. Organizations that have been honored include the Veterans Equity Center (VEC) in San Francisco and the Filipino Association of Singapore (FAS). They are not, however, the only Philippine diaspora diplomats who deserve recognition and encouragement, as this book has revealed. There are millions of Bagong Bayani heroes and heroines out there with valuable lessons to share not just to the Philippines but to the rest of the community of nations.

Each chapter of this book discusses soft power approaches to international relations that are relevant to both diaspora states, like the Philippines and Bangladesh, and to hard power countries like the U.S. and the United Kingdom, as well as to advanced developing states like Singapore and the United Arab Emirates.

Conceptually, the biggest lessons of this volume loop us back to my scholarly conversations with writers in the various schools of international relations and beyond. Through this book, I share my own migrant observations and field research to cover what Professors Putnam, Huntington, Nye and others have inadvertently neglected.

Apparently, eminent scholar Samuel Huntington's 1996 prophesy of an impending "clash of civilizations" cannot be averted solely by the school of realism's prescriptions which revolve around "alliances of large, hegemonic armies, navies, and air forces." Neither can it be prevented by the school of liberalism's leaning towards "economic cooperation founded on high productivity, obsession for profits, monetary wealth, and the almighty GNP." The school of political idealism's calls for more "sister city ties, scholar and student cultural exchanges, study tours, development assistance, press and propaganda," are likewise inadequate. So is Nye's and his neoliberalism's suggestion of more state-initiated public diplomacy anchored on influential state actors and the complex interdependence of nongovernmental organizations (NGOs) and multinational corporations (MNCs).

As I have discussed in this book, the "clash of civilizations" can be successfully mitigated only when countries and cities recognize the citizenship and transnational socio-cultural capital (missed out by Putnam's *Bowling Alone* expose) emanating from hundreds of millions of global migrants— not governments not corporations. Diasporas are at the forefront of people-powered diplomacy. When this is recognized then the love and respect for both baseball and *balut* are possible. The case studies I have presented in this book have provided many illustrations of how Philippine diaspora diplomats have been able to accomplish this task by exerting their influence on their places of worship, work, and welfare via their spirit, mind, and heart.

These stories from the Filipino diaspora illustrate that diaspora diplomacy can thrive in liberal or conservative political systems, hot or cold weather, religious or secular states, and in both developed or developing country contexts. It can be part of the contemporary migration process, both temporary and permanent, and institutionalized or informal. It does not have to be always government-legislated or initiated by politicians since it can be driven, directed, and sustained by the energy and charisma of a broad range of migrants, from young pastors to aging seniors. It is anchored on the migrant attitudes of respect, harmony, self-help, and social justice. Diaspora diplomacy is mutually beneficial for the old homeland and the new home base, and not mere propaganda or coercive. Summarized in Figure 8.1 and elaborated on thereafter are my specific findings.

Figure 8.1
Soft Power through Philippine migration

Kasamahan Filipinization	Bayanihan Filipinization
Influence by praying, working, organizing	Influence by acting, sending, helping
Renewing American Christian churches	Lobbying the U.S. Congress

Kasamahan Filipinization	Bayanihan Filipinization
Engineering and caring from downtown to the Silicon Valley	Earning and shopping at Serramonte Mall
Replenishing American social capital	Educating minds and hearts to change the world
Saving the Queen's church	Introducing a new Christmas tradition
Nursing the sick and caring for the elderly	Sprucing and spicing menus
Blending diversity, creed, and charity	Mixing youth, charisma, and advocacy
Spreading inter-faith respect in the Middle East	Shepherding an evangelical flock in Arabian Peninsula
Securing the ports of the Persian Gulf	Diversifying Emirati cuisine
Schooling the next generation	Dribbling basketballs on the sand
Serving God in South Asia	Expanding the spiritual base at Banani
Ensuring corporate social responsibility	Administering world-class education
Jazzing up Bangla entertainment	Shopping, shipping, remitting, and networking
Planting God and country	Investing in miracles at the lion city
Powering Singaporean families and firms	Facing the media and the academy
Commemorating Philippine independence	Forming skills training programs for migrants

In Filipinizing major cities within their two former colonizers, the U.S. and UK, Filipino diaspora diplomats illustrate the power of patience, prayer, harmony, and peace over colonizing armadas, squadrons, and battalions. Yes, one can argue that the British and American naval victories to conquer Manila were not without death and bloodshed, but were the death and destruction necessary?

Millions of Filipinos have arrived in San Francisco International and Heathrow airports without human and infrastructural casualties. Instead, they slowly and surreptitiously "injected" themselves into London's and San Francisco's welcoming Achilles heel—their teetering spiritual foundations.

The bible relates the story of David's cunning and character in defeating the arrogant behemoth Goliath. Similarly, Filipino migrant faithful already understand that momentum is on their side so they know that to assert their presence in their churches, they need not be too aggressive and demanding. By the sheer force of their numbers and baptism to faith, leaders of the powerful Church of England, the Catholic Church, as well as the Protestant and evangelical Christian churches have had no choice but to take notice, accommodate them, and eventually integrate their Filipino religious practices, music, and even liturgies. In some cases, they have even been granted permission by political and spiritual leaders to take over emptying churches.

As a result of their soft power influence, San Francisco and London Catholic churches have become more ethnically and decoratively diverse. New folks mean new saints, new devotions, new pastors, new readers, new hymns, new languages, and new traditions like *Simbang Gabi*, nine-day novena Christmas masses held at nine different London, San Francisco, and Singapore churches every December.

Not to be outdone by the Catholics, the independent Iglesia ni Cristo has introduced Grand Evangelical Missions (GEM) into the San Francisco Bay Area while the Philippine Independent Church and the Church of England have forged an Aglipayan-Anglican alliance with the creation of a Filipino

Chaplaincy in the heart of London. Some Filipino churches have even been able use their new-found influence to place local Filipino social justice concerns as well as Philippine issues on the agenda of major congregational conferences and into city halls and even the U.S. Congress. They have become influential church pastors, bishops, and lay leaders affecting everything from schedules, languages, music, and allowable practices. Catholic and evangelical church spaces and religious programming at Asia's economic powerhouse, Singapore, have had parallel influences from the more than a hundred thousand Filipino diaspora diplomats visibly investing in miracles every Sunday in the tiny city-state.

In the Middle East and South Asia, Filipino diaspora diplomats have been very discreet and respectful in introducing their *bayanihan* and *kasamahan* religious influence even with their growing numbers in Islamic states. As a result, these modern-day tentmakers have succeeded in making spiritual inroads in places and spaces where centuries of highly-structured western missionizing and mobilizing, sometimes backed by the force of armies and finances, have faltered and even failed.

In Dubai, the Catholic churches Filipino diaspora diplomats attend or establish are not only spaces where Filipino masses, vigils, novenas, and devotions thrive. They are also venues for spreading values of interfaith respect and tolerance. Filipino migrant faithful in Dubai and Dhaka initiate ecumenical prayers with Muslim brothers and sisters since there are more than five million Muslims in the Philippines. Moreover, Filipino Catholic priests and evangelical Christian pastors are more acceptable to Dubai's moderate Muslim religious and political leaders. A Caucasian pastor, for example, who already stands out in terms physical appearance would often create ripples because of his/her liberal rhetoric.

Filipino pastors, on the other hand, are seen as more Asian, responsible, harmonious, respectful and less threatening. They are not seen as extensions of western hegemony and pop culture domination since they also come from a developing Asian country. Thus, they are able to effectively shepherd active Catholic and evangelical flocks in the Arabian Peninsula. Filipinos in Dhaka, who are mostly Catholics, do the same. They emulate the local Bangladeshi Catholics and have thus learned to be very conscious, careful, and respectful of their Islamic surroundings. Moreover, they show themselves as humane neighbors by doing volunteer work at local Dhaka charities, particularly at the convent of the Sisters of Charity. They help a *kababayan* who is religious sister. At Banani Church, they do not just attend the English services, they also lend themselves as lectors, collectors, and choir singers and musicians. Filipino diaspora diplomats used extreme patience and lots of prayers to secure permission from Islamic political and religious leaders to build the Our Lady of Perpetual Help Church in Fujairah and Banani Church in Dhaka.

Through their occupational influences, Filipino diaspora diplomats have demonstrated the power of their *kasamahan* and *bayanihan* perspiration, perseverance and performance. Although they are heavily impacted by market forces, many of them look beyond globalization and the corporate bottom line to increase productivity and profits. They are focused on their goal to take care of their families and hometowns. This requires regularly sending money and balikbayan boxes. The majority of them are in supporting occupational roles as service and care workers. They are not bankers or investors but they still wield much influence. Global economic growth will be at a standstill if they all take a vacation at the same time.

Filipino diaspora diplomats are the nurses and caregivers providing much needed 24/7 patient care in London and San Francisco hospitals, homes, clinics and health care facilities. They are the domestic helpers in Singapore who enable families to earn double incomes and increase productivity while they do the household chores and take care of the children. They are both the retail clerks and shoppers at San Francisco, London, and Dubai's world-class malls. Some of them are technicians and engineers with information and technology companies in Singapore, Dhaka, and San Francisco. They maintain the efficient operations of Dubai's world-class ports. They ensure the high quality and humane production standards of the clothes that are made in Dhaka's thousands of garment factories and export-processing zones which will eventually be sold in the brand-name shops in London, Dubai, Singapore, and San Francisco. Some of them help spruce and spice up recipes in London hotels, cafes, patisseries, and restaurants as well as diversify Dubai's food scene. Some diaspora diplomats have stood out and helped Dhaka reach world-class technical education standards, while in Singapore they are the news presenters and topic experts facing the cameras of local and international news networks. Their occupational soft power influence is quite pervasive and broad, reaching more than a thousand cities.

Filipino diaspora diplomats do not just influence spaces of work and worship in San Francisco, London, Dubai, Dhaka, and Singapore. They demonstrate and display the power and influence of their passion-driven *kasamahan* associations and their *bayanihan* social justice concerns over the rhetoric of presidents and the promises of politicians.

In San Francisco, Filipino immigrant professionals and workers as well as church members have been contributing new and colorful social capital to the fabric of American cities and communities for more than a century. Its educational institutions have Philippine-trained mentors and teachers helping educate minds, hearts, and spirits to change the world.

In London, diaspora diplomats organize one of the most well attended Simbang Gabi traditions outside the Philippines. No other contemporary ethnic group has been more welcomed by the British Catholic church than Filipino migrant Catholics and their various organizations, which are at the core of Philippine cultural commemorations and celebrations. First- and second-generation Filipino Brits have also established organizations that are not only concerned with infusing Philippine culture into London society but also advocating for reforms in the motherland.

In Dubai, Filipino men and women migrants are respectfully and peacefully helping Islamic UAE internationalize and become more acceptable to the global community. They educate the next generation of diaspora diplomats not just in the many Philippine international schools but through the clean-up drives and charities organized by their hometown associations, professional associations, as well as fraternities and colleges alumni associations. Their community leaders have been able to introduce basketball diplomacy to the Middle East region more pervasively than the U.S. National Basketball Association.

Aside from schools and sports, they assist developing cities like Dhaka become world-class and modern, and not just through economic globalization. Energetic Filipino diaspora diplomats are helping the city achieve this by jazzing up Bangla entertainment. They weave western but still Asian-acceptable music and performances in Dhaka's five-star hotels, cafes, restaurants, and bars. They have also done this successfully in the United Arab Emirates.

As it is in San Francisco, Singapore, London, and Dubai, among their major associational pastimes and networking activities are to shop, ship, and remit for family and friends in the Philippines. The inevitability and frequency of their social interactions at these places is even higher than the formal gatherings, like Philippine Independence Day commemorations, organized by the Philippine Embassy and the Philippine Society of Bangladesh, their only ethnic association in Dhaka.

In Singapore, Filipinos form organizations that administer world-class migrant skills training programs that benefit not only Filipinos but also other migrants from Sri Lanka, Thailand, China, Indonesia, Bangladesh, and India. The Filipino Association of Singapore, the Philippine Embassy and its allied organizations have been holding the longest commemoration – more than a month -- of Philippine independence outside of the Philippines for decades. It has become more visible as a cultural and community event than America's July 4th celebrations not just in Singapore but also in London, Dubai, and Dhaka.

I strongly believe that the capacity of the Philippines to operationalize democratization through nonviolent people power mobilization has gone beyond its domestic confines into the international sphere through one of the world's largest contemporary diasporas. These lessons learned from the Philippine diaspora are relevant to multiple stakeholders of various levels of analysis, including: developed countries, aside from the U.S. and the UK; advanced developing countries, beyond Singapore and the United Arab Emirates; less developed migrant sending countries, other than Bangladesh; faith-based, migrant labor, and human rights civil society organizations; international governmental and non-governmental agencies; and multinational business enterprises.

This book asserts that global migrants could:

(1) Play a key role in public diplomacy alongside nation state efforts particularly in spreading knowledge about Philippine culture which achieves mutual benefits for country of origin and country of destination or immigration;

(2) Act not only as diplomats, but as missionaries – spreading and influencing the practice of faith and religion in close to 200 countries;

(3) Earn money while transferring business, technical, service and other skills to recipient states which, in turn, allow them to send back money not only for family necessities but nation state needs, thus reducing dependency from foreign aid and foreign investments; and

(4) Infuse much-needed social, spiritual, organizational, and civic diversity into the multicultural ethnoscape of global cities and communities supplementing existing ones and replenishing what has been lost.

To President Obama and Secretary of State Clinton, I would like to point out that diaspora diplomacy is more mutually beneficial and influential than traditional public diplomacy. Thus, the U.S. needs to look beyond its traditional soft power approaches like sister city relations, governmental, non-governmental, and corporate philanthropies, American international schools, Voice of America broadcasts, McDonaldization, brand recognition, pop culture, educational exchanges, and English language training programs. America needs to use its own under-utilized, multi-ethnic diaspora. The U.S. should also learn to acknowledge the religious, occupational and associational domestic and international influences of its more than 1.4 million Arab and eight million Muslim diaspora diplomats living, working, worshipping, and socializing in its thousands of cities and towns.

Based on a very rough State Department estimate, America itself has a diaspora of around three to six million people. The U.S. Department of Commerce places large clusters of them in European countries--UK, France, Italy, and Germany--but there are also American diaspora communities in East Asia, South Asia, and the Middle East. They could be used to move the U.S. from its predominantly hard power approach to diplomacy to a softer one. Andy Sundberg, the founding director of the nonprofit advocacy group American Citizens Abroad, says he's been playing Don Quixote for thirty-five years trying to persuade the U. S. government to recognize the overseas-American community.

References

Ang, D. (2008). "Bangladesh calls for closer ties with RP." *Manila Times*. November 29, 2008. (http://www.manilatimes.net/national/2008/nov/29/yehey/top stories/20081129top8.html)

Armistead, E. (2004). *Information Operations: Warfare and the Hard Reality of Soft Power*. Dulles, VA: Brassey's.

Bagley, C., Madrid, S., Bolitho, F. (1997). "Stress factors and mental health adjustment of Filipino domestic workers in Hong Kong." *International Social Work*, 40(4), 373-382.

Barnett, T. (2009). *Great Powers: America and the World After Bush*. New York: Penguin.

Battistella, G. (1995). "Philippine overseas labour: From export to management." *ASEAN Economic Bulletin*, 12(2), 257.

Bayne, N. and Woolcock, S., editors (2007). *The New Economic Diplomacy* (Global Finance). Aldershot, UK: Ashgate.

Bonus, R. (2000). *Locating Filipino Americans: Ethnicity and the Cultural Politics of Space*. Philadelphia, PA: Temple University Press.

Bowler, P. J. (2001). *Reconciling Science and Religion: The debate in early-twentieth-century Britain*. Chicago, IL: University of Chicago Press.

Brown, C. (2009). *The Death of Christian Britain: Understanding secularization 1800-2000*. New York: Routledge.

Bruce, S. (2001). "Christianity in Britain, R.I.P.", *Sociology of Religion*, 62:2, 191-203

Business Processing Association of the Philippines (2007). *Offshoring and Outsourcing Philippines: Roadmap 2010*. Manila: BPAP.

Business World. (2003). "Philippines bags special awards (Corporate Social Responsibility)." *Business World*, Oct 28 issue, p. 38.

Campbell, K (2004). "The end of alliances? not so fast". *The Washington Quarterly*, 27 (2): 151-163.

Carr, E. H., (1981). *The Twenty Year's Crisis: An Introduction to the Study of International Relations.* New York: Palgrave.

Chertoff, M. (2008). "Preventing terrorism: a case for soft power." *Harvard International Review, 30*(2), 14-17.

Cho, Y. N., Jong, H. J. (2008). "China's soft power: discussions, resources, and prospects." *Asian Survey, 48*(3), 453-472.

Chowdhury, M. R. and Kabir, A. (2000). "Social responsibility of business: a study with special reference to selected enterprises of CEPZ." *Journal of the Institute of Bangladesh Studies*, 23: 235-248.

Choy, C. (2003). *Empire of Care: Nursing and Migration in Filipino American History.* Durham, NC: Duke University Press.

Claro, R. (2003). *A Higher Purpose: For Your Overseas Job.* Makati, Philippines: Crossover Books.

Constable, N. (1997). *Maid to Order in Hong Kong: Stories of Filipina Workers.* Ithaca, NY: Cornell University Press.

Cornelio, J. (2007). "The minister is lay: social organization in new paradigm Christianity." *Global Missiology.* Online: http://www.globalmissiology. org/english/docs_pdf/dynamics/The%20Minister%20is%20Lay%20 -%209%2007%20GGS.pdf

Cornelio, J. (2008). "New paradigm Christianity and commitment-formation: the case of Hope Filipino (Singapore)." In Abby Day, editor, *Religion and the Individual: Belief, Practice, Identity.* Aldershot, UK: Ashgate.

Corraya, K. (2007). *The Catholic Directory of Bangladesh 2007.* Dhaka: Pratibeshi Prokashoni.

Cowan. G. and Cull, N. J. editors, (2008). "Special issue: public diplomacy in a changing world." *The Annals of the American Academy of Political and Social Science*. March 2008, Volume 616, No. 1.

De Gouveia, P.F. and Plumridge, H. (2005). *European Infopolitik: Developing EU Public Diplomacy Strategy*. London: Foreign Policy Centre.

Ding, S. (2008). *The Dragon's Hidden Wings: How China Rises with Its Soft Power*. Lanham, MD: Rowman & Littlefield-Lexington.

Djerejian, E. P. (2007). *Changing Minds, Winning Peace: A New Strategic Direction for U.S. Public Diplomacy in the Arab & Muslim World*. Washington, DC.: Crossbow Books

Espiritu, Y. L. (2003). *Home Bound: Filipino American Lives across Cultures*. Berkeley, CA: University of California Press.

Filsg.com

Foreign Policy Centre (2005). *Norwegian Public Diplomacy*. London: Foreign Policy Centre.

Fraser, M. (2005). *Weapons of Mass Distraction: Soft Power and American Empire*. New York: St. Martin's.

Gescher, J. M. (2002). "Adding value: dimension of corporate social responsibility," *China Review*, Spring 21: 21-23.

Gill, R. (2003). *The 'Empty' Church Revisited*. Aldershot, UK: Ashgate Publishing.

Gledhill, R. (2008). "Churchgoing on its knees as Christianity falls out of favour." *The Times*. May 8, 2008, p. 36.

Goldfarb, R., Havrylyshyn, O., Mangum, S. (1984). "Can remittances compensate for manpower outflows: the case of Philippine physicians." *Journal of Development Economics*, 15(1,2,3), 1.

Gonzalez, J. (1998). *Philippine Labour Migration: Critical Dimensions of Public Policy*. Singapore: Institute of Southeast Asian Studies.

Gonzalez, J. (2001). *Countries of the World: Philippines*. Milwaukee, WI: Gareth Stevens Publishing.

Gonzalez, J. (2009). *Filipino American Faith in Action: Immigration, Religion, and Civic Engagement*. New York: New York University Press.

Goodnewspilipinas.com

Graffy, C. P. (2008). "Trade, climate change and soft power: does America have friends in Europe?" *Hampton Roads International Security Quarterly. 3(2008)*: 1619.

Graham, S. E. (2008). "US public diplomacy in the Asia Pacific: opportunities and challenges in a time of transition. " *Place Branding and Public Diplomacy: Special Issue: National Image Management in Asia, 4*(4), 336-356.

Gupta, A. K. (2008). "Commentary on India's soft power and diaspora." *International Journal on World Peace, 25*(3), 61-68.

Hampson, M. (2006). *Last Rites: The End of the Church of England*. London: Granta Books.

Holland, Tom (2002). "Ethics pay in the long run." *Far Eastern Economic Review*, 165(15): 49-51.

Hui, Y. F. ed. (2009). "Special focus: the most influential books of Southeast Asian studies." *Sojourn* 24(1), April issue.

Huntington, S. (1996). *The Clash of Civilizations and the Remaking of World Order*. New York: Simon and Schuster.

Ignacio, E. N. (2005). *Building Diaspora: Filipino Cultural Community Formation on the Internet*. New Brunswick, NJ: Rutgers University Press.

Ilgen, T. (2006). *Hard Power, Soft Power and the Future of Transatlantic Relations*. Burlington, VT: Ashgate.

Kahwaji, R. (2004). "U.S.-Arab cooperation in the Gulf: are both sides working from the same script." *Middle East Policy*, 11(3): 52-62.

Kane, R. G. (2008). "Charm offensive: how China's soft power is transforming the world/Asia, America, and the transformation of geopolitics/ securing Japan: Tokyo's grand strategy and the future of East Asia." *Orbis, 52*(4), 702.

Karns, M. P.   (2008). "Multilateralism matters even more." *SAIS Review, 28*(2), 3-15.

Keohane, R. and Nye, J. (1989). *Power and Interdependence: World Politics in Transition.* Boston: Little Brown.

Kiehl, W. P., editor (2006). *America's Dialogue with the World.* Washington, DC: Public Diplomacy Council.

Kurlantzick, J. (2008). *Charm Offensive: How China's Soft Power Is Transforming the World.* New Haven: Yale University.

Lee, A., Pang, A., Sunico, R., and Yuson, A., Editors, (2002). *Love Gathers All: The Philippine-Singapore Anthology of Love Poetry.* Manila and Singapore: Anvil Publishing and Ethos Books.

Lennon, A. T., editor (2003). *The Battle for Hearts and Minds: Using Soft Power to Undermine Terrorist Networks.* Cambridge: Massachusetts Institute of Technology Press.

Leonard, M. (2003). *Public Diplomacy and the Middle East.* London: Foreign Policy Centre.

Leonard, M., Small, A., and Rose, M. (2005). *British Public Diplomacy in the Age of Schisms.* London: Foreign Policy Centre.

Lewer, N. (2009). *Non-Lethal Weapons and Conflict Resolution: A Soft Power Approach.* New York: Routledge

Lord, C. (2006). *Losing Hearts and Minds?: Public Diplomacy and Strategic Influence in the Age of Terror.* Santa Barbara, CA: Greenwood.

Lorente, B., Piper, N., Hua, S., Yeoh, B. (2005). *Asian Migrations: Sojourning, Displacement, Homecoming and Other Travels*. Singapore: Singapore University Press.

Magstadt, T. (2009). *The European Union on the World Stage: Sovereignty, Soft Power, and the Search for Consensus*. Westwood Hill, KS: BookSurge.

Manalansan, M. (2003). *Global Divas: Filipino Gay Men in the Diaspora*. Durham: Duke University Press.

Martin, Philip L. (1993). "Migration and trade: the case of the Philippines." *International Migration Review*, 27(3), 639.

Matsuda, T. (2007). *Soft Power and Its Perils: U.S. Cultural Policy in Early Postwar Japan and Permanent Dependency*. Stanford: Stanford University Press.

Melissen, J., Lee, D., and Sharp, P., editors, (2007). *The New Public Diplomacy: Soft Power in International Relations*. New York: Palgrave Macmillan.

Moller, B., editor, (2001). *Oil and Water: Cooperative Security in the Persian Gulf*. London: Tauris.

Morgenthau, H. (1993). *Politics Among Nations*. New York: McGraw-Hill.

Morris, R., editor, (2009). *Church and State in 21st Century Britain: The Future of Church Establishment*. London: Palgrave Macmillan.

Nye, J. S. (2002). *The Paradox of American Power: Why the World's Only Superpower Can't Go It Alone*. New York: Oxford University Press.

Nye, J. S. (2005). *Soft Power: The Means to Success in World Politics*. New York: PublicAffairs.

Nye, J. S. (2008). *The Powers to Lead*. New York: Oxford University Press.

Osteria, T. (1994). *Filipino Female Labor Migration to Japan: Economic Causes and Consequences*. Manila: De La Salle University Press.

Palongpalong, A. (1992). *Forgotten Neighbors: The Philippines' Relations with South Asia*. Manila: Center for Research and Communication.

Pantoja, L., Tira, S., Wan, E., editors, (2004). *Scattered: The Filipino Global Presence*. Manila: Filipino International Network.

Parreñas, R. (2001). *Servants of Globalization: Women, Migration, and Domestic Work*. Stanford: Stanford University Press.

Parreñas, R. (2008). *The Force of Domesticity: Filipina Migrants and Globalization*. New York: New York University Press.

Philippine Overseas Employment Agency Report (2008). *2007 Overseas Employment Statistics*. Manila: POEA.

philippinegenerations.blogspot.com/2008/08/philippine-chef-association-presents.html

PinoySG.com

Potter, L. and Sick, G. (2002). *Security in the Persian Gulf: Origins, Obstacles, and the Search for Consensus*. New York: Palgrave and MacMillan.

Preview this book

Putnam, R. (2000). *Bowling Alone: The Collapse and Revival of American Community*. New York: Simon and Schuster.

Putnam, R. (Ed.). (2004). *Democracies in Flux: The Evolution of Social Capital in Contemporary Society*. New York: Oxford University Press.

Rafael, V. (2000). *White Love and Other Events in Filipino History*. Durham: Duke University Press.

Richmond, Y. (2008). *Practicing Public Diplomacy: A Cold War Odyssey*. New York and Oxford: Berghahn Books.

Richter, J. (2001). *Holding Corporations Accountable: Corporate Conduct, International Codes and Citizen Action*. London and New York: Zed Books.

Rodriguez, E. (1998). "International migration and income distribution in the Philippines." *Economic Development and Cultural Change*, 46(2), 329-350.

Roman, F. L. (2002). "Managing corporate governance: legal/regulatory environment and corporate governance practices in the Philippines." Conference presentation at the 2nd Asian Corporate Governance Conference in Seoul, South Korea, Asian Institute of Corporate Governance, May 16-17, 2002.

Rufino, M. V. (2000). "Beyond brushstrokes: artistic expressions and corporate social responsibility." *Business World* (Philippines), Sept 11 issue, p. 48-49.

Rugh, W. (2005). *American Encounters with Arabs: The "Soft Power" of U.S. Public Diplomacy in the Middle East*. Westport, CT: Praeger.

Rugh, W.A., editor (2004). *Engaging the Arab and Islamic Worlds Through Public Diplomacy*. Washington, DC: Public Diplomacy Council.

San Pablo-Baviera, A. and Yu-Jose, L., editors (1998). *Philippine External Relations: A Centennial Vista*. Manila: Foreign Service Institute.

Satloff, R. (2004). *The Battle of Ideas in the War on Terror: Essays on U.S. Public Diplomacy in the Middle East*. Washington, DC: Washington Institute for Near East Policy.

Seib, P. M. (2009). *Toward a New Public Diplomacy: Redirecting U.S. Foreign Policy*. New York: Palgrave Macmillan.

Snow, N. and Taylor, P., editors (2008). *Routledge Handbook of Public Diplomacy*. New York: Routledge.

Sriramesh, K. (2009). *The Global Public Relations Handbook Revised Edition: Theory, Research, and Practice*. New York: Routledge.

Starr, D. (2009). "Chinese language education in Europe: the Confucius Institutes." *European Journal of Education, 44*(1), 65.

Stretton, A. W. (1981). "The building industry and urbanization in Third World countries: a Philippine case study." *Economic Development and Cultural Change*, 29(2), 325.

Sun, H. H. (2008). International political marketing: a case study of United States soft power and public diplomacy. *Journal of Public Affairs*, 8(3), 165.

Thucydides' (431 B. C. E.). *History of the Peloponnesian War.* Translated to English by R. Crawley http://classics.mit.edu/Thucydides/pelopwar.html

Tiongson, A., Gutierrez, E., Gutierrez, R. editors (2006). *Positively No Filipinos Allowed Building Communities and Discourse.* Philadelphia: Temple University Press.

Troubnikoff, A. (2003). *Trafficking in Women and Children: Current Issues and Developments.* New York: Nova Science.

Tzu, S. (undated). *Art of War.* Translated to English by L. Giles (1910) http://www.chinapage.com/sunzi-e.html

U.S. Census Bureau (2004). *American Community Survey.* Washington, DC: U.S. Census Bureau.

U.S. Department of State (2007). *Bureau of East Asian and Pacific Affairs Staff Report.* May 2007.

U.S. State Department (2008). *2007 Human Trafficking Report.* Washington, DC: U.S. State Department.

United States Conference of Catholic Bishops (2003). *Office for the Pastoral Care of Migrants and Refugees Report.* Washington, DC. USCCB.

Vergara, B. (2009). *Pinoy Capital: The Filipino Nation in Daly City.* Philadelphia: Temple University Press.

Waller, J.M. (2007). *Fighting the War of Ideas like a Real War.* Washington, DC: Institute of World Politics.

Waller, J.M., editor (2007). *The Public Diplomacy Reader*. Washington, DC: Institute of World Politics.

Waltz, K. (1959). *Man, the State, and War: A Theoretical Analysis*. New York: Columbia University Press.

Wang, H., Lu, Y. (2008). "The conception of soft power and its policy implications: a comparative study of China and Taiwan." *Journal of Contemporary China, 17* (56), 425.

Watanabe, Y., and McConnell, D., editors, (2008). *Soft Power Superpowers: Cultural and National Assets of Japan and the United States*. New York: M.E. Sharpe.

Wright, S. (2007). *The United States and Persian Gulf Security: The Foundations of the War on Terror*. Ithaca, NY: Ithaca Press.

www.asef.org

www.bayanihancentre.org

www.catholic.org.sg/acmi/

www.centreforfilipinos.org

www.cfo-pso.org.ph

www.churchmodel.org.uk

www.churchsociety.org

www.dsj.org

www.geocities.com/CollegePark/Campus/9782/)

www.geocities.com/elshaddai_dwxi_ppfi/

www.graceaog.org

www.hopesingapore.org.sg

www.ibc-fc.org

www.ibcs.org

www.luckyplazashopping.com

www.migrants.org.sg

www.nccs.org.sg

www.oakdiocese.org

www.ofwpinoystar.com.sg

www.philippinecentre.com

www.philjury.com

www.pinoysg.com

www.sfarchdiocese.org

www.sfc-singapore.org

www.thelivingwordfellowship.com

www.usccb.org

www.veritas.org.sg

www.whychurch.org.uk

www.wordfortheworld.com

Yeoh, B., Huang, S., and Gonzalez, J. (1999). "Migrant female domestic workers: debating the economic, social, and political Impacts in Singapore." *International Migration Review*, 33 (1).

Zaharna, R. (2009). *Strategic US Public Diplomacy in a Global Communication Era: From Battles to Bridges*. New York: Palgrave Macmillan.

About the author

Joaquin Jay Gonzalez III, Ph.D., is Associate Professor of Politics, Chair of the Asian Studies Program, and Director of the Maria Elena Philippine Studies Program at the University of San Francisco. He has authored or co-authored several books, including *Filipino American Faith in Action* (New York University Press) and *Religion at the Corner of Bliss and Nirvana* (Duke University Press). After the horrific events of 9/11, Dr. Gonzalez was appointed Mayor George Christopher Professor of Public Administration at Golden Gate University and Commissioner of Immigrant Rights for the City and County of San Francisco.

CPSIA information can be obtained at www.ICGtesting.com
Printed in the USA
BVOW030711311212

309479BV00006B/9/P